DYNAMICS OF DALITS

DYNAMICS OF DALITS

Old Issues and New Challenges

Edited by

K.B. Dutta

AKANSHA PUBLISHING HOUSE
NEW DELHI - 110 059 (INDIA)

AKANSHA PUBLISHING HOUSE
R-37B, Vani Vihar, Uttam Nagar
New Delhi - 110 059
E-mail: ektabooks@yahoo.com

Showroom
4649/21B, Ansari Road
Daryaganj, New Delhi - 110 002
Phones: 9212065579, 9811582579

Dynamics of Dalits

First Published, 2005
ISBN 81-87606-95-9

PRINTED IN INDIA

Published by M.P. Misra for Akansha Publishing House, New Delhi - 110 059 and Printed at Tarun Offset Press, Delhi.

Dedicated
to
Dr. B.R. Ambedkar
The Great Humanitarian & Champion
Who strived for the cause of Dalits
&
The Veteran Dalit Scholars
Who have been incessantly raising Dalit voice

Contents

Preface

Dalits are those ill-treated, humiliated, even discarded common civil rights people mainly belonging to lowest rung of Hindu caste system. They have been discriminated in all walks of life for centuries and were compelled to lead an animal-like life. Variously known as untouchables, Harijans and Scheduled Castes, they remain victims of all sorts. They were assigned menial works like shoe-making, scavenging all dirty jobs etc.

Literally the term 'Dalit' in Sanskrit means 'oppressed' or 'broken'. The word 'Dalit' has gained wide circulation after upheaval of caste-based politics and political parties in India. It is a very recent development. Probably, it was used in the 1930s as a Hindi and Marathi translation of 'Depressed Classes', the term the British used for what are now officially called the Scheduled Castes. Since the early 1970s, the word has come into increasingly wider use in the press and in common parlance where it is normally used in the original, narrower, caste-based sense. The word was also used by B.R. Ambedkar in his Marathi speeches.

As enshrined in the Constitution, India is a Welfare State, committed to the welfare and development of its people in general and of vulnerable sections Dalits in particular. Preamble, Directive Principles of State Policy, Fundamental Rights and specific sections, namely Articles 38, 39 and 46 in the Constitution of India stand testimony to the commitment of the State to its people. Welfare is not a matter of charity. Welfare programmes in the beginning were directed to provide a few basic curative and rehabilitative services. Over the years, a developmental orientation in contrast to curative and custodial approach was given to welfare programmes of the state.

The Constitution prescribed protection and safeguards for scheduled castes, scheduled tribes and other weaker sections either specially or by way of insisting on their general rights as citizens with the object of promoting their educational and economic interests and removing social disabilities they are subjected to. With a view to effectively deal with crimes against scheduled castes and scheduled tribes and to tone up administrative machinery to tackle the vital issues, comprehensive guidelines containing precautionary, preventive, punitive and rehabilitative measures exist which states/union territories have to follow.

A number of voluntary organisations also promote welfare of Dalits and scheduled tribes. Among them, the important organisations of all India character are: Harijan Sevak Sangh, Delhi; Indian Red Cross Society, New Delhi; Ramakrishna Mission, Narendrapur; Bharatiya Adimjati Sevak Sangh, New Delhi; Ramkrishna Missions, Puri, Silchar and Purulia; Bharatiya Samaj Unnati Mandal, Bhivandi in Maharashtra; Servants of Society, Pune, Maharashtra etc.

Legislation against Untouchability; Special Central Assistance; Coaching and Allied Scheme; Girls Hostels for SCs; Boys Hostels for SCs; Book Bank Scheme; Pre-Matric Scholarships; Post-Matric Scholarship for SC/ST Students; Liberation and Rehabilitation of Scavengers; National Overseas Scholarship and Passage Grants for Higher Studies; Research and Training Relating to Scheduled Castes Development etc., are some of the official welfare measures while State Scheduled Castes Development Corporation; Baba Saheb Dr. Ambedkar Foundation; National Scheduled Castes and Scheduled Tribes Finance and Development Corporation; National Commission for SCs and STs etc., are some of the institutional setups meant for the purpose.

No doubt, with the upsurging wave of awakening among Dalit masses, some improvement is apparently seen there. But so far these measures have not made them self-dependent which is the real need of time. Baba Saheb B.R. Ambedkar was the champion who faught valiantly for the cause of Dalits. Maharashtra, Madras (Tamil Nadu), Andhra Pradesh, Kerala were the states who stood in forefront for advocating the upliftment of Dalits. Later in other states this upsurge was seen. Mahatma Jotiba Phule, Ramaswami Naicker, Periyar and others are some of staunch veterans. In the field of politics, after Babasaheb, Babu Jagjivan Ram and more recently Kanshi Ram, Mayavati, Ramvilas Paswan, Meira Kumar, S.K. Shinde and many more have made visible the presence of Dalits. But one thing to be noted from the recent developments is that Dalit movement, seems, has lost in bewilderness due to personal ambitions of so-called Dalit politicians. Again the question still remains unanswered how to uplift Dalit mass in the real spirit? Really the root cause of the evil is in the abject poverty and other socio-economic conditions. As such remedy lies in alleviating the root causes. Remember! not the retaliation but self-strengthening, equipping oneself with the vigour for common cause will serve the cause of promoting interests of Dalits. Society is always made of a composite fabric. Instead of distorting the basic texture, it is wise to make weak yarns more strong.

In the era of globalisation, the existing statutory measures of reservation for Dalits will prove futile. With the ongoing privatisation process the situation will be grim. What next?

The present book contains well-researched material on Dynamics of Dalits, and vital issues pertaining to them. The entire information is gathered under thirteen chapters e.g. Dalits and Dalit movements, problems of untouchables; Dalits and economic policy; sociological analysis of Dalit movements; process of Dalitisation; Harijan Sevak Sangh; Satyashodhak Samaj; social justice; Gandhian view on untouchables; impact of new economic policy; case study of rural Dalit masses; higher education etc. Supported by the facts and findings derived from various authoritative sources, e.g. books, journals, official documents and individual researches of different scholars, this book will prove informative and useful for scholars and laymen alike.

We owe a deep sense of gratitude to all those whose writings are reproduced here. The real credit for this compilation goes to them all, particularly to Dalit scholars who have been incessantly vocal and instrumental in raising the Dalit voice. To make the book more comprehensive we have drawn case studies made by different scholars. We acknowledge great indebtedness to them for sharing their views. Efforts are made to acknowledge them individually. Whose name(s) could not be traced, we owe gratitude to them also. This is technical limitation and unintentional. We are equally thankful to our near and dears for their inspiration. Mr. M.P. Misra deserves all appreciation for bringing out this book.

—KBD

1

Dalits and Dalit Movements: An Introduction

"Bowed by the weight of centuries he leans
Upon his hoe and gazes on the ground,
The emptiness of ages in his face,
And on his back the burden of the world,
Who made him dead to rapture and despair,
A thing that grieves not and that never hopes.
Stolid and stunned, a brother to the ox?
Who loosened and let down this brutal jaw?
Whose was the hand that slanted back this brow?
Whose breath blew out the light within his brain?

"Through this dread shape humanity betrayed,
Plundered, profaned and disinherited.
Cries protest to the Judges of the World,
A protest that is also prophecy."

—*Edwin Markham*

The word 'Dalit' has gained wide circulation after upheaval of caste-based politics and political parties in India. Its a very recent development. Literally the term 'Dalit' in Sanskrit means 'oppressed' or 'broken'. Apparently it was used in the 1930s as a Hindi and Marathi translation of 'Depressed Classes', the term the British used for what are now called the Scheduled Castes. Since the early 1970s, the word has come into increasingly wider usage in the press and in common parlance where it is normally used in the original, narrower, caste-based sense. The word was also used by B.R. Ambedkar in his Marathi speeches. In *The Untouchables*, published in 1948,

Ambedkar chose the term 'broken men', an English translation of 'Dalit', to refer to the original ancestors of the Untouchables for reasons which must have been self-evident because he did not explain them. The Dalit Panthers revived the term and in their 1973 manifesto expanded its referents to include the Scheduled Tribes, 'neo-Buddhists, the working people, the landless and poor peasants, women, and all those who are being exploited politically, economically and in the name of religion' (Omvedt, 1995: 72). There has thus been a narrow definition, based on the criterion of caste alone, and a broader one to encompass all those considered to be either similarly placed or natural allies.

Scholars, using a class analysis of Indian society subsume Dalits within such class or occupational categories as peasants, agricultural labour, factory workers, students, and the like. This can be seen in most Marxist historical writings, the subaltern studies volumes, and to a lesser degree, in the Dalit Panther manifesto. To those using a communal analysis of caste, Dalits are the people within Hindu society who belong to those castes which Hindu religion considers to be polluting by virtue of hereditary occupation.

Dalits were listed in the chapters of the census devoted to castes and tribes. The 1881 Census simply described and enumerated castes in the various provinces and states. Varna categories were often used to group them and so the Dalit *jatis* generally appeared at or near the end of the lists. The 1891 Census, on the other hand, adopted a standard classification of castes according to the occupation assigned to each by tradition. Dalit castes were thus included within such occupational categories as field labourers, leather-workers, scavengers, watchmen and village menials. The 1901 Census classified Hindu castes in order of social precedence 'as recognised by native public opinion' (Pradhan, 1986: 197).

The 1911 Census provided a separate enumeration of those castes and tribes which either did not conform to or were excluded from certain aspects of what was considered to be generic Hindu religion. Ten criteria were used to determine whether a caste or tribe was, to quote Ambedkar, 'one hundred per cent Hindu' or not (Ambedkar, 1969: 92). The five which applied to Dalits pertained to the denial both of various services by Brahmana priests and access to the interior of temples, to causing pollution by proximity or contact, as well as to the Dalit practice of eating beef and not revering the cow (Pradhan, 1986: 197). However, under special instructions from the Government of India which wanted more information about them, an entire appendix of 30 pages in the 1931 Census was devoted to what J.H. Hutton, the Census Commissioner, chose to call the 'exterior castes'.

Hutton's instructions to the various superintendents of census operations advised them to develop their own criteria in determining which castes should or should not be included, since such criteria might vary throughout India. 'It is not intended that the term should have any reference to occupation as such but to those castes which by reason of their traditional position in Hindu society are denied access to temples, for instance, or have to use separate wells or are not allowed to sit inside a school house but have to remain outside or which suffer similar social disabilities' (Hutton, 1933: 417).

Later in his report Hutton did ponder two criteria which would indicate that pollution, and hence interaction with high-caste Hindus, might be a consequence of a caste's socio-economic position (ignorance, illiteracy, poverty) or occupation, both of which are changeable, rather than of its traditional position in Hindu society, which was not, but he did not consider those criteria to be functionally operative. He placed their disabilities into three categories:

> Firstly, that under which they are barred from public utilities, such as, the use of roads and tanks, and secondly, their religious disabilities which debar them from the use of temples, burning grounds, *mats* and some other institutions. In addition to the above, but arising out of the second of

> these, there are the disabilities involved in relation with private individuals, such as the services of barbers and the admission to tea-shops, hotels or theatres owned by private individuals (Hutton, 1933: 482).

This enterpretation was largely supported by contemporary witnesses. On the one hand, Dr Ambedkar had testified before the Simon Commission in 1928 that the Bombay labour unions wished to preserve caste distinctions, while at a Bihar Depressed Classes Conference in 1937, Jagjivan Ram said that members of the Kisan Sabha were exploiters of the Dalits (Webster, 1994: 127). From their Dalit perspective, caste was much more powerful than class. On the other hand, not only Gandhi's anti-untouchability and Harijan uplift campaigns, which sought to remove the stigma of inherited pollution and change patterns of social interaction, but also the opposition which his campaigns aroused bore eloquent testimony to Hutton's understanding of what set Dalits apart from other Indians of the same social class. A number of recent sociological studies indicate that, despite all the changes which have occurred in the past 80 years, this continues to be what sets Dalits apart. The assumption underlying the Government of India's constitutionally mandated compensatory discrimination policy has been that if Dalits can raise their class status through the educational, employment and political opportunities opened up to them, then their caste status, defined in terms of interaction with people belonging to other castes, will also be raised. This assumption has, however, proven to be only partially true.

Thus, class analysis not only fails to take account of the basic contradiction and oppression which Dalits face, but also conceals these by using categories which divert attention away from them. It is no accident that historians using class analysis have largely ignored the Dalits, while those who have written histories of the Dalits do not make class analysis the basic framework of their histories.

As noted earlier, the Census saw caste as a religiously

sanctioned Hindu pattern of social organisation. The Muslim pattern was seen as primarily tribal, at least at its upper levels. Census reports often provided statistics on the religious affiliations of members of various castes, thus opening up the possibility that caste might not be a strictly Hindu phenomenon. When the 1911 Census had to determine which Hindu castes and tribes had to be enumerated separately for reasons of non-conformity or exclusion, religious criteria were used.

The 1931 Census treated the 'exterior castes' as Hindu castes because 'they worship the same deities and, though refused entry to the temples, boxes are placed outside, at the limits to which they can approach, to receive their offerings' (Hutton, 1933: 484). Thus Hutton's entire appendix is devoted first to those disabilities which high-caste Hindus impose upon their co-religionists that define the latter as 'exterior castes' and then to naming the castes so defined. It is significant that 'it was decided that Muslims and Christians should be excluded from the term "depressed class"'. The reason for the decision may have been practical, but the decision had a very definite ideological dimension. It was in keeping with that kind of thinking which the British government used when introducing separate electorates for Muslims in the 1909 Constitution, extending them to Sikhs in the Punjab and Indian Christians in the Madras Presidency in the 1919 Constitution, and continuing them in the 1935 Constitution. The fundamental divisions within Indian society are religious; each religious community constitutes a watertight compartment; each has its own distinct social patterns, religious beliefs, and political interests which require that each community be represented by co-religionists of its own choosing. Thus, despite evidence to the contrary (Hutton, 1933), the stigma of untouchability and its accompanying disabilities were seen as affecting relationships only among Hindus. The Order in Council specifying the Scheduled Castes referred to in the 1935 Constitution, turned this communal view of caste into law by specifically stating that 'no Indian Christian shall be deemed to be a member of any Scheduled Caste'. While Mahatama Gandhi was also wedded to this communal view of caste; not only his fast in response to the Communal Award but also his scrupulousness in having the Harijan Sevak Sangh confine its uplift activities to Hindu Harijans was based on this premise. Ambedkar, came to the opposite conclusion; while agreeing that Hindu religion was clearly a, if not the major source of Dalit oppression, he did not consider the Dalits themselves to be Hindus.

The same communal view of caste which initially defined the Scheduled Castes in 1936 was stated even more strongly in the President's Constitution (Scheduled Castes) Order No. 19 of 1950 which designated these castes to be considered Scheduled Castes in the Constitution of independent India. It stated that *'no person who professes a religion different from the Hindu religion shall be deemed to be a member of a Scheduled Caste'*. This was amended in 1956 to include the Sikhs and in 1990 to include the Buddhists. Moreover, in 1985, this religious criterion for determining caste membership was upheld by the Supreme Court which argued that caste was a peculiarly Hindu phenomenon. When one moves out of the Hindu community into the Christian community, then one must show equal disabilities and backwardness within the Christian *community* in order to be considered a member of the Scheduled Castes according to the Constitution.

Social scientists have also based their work on this set of assumptions by consciously or unconsciously applying a religious in addition to a caste criterion to determine whether or not a person is a Dalit. This is understandable. The colonial government, through the provision of separate electorates as well as in its Census procedures and categories, had shaped the history about which historians now write in those terms, and the government of independent India, while dropping communal electorates, continues to use the old categories in areas of 'social policy'. Kamble, Gupta, Pradhan and Trilok

Nath in their histories of the pre-independence Dalit movement treated those Dalits who converted to other religions as no longer Dalits and therefore no longer part of the history of the Dalit movement, whereas Mark Juergensmeyer (1982) included Christian Dalits in his history of the movement against untouchability in the Punjab.

Most sociologists and political scientists in studying Dalits since Independence confine their samples to Hindu and, where relevant, Buddhist Dalits. Suma Chitnis, included Christians and Sikhs as well in her national survey on the grounds both that conversion had not changed their situation and that several state governments had recognised this.

Historical research of the Dalit Christians indicates that this 'communal' framework of analysis does not do justice to the complexity of either Dalit social reality or the modern Dalit movement. In fact, it breaks down at three crucial points. The first is in its assumption that the social consequences of conversion to Christianity were the same for Dalits as for members of the higher castes. In fact they were quite different. Back in the last quarter of the 19th century and the first quarter of 20th century when most of the Dalit mass conversions occurred, high-caste people were completely cut off from family and caste (*jati*) upon conversion to Christianity. For them, the Supreme Court's assumption proved to be substantially correct; they moved out of their *jati* community into the Christian community and were to be governed only by the latter's norms. However, this did not happen to Dalit converts. They were not outcasted but almost always continued to live with their caste fellows on the periphery of the village or, in the South, in the *cheri* outside the village. They also continued to marry within their own *jatis*, preferably with coreligionists. Moreover, their place in the village economy and social system was not altered by conversion, as immediate persecution was designed to point out! This is not to suggest that conversion produced no strains in self-understanding and social relationships or no alterations in the lifestyles and attitudes of the converts. It is to say that these strains and alterations occurred without totally changing their social identity and relationships within the village.

In 1919, Christians in the Madras Presidency, where the vast majority of Dalit Christians lived, were granted separate electorates. Dalit Christians there were placed in the Christian rather than in the general constituency. (Elsewhere in India all Christians were part of the general constituency until 1935.) There is not much evidence of Dalit Christian political activism during this period; Ambedkar was right about that. However, what evidence there is indicates that they were more active as Dalits on Dalit issues than as 'Christians' on general 'Christian' issues. They had no voice in the All-India Conference of Indian Christians or other Christian political organisations, and these bodies were as guilty of patronising neglect as were the Congress, other non-Dalit political parties, and the government. Where Dalit Christians were politically active was in Dalit caste associations, and in protesting against caste discrimination within the churches. In fact, in 1929, a deputation of Dalit Christians gave evidence before the Simon Commission in Madras, arguing that they should be put in the general constituency where they expected fairer treatment than they had received in the Christian constituency (Indian Statutory Commission oral evidence, 1929: 14-20). It would seem, therefore, that the modern Dalit movement was not just a movement within the Hindu community alone, but, like the nationalist movement, it included people on all sides of the neat communal boundaries which the British had built up.

Last, the communal framework of analysis breaks down because it accepts as exclusively valid the 'sacral view' of caste according to which castes are treated as 'components in an overarching sacral order of Hindu society' and does not include the more secular associational and organic views of caste, which can be equally oppressive to Dalits (Ambedkar,

1946; Joshi, 1982). Here too, research on caste in the Christian community and churches since Independence, while of uneven quality, is nonetheless instructive.

Caste exists in and affects the Christian community today, even though castes are rarely part of the 'Christian sacral order'. Moreover, caste does not function within the Christian community in the same ways throughout India. Three variables account for virtually all the differences: location (rural vs. urban), region (North vs. South), and denomination (Protestant, Roman Catholic or Syrian Orthodox). Denomination is a significant variable because historically these different branches of the Christian Church have viewed caste differently. The Protestants have been the most consistent in attacking it as part of the Hindu sacral order and in trying to establish among Christians a community without caste. The Roman Catholics adopted an organic view of caste, treating it as simply the Indian system of social stratification, and until recently have chosen to work within its constraints. The same can also be said of the Syrian Orthodox churches which have tended to function as one caste among many in Kerala society rather than as a multi-caste community (Koshy, 1968). Region is an important variable because the patterns of conversion have not been the same in the North as in the South. Whereas in the North a small number of converts from miscellaneous castes as well as from Islam combined with large numbers of converts from only one Dalit caste (e.g., the Chuhras in the Punjab and the Bhangis in Uttar Pradesh) to form the Christian community (Webster, 1976: 46-53, 227-34), in the South large numbers of several castes of differing status converted to form the Christian community.

Thus it has been possible in the South, as it has not been in the North, for two, three or four castes to carry on within the churches the same competition for status and precedence as their Hindu caste fellows were carrying on in other arenas. Location is also a variable because it is generally recognised that caste sanctions are more strictly enforced in rural than in urban settings. One would expect to find caste weakest in urban Protestant congregations in the North and strongest in rural Roman Catholic or Syrian congregations in the South.

In the overwhelming majority of villages where Dalit Christians live, the dominant castes are Hindu and so social identity and social relationships are determined by Hindu rather than by Christian norms and values. There the sacral view of caste still generally prevails; Christian Dalits are simply categorised with other Dalits and treated accordingly. Second, within the urban Christian community caste seems to have been replaced by class in the North, whereas the associational view of caste prevails in the South. There, caste often provides the social networks necessary for getting jobs or winning elections to positions of leadership within the churches. Because Dalit caste networks are less effective than those of the higher castes, Dalits often lose out in the competition (Caplan, 1987: 152-63). Third, those studies of South Indian villages where both the dominant castes and the Dalits are Christians not only indicate that the distinctions of status and precedence on the basis of caste exist but also suggest that considerations of purity and pollution still affect relations between Christians of differing castes.

A communal view of caste imposes a framework for studying the history of the modern Dalit movement which seriously distorts the empirical realities of the Dalit situation and Dalit movement. A more inclusive framework is thus required.

This critical examination of alternate referents for the label, Dalit, indicates that the original definition of who is a Dalit is empirically the soundest one for the historian to work with. Caste alone has determined who is a Dalit, not class or religion. Social stigma and a variety of disabilities were based on caste; these were and, to a significant degree, still are the defining characteristics of a Dalit, even if a Dalit moves up in social class or changes religion.

REFERENCES

Ambedkar, B.R. (1946), *What Congress and Gandhi Have Done to the Untouchables* (Second edition). Bombay: Thacker & Co.

Ambedkar, B.R. (1969), *The Untouchables* (Second edition) Balrampur: Jelavan Mahavir.

Caplan, Lionel (1987), *Class and Culture in Urban India: Fundamentalism in a Christian Community.* Oxford: Oxford University Press.

Chitnis, Suma (1981), *A Long Way to Go: Report on a Survey of Scheduled Caste High School and College Students in Fifteen States of India.* New Delhi: Allied Publishers.

Frykenberg, Rober Eric (1989), 'The Emergence of Modern "Hinduism" as a Concept and as an Institution: A Reappraisal with Special Reference to South India', in Gunther, D. Sontheimer and Hermann Kulke (eds.), *Hinduism Reconsidered.* Delhi: Manohar.

Galanter, Marc (1968), 'Changing Legal Conceptions of Caste', in, Milton Singer and Bernard S. (eds), *Structure and Change in Indian Society.* Chicago: Aldine Publishing Co.

Gupta, S.K. (1985), *The Scheduled Castes in Modern Indian Politics: Their Emergence as a Political Power.* Delhi: Munshiram Manoharlal.

Hutton, J.H. (1933), *Census of India, 1931. Vol. I-India: Part I- Report.* Delhi: Manager of Publications, Government Press, Indian Statutory Commission Oral Evidence. 1929. Fourteenth Meeting, Madras. 1 March.

Joshi, Barbara R. (1982), *Democracy in Search of Equality: Untouchable Politics and Indian Social Change,* Delhi: Hindustan Publishing Corp.

Juergensmeyer, Mark (1982), *Religion as Social Vision: The Movement Against Untouchability in 20th-century Punjab.* Berkeley: University of California Press.

Kamble, J.R. (1979), *Rise and Awakening of Depressed Classes in India.* New Delhi: National Publishing House.

Kananaikil, Jose (1986), *Scheduled Castes in Search of Justice. Part II: The Verdict of the Supreme Court.* New Delhi: Indian Social Institute.

Koilparampil, George (1982), *Caste in the Catholic Community in Kerala,* Kochin: C.I.S.R.

Mathew, Joseph (1986), *Ideology, Protest and Social Mobility: Case Study of Mahars and Pulayas.* New Delhi: Inter-India Publications.

Mosse, C.D.F. (1986), 'Caste, Christianity and Hinduism: A Study of Social Organisation and Religion in Rural Ramnad.' Unpublished D.Phil. Thesis, University of Oxford.

Nath, Trilok (1987), *Politics of the Depressed Classes*. Delhi: Deputy Publications.

Oddie, G.A. (1969), 'Protestant Missions, Caste and Social Change in India', *Indian Economic and Social History Review* VI, September 259-91.

Omvedt, Gail (1994), *Dalits and the Democratic Revolution: Dr. Ambedkar and Dalit Movement in Colonial India*. New Delhi: Sage Publications.

Pradhan, Atul Chandra (1986), *The Emergence of the Depressed Classes*. Bhubaneswar: Bookland International.

Ram, Nandu (1988), *The Mobile Scheduled Castes: Rise of a New Middle Class*. Delhi: Hindustan Publishing Corporation.

Thapar, Romila (1985), 'Syndicated Moksha', *Seminar* 313, September: 14-22.

2

Problem of Untouchables: Gandhi *vs.* Ambedkar Approaches

(A) GANDHIAN APPROACH

Though criticised from different quarters, Gandhiji was very sympathetic to depressed classes and was firm determined to maintain Chaturvarna as the basis of Hindu religion. Gandhi considered the God as the originator of caste system, therefore, it must be maintained. He wanted to keep untouchables away from political platform, by declaring himself as their saviour and representiative at the Round Table Conferences.

While interpreting Gandhiji's attitude towards Dalits (Untouchables), D.R. Jatava writes, "Gandhi and other Congress stalwarts like Patel and Rajendra Prasad wanted Ambedkar and the Depressed classes to surrender to them so that they could be used as tools in the fight against British imperialism for India's political freedom. Ambedkar opposed this move and at the same time wanted the depressed classes to fight against the Hindu social imperialism and the British Political imperialism. He not only wanted among them social upsurge but also political revolt in their own way independently." With respect to the removal of untouchability, one of the political programmes of the Congress, Gandhi said that "without the removal of this curse, swaraj is a meaningless term." By this, according to Ambedkar Gandhi wanted to create the illusions so that these may be used as arguments to support his movement. In the talks with

Ambedkar on 14 August 1931 in Bombay, Gandhi explained to him how in spite of opposition from his colleagues he introduced the removal of untouchability as one of the main programmes of the Congress; but Ambedkar replied, "Congress did nothing beyond giving formal recognition to this problem." He told him that Hindus were not showing signs of change of heart towards the problem of untouchables. He said, "we are not prepared to have faith in great leaders and Mahatmas. Let me be brutally frank about it. History tells that mahatmas like fleeting phantoms raise dust, but no level. Ambedkar also asked, "why should the Congressmen oppose our movement and dub me as traitor? He explained that untouchables could not love this land, could not call it their own land, because of the injustice inflicted on untouchables.

Gandhi claimed that he represented all the sections and all communities including the untouchables. Ambedkar opposed it and asked his men to denounce the attitude of Gandhi. Ambedkar said that Gandhi valued more his reputation as the saviour of the untouchables than his reputation as the champion of swaraj or as protogonist of ahmisa. Ambedkar opines, "As a unifying force Gandhi was a failure."

> All the participators and supporters of the Minorities pact were strongly opposed by Gandhi at the round table conference. He was particularly furious at the recognition given to the untouchables as a separate political entity. With respect to the recognition of separate political entity of untouchables, he said I can understand the claims advanced by other communities; but the claim advanced on behalf of the untouchables that is the unkindest cut of all. It means the perpetual bar sinister. I would not sell the vital interests of the untouchables even for the sake of winning the freedom of India."He warned that the separate electorate and the separate reservation were not the ways to remove that bar sinister. He regarded untouchability as no part of Hinduism. He said, "I would for rather that Hinduism died than that untouchability lived. Gandhiji remarked that "the bitter experiences that he (Ambedkar) had undergone has for the

> moment wraped his judgement." According to Gandhi the claim that Ambedkar represented whole of the untouchables of India was not tenable. He thought that the attitude of Ambedkar would create division of Hinduism.
>
> According to Gandhi, if separate electorates were given, then there would be a division among villagers, the lives of untouchables as villagers would be miserable since villages were the strong holds of Hindu orthodoxy. He thought that the proposal for a special representation of Muslims or Sikhs could be tolerated, but only "as a necessary evil," but separate electorate for the untouchables were positive danger" to the untouchables.According to Gandhi the only way to the problem was to put untouchables on voters' list and give them fundamental rights in the constitution. To Gandhi, untouchability was a stigma on Hindu religion. In the near future it would vanish. But separate electorate to the untouchables will ensure them bondage in perpetuity. Gandhi's view was that the adult franchise combined with a powerful and moral social drive against untouchability was the ture means of liberation. Ambedkar criticised Gandhi when he took fast unto death against safeguards granted to untouchables. Gandhi wanted to nullify them completely— As a result, Poona Pact was concluded according to which, as Ambedkar proved, untouchables were completely disenfranchised. It was embodied in the Government of India's Act, 1935.

As regards Gandhi's joining of untouchable's Temple entry movement Ambedkar said that the Gandhi's aim in joining it was to destroy the basis of the claim of untouchable for political rights by destroying the barrier between them and the Hindus which made them separate from Hindus. He characterised Gandhi's temple entry movement as a strong game of political acrobatics. He remarked, "when the Hindus threaten to defeat the Congress in the election, Gandhi, in order to preserve political power in the hands of the Congress, gives up temple entry." To Jinnah, it was Gandhi who converted Congress into communal body. If the economic conditions of untouchables reformed, then there traditional social usages would automatically be removed. Referring to

'Harijan Fund' started by Gandhi, Ambedkar said that its main object was to enslave untouchable, to the camp of caste Hindus and Congress.

When the untouchables were launching satyagraha campaigns, Gandhi surprised the untouchables by issuing a statement condemning their campaign of satyagraha against the Hindus. He stated that "satyagraha was to be used only against Foreigners. Ambedkar believed that Gandhi did not want the untouchables to organise and be strong. To him, "the Harijan Sevak Sangh under the pretence of service was out to kill the spirit of independence from among the untouchables."

Gandhi made it absolutely clear that removal of untouchability did not mean inter-dining or inter-marriage between the caste Hindu and the untouchables. His anti-untouchability, according to Ambekdar, was that the untouchables would be classified as Shudras instead of ati-Shudras. They were to follow their hereditary professions. Hinduism believed in caste, cow worship upheld the law of Karma, Pre-destination of man's condition in this world accepted the authority of the Shastras, believed in incarnations of God and idols all this is accepted by Gandhism. As per Ambedkar: All that the Gandhism has done is to find a philosophic justification for Hindusim and its dogma.

Ambedkar described the Gandhi age as an age in which people are returning to antiquity; they have ceased to think for themselves, ceased to read and examine the facts of their lives. He referred to the age of Ranade as the age of Renaissance.

Gandhi wanted the untouchables to be led and dragged by the Congress into the battle against British regime, where as Ambedker asked the Untouchables to lead themselves, contribute within the limits of resources available to them, achieve independently, in the struggle for freedom. It was this basic difference in their approaches which subsequently decided the role of Gandhi and Ambedkar with regard to the untouchable's political status *vis-a-vis* other communities during the national movement, in fact, Gandhi called the untouchables 'The slaves of slaves' and curiously enough, he asked them first to first against rulers of the Hindus, i.e., the Britons, in the national movement; and later on, after independence, the Hindus would endeavour to remove their social disabilities.

It is true fact that no depressed class leader of any time did more to sting the conscience of caste Hinduism. Ambedkar and Gandhi both differed in their approach not only with regard to the political rights of the untouchables but in many other respects also. The essence of Ambedkar's movement was the way of self recovery through some vital upheaval from within. The explosive forces needed must be generated within the soul of untouchable community itself. It could not come through gifts and grants from without. It must come from within the depressed people, and their spirit must be kept in the state of revolution so that they could stand by themselves in any sort of adversity.

(B) AMBEDKAR ON CONGRESS POLICY TO THE UNTOUCHABLES

Dr. Ambedkar has criticised the Congress because of the policy which it followed with respect to the problem of the untouchable. He once remarked that no untouchable became president of the Congress from 1885 to 1940. It was 1916, when some attention was paid to the pitiable condition of untouchables in socio-religious field. There was no political recognition of untouchable in India upto 1917. For the first time in the political history of India, the representation of the Untouchable put forth their grievances before Lord E. Montague. In 1917, Ambedkar who was ordinary figure in India's power politics, asked the existing organisations of untouchables to stand by themselves. Some important institutions like the Panchama Kavli Abhivarthi-Abhimanu Sangha, the Madras Adi-Dravid Jan Sangh, the Bengal

Untouchable Classes Organisation, and the Depressed Classes Mission of India, appeared before Montague to explain their miserable position and grievances. These organisations appealed to the British Government to save the untouchables from the age long thraldom of caste Hindus. Sir N.G. Chandavarkar, the president of the Depressed Classes Mission, too, sought an interview with Montague and asked for the removal of social and political disabilities of untouchables.

From the time of this event onward, the cause of untouchables started to be recognised in India's politics Congress men soon became conscious of their existence, who uptill now considered their social misery as being beyond the domain and deliberation of Congress session. The Congress's new found love for Depressed classes, however, emanated from an ulterior motive of winning their support and cooperation for the Congress-League scheme in which, no notice was taken of political existance of untouchables.

Mrs. Besant, the president of Indian National Congress advocated a practical policy for uplifting the untouchables without neglecting them any more in social and political process of the country in 1917. In fact, under presidentship of Mrs. Besant, "The Congress broke is long standing rule of ignoring social questions. Having the Lucknow pact in mind, at its Calcutta session in December 1917, under her presidentship, the Congress, therefore, passed the following resolution, "the Congress urges upon the people of India the necessity, justice and righteousness of removing all disabilities imposed by custom upon the Depressed classes, the disabilities being of a most vexatious and oppressive character, subjecting those classes to considerable hardship and inconveniene."

Naturally a question arises: why Congress decided to pass such a resolution in 1917 after a lapse of three decades since its inception in 1885? What made it thinks about cognizance of the poor untouchables ? According to Ambedkar, there were two main reason of the passing this resolution by Congress. In view of Montagu's announced policy of "gradual development of self-governing institutions" the Congress had its own scheme and it wanted the support of all Depressed classes so that British Government could accept its proposals. This was the first reason and secondly, it enlisted services of N.G. Chandavarkar, a Brahmin, an expresident of the Congress (Lahore : 1900) for mobilishing the depressed classes to support the scheme. He was also the president of the Depressed Classes Mission of India. It was, as a result of his influence that a section of the Depressed Classes agreed to support the Congress. It was, however, not unconditioning support. Sir Chandavakar and his Depressed classes friends agreed to support on the condition that Congress passed a resolution for removal of the social disabilities of the untouchables. The Congress resolution thus was a fulfilment of its part of the contract with the Depressed classes which was negotiated through Sir Naryana Chandavakar."

There was a large section of Depressed classes which, did not like to give any support to the C.-L. Scheme. It contained nothing for untouchables. The meeting of depressed classes under the chairmanship of Bapuji Namdeo Bagade on Nov. 20, 1917, opposed it and resolved that the Indian administration should largely be under the control of British till all classes, especially the depressed classes, rise up to a condition to effectively participate in the affairs of the country. It was really due to this blow to the C.L. Scheme that the Hindu leaders started thinking and recognising the existence of untouchables. It was, however, Ambedkar, who could know, that how the Congress had befooled the Depressed classes by its resolution of 1917. What happened to the Resolution ? No one knew it. The Congress forgot the Resolution the day it was passed. There was an ulterior motive behind the Congress Resolution. That motive was not a spiritual motive. It was a political motive," said Ambedkar the Congress Resolution was an expedient which was not seriously implemented." Its main objective was political and constitutional rather than social and religious.

In exchange for giving its support to the Congress-League Scheme, the depressed classes Mission of India had passed a resolution calling upon the higher castes, who claimed political right, to take steps for the purpose of removing the blot of degradation from depressed classes, which has subjected these classes to the worst of treatment in their own country." What did the Congress do to give effect to this demand of depressed classes ? In return Congress was bound to organise a drive against untouchability to give effect to the sentiments expressed in its resolution of 1917. According to Ambedkar the passing of resolution, at the instance of Gandhi was in fact a heartless transaction and entirely opposed to the declared policy of Congress.

Depressed Classes Mission of India held its first All India Depressed Classes Conference on March 23-24,1918, under the presidentship of Maharaja Sayaji Rao Gaekwad of Baroda, and attended by eminent personality like Vithalbhai Patel, M.R. Jayakar, B.C. Pal, B.G. Tilak, A.V.Thackkar and G.S. Khaparde. It asked whole of India, including the Caste Hindu to remove the blot of untouchability. Tilak made a fervent appeal not to tolerate untouchability. At the same time, he did not sign an All India Anti-untouchability Mainfesto.

With regard to an agitation by lower castes for separate representation in Indian legislatures, Tilak said, "their business was to obey the laws and not to aspire for power to make laws." How then could be have signed the pledge not to observe untouchability, though he had spoken fervently against it earlier ?

The social reform conference was an eye sore to the Congressmen who belonged to the anti-social reform sections. Ambedkar remarked that the opposition to the Social Reform Conference was headed by no other person than Tilak to a slogan 'Swaraj is my birth right" of Tilak, Ambedkar said, "Had he born among untouchables he would have demanded" Removing untouchability is my birth right."

The Congress under Gandhi, began a programme of social emancipation of the Depressed classes, to that effect, the Congress Working Committee (C.W.C.) in its February meeting (1922), at Bandoli passed an important resolution to organise the" Depressed classes for a better life, to improve their social, mental and moral condition, to induce them to send their children to national school and to provide for them the basic facilities which the other citizens enjoy. But the C.W.C. had no real interest in their emancipation. Therefore, the year 1922 passed without any solid work for their emancipation.

The Congress Working Committee Resolution (1922) requested All India Hindu Mahasabha to take up the work of abolishing untouchability and remove the evil from amidst the Hindu community. Criticising the step of C.W.C, Ambedkar said," If there is any body which is quite unfit for addressing itself to the problems of untouchables it is the Hindu Mahasabha. It is not a social reform association. It is purely political organisation." In nutshell, it was to represent the Hindu Nationalism by opposing Muslim communalism.

Was it not to add insult to injury by relegating the work of the uplift of untouchables to such a body which has even today, no relevance to untouchable's social aspirations. The fact, however, is that the Congress wanted to get rid of the problems of the untouchables. For, it did not wish to invite wrath of the caste Hindu. But at the same time, it wanted to make their issue an appendage to its constructive programme without antagonising the orthodox Hindu elements in the nationalist movement. Whilst, therefore, the Congress thought, that in places where the prejudice against the untouchables was still strong, separate schools and separate well must be maintained out of the Congress funds. However, every effort should be made to draw such children to national schools and to the to allow them to use the common well. But the Congress did not spend even one per cent of the crores of rupees it had collected, on the amelioration of socio-economic conditions of the depressed classes. Instead, the Congress spent the public money from Tilak Swaraj Fund for nursing their own constituencies without any qualms of conscience. Gandhi was a witness to all that was openly plundered out of the Tilak Swaraj Fund.

Why could Gandhi not save a large part of this Fund organised loot by Congress leader, for the benefit of poor untouchables, Gandhi's arguments were remarkable for their subtletey and sophistry.

In Nov. 1918, the Congress condemned the Mont-Ford Report as disappointing and unsatisfactory. It was very significant one from the point of view of the depressed classes. This Report had recognised for the first time, the existance of the untouchables. The Report had admitted that in India, some stronger and cleverer elements were oppressing the weaker classes, and until it was clear that the interests of the oppressed could be safely represented and considered in Legislative Councils, the British must retain power to protect them.

In 1919, Ambedkar explained to the South borough Committee dealing with franchise in the light of Mont-Ford Reforms, the horrible conditions of untouchables and demanded separate electorate with reserved seats in proportion to their population. A few days latter, he also spelled out his views on the demand for home rule. He argued that before demanding home rule, it was the duty of caste Hindus to bring the lower and depressed classes on a ladder of social equality, for they belonged to the same religion, country and society, and had the same aspirations for liberty and home rule. Home Rule was as much the birth right of a Brahmin as that of an untouchable without their elevation in social esteem, the day on which India would have Home rule was distant. In other words, the South borough Committee too recognised the separate political existence of untouchables and strongly recommended that the measures should be taken to protect the interests of the Depressed classes in the ensuing constitutional reforms.

The Government of India Act (1919) for the first time in Indian history recognised the politic-constitutional existance of the Depressed classes. But this Act proved to be a failure in the sense that the objective for the sake of which it was introduced was not realised, there was no real transfer of power to people, no genuine responsible government even in the limited sphere of transferred subject."

Gandhi after having declared himself as a leader of untouchable in 1920, asked them to follow him in the national movement. According to Ambedkar, the Mahatma wanted to make the Panchmas his devout disciples and use them in (as the tools of) caste Hindus fight against the British imperilism. It was, indeed, a fact that "Congress and Gandhi saw the need to gaining the political support of untouchables, if only to assure their being counted as Hindus in the calculations for communal representations in the reformed legislatures, Gandhi asked the caste Hindus to undertake the work of removal of untouchability.

At this time Ambedkar, stressed more an political progress of untouchable, "He was right in stating that progress for the depressed classes after 1920 was a political, not a social issue."Ambedkar asked the untouchables, first not to be beguiled by the Congress and Gandhi and secondly to realise their own responsibility to rise in life, this may appear a minor point of variance, but it reflected the deeper ideological-differences involving the relative worth of the two different approaches during the national movement.

Government of India Act, 1935 gave the right of vote to only about 10 per cent of people of the country. Ambedkar analysed the results of 1937 election and came to the conclusion that Congress was not a majority party—the Congress not even obtained 50 per cent of votes. According to Ambedkar the Congress claim to represent all classes and communities was a hollow one, with no foundation in fact. The system of joint electorates and reserved seats which was in operation was a system of two member constituency. The Hindus under the Congress were so completely organised that there was no possibility of electoral contest and consequent waste of votes. The result was that the system helped the Hindus to win the reserved seats and worked against the Scheduled Castes.

According to Ambedkar the number of seats captured by a party was not always in proportion to the number of votes caste in favour of the party and often a party carried a majority of seats with minority of votes. This was particularly true when the singular member constituency system prevailed as it did in India. Ambedkar showed that the untouchables candidates triumphed over the Congress because they got 10 per cent votes of their community in the primary elections.

The Congress aimed at re-establishing a democratic form of government. It wanted democratic form of government based on adult franchise with no safeguards for untouchables. Ambedkar remarked that if there were no guarantees to the untouchables, the result would be that the Hindu Communal majority would not only capture the legislature, the executive and the administration, but these would be over run by the Hindu communal majority. As a result, these powerful organs of State, instead of protecting the minorities would become the tools of the Hindu Communal majority doing its bidding. He maintained that the Hindu Communal majority was the backbone of the Congress, and the Congress, therefore, was bound to protect its rights. The social psychology of the Hindu Communal majority was dominated by the dogma which recognised not merely inequality but graded inequality as the rule governing the inter-relationship among the various communities. According to Ambedkar, "This dogma of graded inequality is absolutely inimical to liberty and fraternity. He was of the opinion that the political safeguards to counteract the evil of graded inequality were quarantees for minimum representation in the legislature, the executive and the public services. He remarked that these demands of the Scheduled Castes were rediculed by the Congress as "communalism" and the leaders of the untouchables were represented as "job hunters."

Ambedkar wanted to refer the dispute between Hindus and untouchables to an international board of arbitration. Ambedkar maintained firmly that the untouchables were a separate element in the national life of India he said, "They are distinct and separate from Hindus. What the Congress believed was just contrary to his views. According to Ambedkar European nationalities were Christians by religion, still they were different. Whites and Negroes were both Christains, but they formed different Communities. Indian Christians, Anglo-Indian and Europeans followed the same religion, still they did not form a single community. Sikhs, Mazbi Sikhs, Ramadasia Sikhs—all professed Sikhism, but it was accepted that they did not form one community.

Ambedkar expressed his view that the Congress was failure in realising that the fundamental issue for settling the question whether to grant or not to grant constitutional safeguards was union *versus* separation of social group in the population. Muslims and Christians were given political recognition because they formed, in fact, separate elements from Hindus. He remarked: Hindus and social union are incompatible. If Hindus wish to be one they will have to discard Hindusim. Hinduism is the greatest obstacle to Hindu Unity.The problem was to achieve liberty and equality for a minority from the hands of a hostile majority, Therefore, essentially the problem of untouchables was fundamentally a political problem.

According to Ambedkar, the system of untouchability was a gold mine to the Hindus he said "Untouchability was not only a of unmitigated economic exploitation, but it was also a system of uncontrolled economic exploitation. This was because there was no independent public opinion to condemn it and there was no impartial machinary of administration to restrian it. Hindus belonged to the exploiting class." Ambedkar thought that Swaraj instead of putting an end to untouchability, might extent its life. He was of the view that in Swaraj the untouchables would get no privileges but the perpetuation of slavery.

The leftists and radical parties of Europe and America were also criticised by Ambedkar for giving blind and unquestioned support to the Congress which was admittedly run by capitalists, landlords, money-lenders and reactionaries. The press correspondents of journals were almost always from the Congress camp. A foreigner believed that the Congress had the representative character and it was fighting for India. But he maintained that the 1937 election showed that the Congress did not represent the nation. A foreigner never thought of distinction between freedom of country and freedom of people in the country. India might become free but the people of India (like untoucbales) might not become free. He asked, "is it necessary to tell them that to support Congress is to let tyranny have freedom to enslave?"

Ambedkar visualised the Brahamin-Bania class as a governing class in India instead of Brahmin Kshatirya combine as it used to be. He said, "This class would not disappear by magic of Swaraj". In proportion to their numbers the Brahmins had secured overwhelming representation. The representative of Bania was also over whelming. He held that Swaraj would not be government by people, but it would be a government run by the governing class, and in trie absence of government by the people, government for the people would be of what the governing class would choose to make of it. Whenever servile classes asked for reservation in legislatures, the executives or the Public service, the governing class raised the cry of "nationalism in danger." Far from sacrificing its privileges for nationalism, it was exploiting nationalism to preserve them.

Ambedkar pointed out that, "the fight for freedom" led by the governing class was, from the point of view of the servile classes, selfish struggle. The freedom which the governing class in India was struggling for was freedom to rule the servile classes. What it wanted was the freedom for the Master race to rule the subject race which was nothing but the nazi or Nietzschean doctrine of freedom for superman to rule the common man. The governing class was aware that a political campaign on class ideologies, class interests, class issues and class conflicts, would toll its death knell. It knew that the most effective way of side tracking the servile classes and fooling them was to play upon the sentiment of nationalism and national unity and realised that the Congress platform was the only platform that could most effectively safeguard the interests of the governing classes. For if there was any platform from which all talks of conflict between rich and poor. Brahmin and non-Brahmin, land lord and tenant, creditor and debtor, which did riot suit the governing classes was debarred, it was the Congress platform. The Congress was not only bound to preach nationalism and national unity which was what the governing classes wanted and on which its safety entirely depended but also prohibited the preaching of any other ideology inconsistant with nationalism from its platfrom.To Ambedkar, the reservations demanded by servile classes were, in fact, controls over the power of the governing classes.

After the resignation of the Congress ministries in November, 1939, Jinnah called on Muslims throughout India to observe "Deliverance Day" on 22 December 1939. Ambedkar declared that he would like to join Jinnah in celebrating the Deliverence Day. He however, explained that it was not an anti-Hindu move, it was anti-Congress and therefore purely political. He and his independent labour party also participated in it. In a statement to the press, he asked for the appointment of a Royal Commission to investigate the cases of tyranny and oppression by the Congress Ministries.

Ambedkar bitterly criticised the Congress for its policy of non-inclusion of the representatives of minorities in its cabinet. One of the reasons given for it by the Congress was that a cabinet must be the party cabinet if it was to take collective responsibility. The minorities could be included in the cabinet only when they were prepared to join the Congress and sign its pledge According to Ambedkar it was a part of Congress policy not to admit the right of untouchables to be represented in the cabinet and this policy head the support of Gandhiji. He showed that amongst the candidates selected by the Congress for the legislature, the candidates from Brahmin and other allied communities were the most highly educated, the candidates from non-Brahmins were moderately educated; the candidates from untouchables were just above literates. It was designed to allow none but Brahmins and allied castes to form the main part of ministry and to secure for them the support of a docile unintelligent crowd of non-Brahmins and untouchables who would be no rivals but would be content to follow the lead for no other consideration except that of having been raised to the status of members of the legislatures.

Ambedkar in a public meeting in 1937 had denounced the Congress as a tool in the hands of the capitalists; and remarked that it was looking against the interest of workers and peasants. In a conference of peasant of Mahad in 1938, he attacked the Bombay ministry as a tool in the hands of Sardar Patel and Gujarati capitalists. They were the enemies of Maharashtra the untouchables. On being persuaded by the peasant leader from Bihar in 1938, to join the Congress to form a united front against imperialism, Ambedkar replied that he would be glad to liquidate the Independent Labour Party and join the Congress party, if the Congress decided to fight imperialism. But he said that the Congress was using the constitutional machinery to advance the interests of the capitalists and other vested interests by sacrificing the interests of peasants and workers, and therefore, he could not join such an organisation. Ambedkar charged that Nehru government and the Congress party had failed to give to the people a pure and incorruptible administration. He accused the Congress of not providing food and clothing to the people; and said that the Congress failed to give to the people an administration free from corruption, bribery, nepotism and favouritism. What stood in its way, according to him, was the Congress itself, because it did not believe in purity of administration. He charged that the Congress was being conducted on the basis of personal allegiance.

REFERENCES

Ahir, D.C. (1979), *Gandhi And Ambedkar,* Jalandar, p. 29.

Ambedkar, B.R. (1970), *'Federation Versus Freedom' Bheem Patrika (Jalandar).*

Ambedkar, B.R. (1946), *What Congress and Gandhi have done to untouchable,* Thacker, (Bombay).

Ambedker, B.R. (1948), *'Pakistan or Partition of India'* Tacker & Co. Ltd., Bombay, IIIrd Edition, p.28.

Ambedker, B.R. (1982), *'Poona Pact'* Buddhist Publishing House, Jalandhar.

Babu jagjivan Ram: Jivan Aur Vijaktiwa, Depressed Classes League Publication, New Delhi, 1956, p. 104.

Bose/Ratwardhan (1967), *Gandhi in Indian Politics,* Lalvani(Bombay), p. 33.

Covett, V.A. (1972), *History of the Indian Nationalist Movement,* p. 30.

Extract from the 5th *Despatch of Government of India, dated 23rd April 1919 on the report of Southborough Committee on Franchise.*

Frank Mordes (1973), 'Witness to An Erd; *Holt* (NY), pp. 47-48.

Heimsath, C.H. (1964), *Indian Nationalism and Hindu Social Reform.* Princeton (New Jersay), p.342.

Issae, Horld R. (1965), *'India's Ex-untouchables',* Bombay Asia Publishing House, p.40.

Jatav, D.R. (1979), *Dr. Ambedkar's Role in National Movement,* Buddha Sahitya Sammelana. New Delhi.

Jatav, D.R. (1975), *'To the critics of Dr Ambedkar*, Jan Utthan Parishad, New Delhi.

Jatav, D.R., (1979), *Dr. Ambedkar's Role in National Movement*, Buddha Sahitya Sammelan.

Keer, D. (1962), *'Dr. Ambedkar: Life and Mission'*, Popular (Bombay).

Natarajan, S. (1959), *A Century of Social Reform in India*, Asia (New Delhi).

Rajgopalachari C (1946), *Ambedker Refuted*, Hind Kitab, Bombay, p.8.

Santhanam, K. (1946), *Ambedkar's, Attack*, The Hindustan Press, New Delhi, p.34.

3

Dalits and Economic Policy

Before the collapse of communism in Soviet Union, debates on economic policy had a clear 'left-right', progressive-conservative line-up. Socialists and progressives pushed for more role for the state, if not in building socialism then at least in assuring welfare where markets failed, while rightists hailed the market. Those days are gone. Today the most notorious reactionaries on social issues, from Pat Buchanan to Zhirinovsky, join with old leftists and trade unionists in calling for protectionism. The former socialist countries are forging a path towards capitalism, the Asian ones are under the leadership of their communist parties. On the other hand, fervent free-marketers such as the 'Freshmen Republicans' of New Gingrich in the USA have discovered the virtues of at least some subsidies. In India, the BJP and CPI(M) alike have opposed 'Dunkel' tooth and nail while in opposition, but have promised that 'reforms will not stop' while in power: the effective debate now is only over the speed and type of reforms. Socialism is seemingly dead, but the market has hardly triumphed, welfare survives, and people everywhere behold the doings of their political classes and intellectual leaders with scorn and puzzlement. Rethinking is clearly necessary.

Ambedkar's Economic Theory: The Stage of Economic Traditionalism

Ambedkar—even more than Marx—was primarily a political activist, though with a Ph.D. in economics. He had little time for deep academic research, but was immersed in the turmoil of his times. This is reflected in his economic thinking, which broadly went through three stages. The first was in his early, more academic economic writings of the 1920s (especially *The Problem of the Rupee* and *The Evolution of Provincial Finance in British India* [Moon, 1990c]) which gave strong anti-imperialist but fairly orthodox liberal economic assessments of British rule. The second was in the 1930s and 1940s when as a central figure in the social and national movements of the period he was heavily influenced by traditional Marxism in the field of economics, a period that climaxed with the slogans of 'state socialism'. During this period Ambedkar used a kind of 'dual systems' approach in which Brahmanism and capitalism were seen as parallel systems of exploitation. The third period was towards the end of his life, marked by his historical researches on caste, Hinduism and Buddhism, when he sought a total alternative in Buddhist philosophy.

In the 1920s, as a professor at Sydenham College, Ambedkar spent his time reading and working and preparing the base for a surging Dalit movement. This included the organisation of the Bahishkrut Hitakarni Sabha and the first great campaign (later to be memorialised as 'Untouchable Liberation Day') for water in the Mahad tank satyagraha. This organising of Mahad tank satyagraha in the Konkan region, it might be noted, was in an area that was later to become a centre for a united Mahar-Kunbi movement against the Khoti landlord system. But, with a pace somewhat lower than that of later years, Ambedkar found time for two major economic treatises. Both followed fairly conventional economic thinking, and both also had important similarities with the Indian economic nationalists—with the *Evolution of Finances* taking a harsh stand against much of British policy.

The *Problem of the Rupee* was the book that justified Narendra Jadhav's contention that Ambedkar would have supported devaluation. In the final sections of the book, Ambedkar dealt with the devaluation controversy of his day. Strikingly, at that time it was the Indian bourgeoise who wanted a low rupee against the pound, while the British bureaucracy wanted a high rupee—the first, undoubtedly because they were primarily in an industry which had been a world leader from the very beginning (the textile industry), the second at least partly because of personal interests which would have preferred to be able to buy more pounds from their rupee salaries when they retired.

Ambedkar's own position was to argue for a moderately low rupee. In the course of his discussion, however, he did something which few in the devaluation debate of the 1990s had done: he gave a class analysis of the (at least temporary) effects of devaluation—arguing that entrepreneurs and the self-employed (from businessmen and farmers) would benefit from a low rupee, while wage and salary owners (from bureaucrats to daily labourers) would benefit from a high one which would keep consumer goods cheaper. Ambedkar's recommendation was therefore one which he consciously saw as a compromise between workers and capitalists—a devalued rupee but not quite as much as the Indian bourgeoisie would have liked.

Against Brahmanism and Capitalism

Ambedkar did not remain a 'conventional economist' for long. In the 1930s and 1940s, under the impact of a mass upsurge, the pressure of the Great Depression and the evidently successful economic progress of the USSR and the working-class radicalism this gave birth to, he turned to the left. This was the period when his Dalit-based Independent Labour Party joined with communists to organise peasants and workers and he formulated the struggle as being against both 'capitalism' and 'Brahmanism'. In the largest peasant march of the 1930s, organised to demand abolition of the Khoti landlord system in the Konkan, he had told the rally that 'in regard to the toiler's class struggle, I feel the Communist philosophy to be closer to us' (*Janata,* 15 January 1938). Later that year at a conference of Dalit railroad workers, he said,

> There are in my view two enemies which the workers of this country have to deal with. The two enemies are Brahmanism and Capitalism.... By Brahmanism I do not mean the power, privileges and interests of the Brahmins as a community. By Brahmanism I mean the negation of the spirit of Liberty, Equality and Fraternity. In that sense it is rampant in all classes and is not confined to the Brahmins alone though they have been the originators of it' (reported in *The Times of India,* 14 February 1938).

These were years in which the pages of *Janata,* Ambedkar's weekly, were filled with reports of the struggles of workers and peasants against 'capitalists and landlords' as well as the fights of Dalits against atrocities. Ambedkar did not have much time for theoretical writing in this period of tumultuous organising, but his programmes and speeches indicate that he accepted broadly the Marxist analysis of class struggle so far as economic issues were concerned. What this led to, though, was a kind of *dual systems theory* which saw capitalism and Brahmanism (casteism) as separate systems of exploitation, the one to be fought by class struggle, the other by caste struggle.

The climax of this approach in many ways came with the writing of *States and Minorities* (Moon, 1990a), proposed to be a draft of sections of the Constitution. Here Ambedkar gave a severe critique of capitalism and called for the nationalisation of land and basic industries, explicitly calling this 'state socialism'. In a sense the term 'state socialism' indicated his difference with the communists, in that in contrast to a revolution under 'working class leadership', state ownership was to be written into a democratic constitution. At another level, the phrase simply made the assumption of a mechanical Marxism that 'socialism' or collective ownership of the means of production was equivalent to *state* ownership.

However, many problems were there with the 'dual systems' of Brahmanism and capitalism. These became clear in *State and Minorities* itself, which seemed to contain two rather disparate sections, one advocating land nationalisation and state socialism, the other calling for separate village settlements of Dalits. The connection between the two was not clear. The problems of any 'dual systems theory' remained: seeing separate systems of class and caste exploitation left unchallenged by the Marxist assumptions of a class analysis accepted the idea that 'class' dealt with the economic issues while the 'caste' system of exploitation was at a cultural and ideological (superstructural) level. The dual systems of 'capitalism' and 'Brahmanism' provided useful rhetoric and a rule of thumb for analysis, but this left the question of the connection between the two systems completely unresolved. And if other systems of oppression (for instance 'patriarchy' and 'national oppression') were also included, then such an approach simply would yield to an unwieldy amalgam of many disparate 'systems' of exploitation. In other words, the dual systems theory could not give an integrated, holistic explanation. It reflected Ambedkar's initial grappling with Marxism, when he insisted that 'caste' be added to a class approach (and even that it should have priority) but did not develop an overall alternative theory.

Buddhism *versus* Marxism

If 'capitalism and Brahmanism' were the themes of the 1930s and 1940s, the last years of Ambedkar's life were preoccupied with Buddhism, and from time to time with the question of Buddhism and Marxism. But the framework of thinking was different. Whereas in the 1930s and 1940s Ambedkar had tended to see dual systems of exploitation, increasingly he came to give weight to caste and Brahmanism, and to try to theorise these in a way that would provide a unifying theme for the entire society. In the process, he also came to question his earlier acceptance of a mechanical class approach and of 'state socialism' as the solution to economic exploitation. In his search for a 'single system' theory, Ambedkar began to look towards Buddhism as the solution not only to problems of caste but also to economic exploitation.

We do not have to seek far for the reasons for this change. One was 'internal': that is, the logic of a dual systems theory was inadequate in the sense that it gave no idea of the connection between Brahmanism and capitalism. Making 'class' the economic base and 'caste' a political-ideological superstructure tended to give legitimacy to the mechanical Marxist position that the base was primary and that caste was a secondary issue. This was unacceptable to Ambedkar and other Dalit-Bahujan activists.

But the other reason for disillusionment with the existing theory of Marxism was *external,* the result of historical experience. On the one hand Ambedkar had an on-going struggle with the Indian communists, who saw him only as a party bourgeois misleader. On the other hand the world context was changing. In the 1930s and 1940s the revolutionary claims of mechanical Marxism appeared justified by world events; depression, war and revolution abounded and the Soviet Union seemed to be able to achieve both equality and impressive economic growth. By the 1950s these conditions had reversed themselves. Capitalist growth in the West was showing a new dynamism, and its proletariat was becoming integrated into the system. And, the Soviet 'model' was beginning to tarnish; the state was not withering away, it was showing its dictatorial face in a way clear to all. In this context, Ambedkar began to define himself not so much as a socialist but as an equalitarian who was equally devoted to freedom and a moral community life. His earlier definition of 'Brahmanism' had seen it as the negation of the ideals of liberty, equality and fraternity; now he returned to this theme. As his conclusion to a draft essay on Buddha and Marx says:

> Society has been aiming to lay a new foundation as was summarised by the French revolution in three words,

> fraternity, liberty and equality. The French revolution was welcomed because of this slogan. It failed to produce equality. We welcome the Russian revolution because it aims to produce equality. But it cannot be too much emphasized that in producing equality society cannot afford to sacrifice fraternity or liberty. Equality will be of no value without fraternity or liberty. It seems that the three can coexist only if one follows the way of the Buddha. Communism can give one but not all (Moon, 1990b: 462).

What did Ambedkar mean by 'the way of Buddha'? He could not finish the book he proposed on this, but the essay on 'Buddha or Karl Marx' gives some indications of his thinking. The essay begins with an outline of Marxist propositions and states that most of these have been historically invalidated: the proletariat has not become increasingly immiserated and revolutionary; the state has not withered away after revolutions. Marx's assertions of private property as the origin of exploitation and of class conflict remain, in Ambedkar's words, 'a residue of fire, small but still very important' (Moon, 1990b: 444), but now he sees the way to overcome the exploitation of private property in a radically different way. In other words, with this Ambedkar rejects state socialism, nationalisation and the dictatorship of the proletariat as solutions to the problem of exploitation and turns to Buddhism for an alternative. And here he comes up with what may be called a 'moral economy' solution to the problems of exploitation. This was not simply a matter of a stress on non-violence as opposed to violence.

Ambedkar had never rejected Marxism simply because of the role of force in its philosophy; unlike Gandhi he did not see non-violence as an absolute or religiously based principle. In this essay he expands on what he feels is a more practical Buddhist attitude towards violence. His argument is that we cannot (and Buddha did not) renounce force when it is necessary to obtain justice. '[Buddha] certainly would not have exempted property owners from force if force was the only means for that end,' Ambedkar writes (Moon, 1990b:

451). But this kind of force was not necessary, he argues, first because equality and the abolition of private property was achieved in the Bhikku Sangha through voluntary means, and second because morality and a welfare state could ensure that private accumulation of wealth did not lead to impoverishment.

'But Ambedkar assumes here that property and wealth accumulation will continue, though under state regulation. In regard to this, Ambedkar makes an important contrast between Buddhism and Christianity. Christianity gives a high value to poverty and otherworldliness, Buddhism does not—and Ambedkar believes he was superior precisely for this reason: 'There is no Sermon on the Mount to be found in the Buddha's teachings. His teaching is to acquire wealth' (Moon, 1990b: 460). For householders, lawful and moral accumulation of wealth is praised:

> Thus to acquire wealth legitimately and justly, earned by great industry, amassed by strength of the arm and gained by the sweat of the brow is a great blessing. The householder makes himself happy and cheerful and preserves himself full happiness; also makes his parents, wife and children, servants and labourers, friends and companions happy and cheerful, and preserves them full of happiness (Moon, 1990b: 461).

Ambedkar in this essay thus talks of equality but not of 'socialism'. Similarly, in his speech introducing the Indian Constitution, he refers to 'social democracy' rather than socialism (Moon, 1993: 1216). Was he having doubts about the value of socialism as defined in terms of collective ownership of the means of production? Or were these response only due to the situation: after all, a summing up of the debate on the Constitution was not a place to talk of socialist ideals since no one had, at that time, seriously proposed that independent India define itself as socialist. But, if Ambedkar maintained a socialist ideal, it must have been in a very different form than the traditional understanding of socialism at the time. Socialism was defined in terms of 'collective ownership' and Ambedkar's identification of this as 'state ownership' was similar to the confusion shown by all the Marxists of his day. Ambedkar continues to emphasise equality but does not use the word socialism and explicitly rejects the abolition of property by force. 'Equality' is to be maintained by voluntary communism in the Bhikku Sangha, and poverty is to be remedied by the redistributive activities of the state. Thus, by the end of his life Ambedkar can be called a 'socialist' only if socialism is defined in terms of the value of equality, and not as equivalent to the collective ownership of the production means.

Ambedkar and the Moral Economy

Provoked by the failures of 'state socialism' and by the resurgence of issues of identity, culture and spirituality, many socialist activists and theorists are centring their attack on the immorality of commercial capitalism and writing about the need for a 'moral economy'. Ambedkar would have agreed, and the need for 'morality' in the economic and political ordering of society was one of the crucial points of his criticism of the contemporary Marxism.

Today, most of the progressives arguing for a 'moral economy' in the abstract, do so basing themselves on a criticism of the 'immorality' of the 'market economy', and the meaninglessness and destructiveness of 'economic growth for its own sake', also avoid this issue. But the guiding theme for their 'moral economy' is a neo-Gandhian Hinduism, in which 'Indian (Hindu) spirituality' and the 'limitation of needs' are praised. On these points Ambedkar would have thoroughly disagreed. Morality in economic life required, according to him, a firm rejection of the pseudo-morality of traditional 'Hinduism', it had to be grounded in the three revolutionary values of 'liberty, equality and fraternity', and it presumed the overcoming of poverty through the development of human productive forces. Ambedkar sees these as universal ideals and as necessary for the welfare of the Bahujan Samaj.

This is evident in an early essay of Ambedkar, a review of a book by Bertrand Russell. In contrast to the Gandhian notion of 'limitation of needs', Ambedkar never accepted the equation of morality with suffering, poverty, asceticism or renunciation of money and consumption. As he wrote,

> This time-honoured complaint of the moralists against 'love of money' is only a part of their general complaint against the goods of the world and finds its justification in the economic circumstances which gave rise to this particular belief.... At a time when the whole world was living in 'pain economy' as did the ancient world and when the productivity of human labour was extremely low and when no efforts could augment its return, in short when the whole world was living in poverty, it is but natural that moralists should have preached the gospel of poverty and renunciation of worldly pleasures only because they were not to be had (Moon, 1990a: 489).

Ambedkar's moral economy, then, was to be one of abundance and wealth accumulation. His rejection, in *Buddha or Karl Marx,* of the Christian glorification of poverty is consistent with this. It seems at the end of his life he returned to his first insight, 'the trouble...is not with property but with the unequal distribution of it' (ibid.: p. 491).

Once again, when many environmentalists, are preaching an anti-developmentalist ethic and urging a return to traditionalist practices, this basic philosophical outlook is important. Ambedkar would certainly have been aware of the problems of ecological destruction caused by unregulated overproduction, but he would even more certainly have seen the solution to this in a form of *sustainable development*, not a rejection of development as such. Ambedkar here shares with Marx a positive appraisal of economic development—the development of the 'forces of production' and the potentials of wealth, choice and freedom made possible by this. He has no inclination towards the ascetic 'limitation of needs' and rejects what he calls a 'pain economy'. Thus Ambedkar's 'moral economy' which is outlined in a very sketchy way in *Buddha or Karl Marx,* is not contrasted either to a market economy or a planned economy as such but rather presents some alternatives that will make both market and state work for the good of the people.

It has three basic elements: (1) the role of the state was seen to be in providing 'protection' and the removal of poverty; (2) the role of the market was to be in the production and accumulation of wealth by individual householders (modified by moral concerns); and (3) the role of community which would give equality was seen in the development of a voluntaristic equalitarian communism in the Bhikku Sangha.

Ambedkar's Economic Theory and Economic Reforms

One should not make too much of *Buddha* or *Karl Marx;* it provides at most a direction of economic thinking but by no means provides a fully developed economic theory. Would Ambedkar have opposed privatisation or supported liberalisation? Statements at this level remain to a large degree speculation. But it seems clear that a large part of his approach, finally, would have been pragmatic, looking for the most effective combination of state, market and community roles; that he would have been clearly for the kind of globalisation that would aid the Dalits and other sections of the poor to establish their full place in a world heritage; that he would have been concerned both with all-round economic growth and its impact on the poorest and most deprived sections of the community.

[*Note: This chapter is substaintially based on the work of Gail Omvedt.*]

REFERENCES

Bhoyar, Divakar (1994), Dunkel, GATT and Bahujans', *Bahujan Sangharsh.* 30 April.

Chaudhuri, Nagesh (1994), 'What Policy Should We Take Towards Dunkel?' *Bahujan Sangharsh,* 30 April, Editorial.

Kamble, Siddharth (1994), 'What is the Dunkel Draft?' *Bahujan Sangharsh,* 30 April.

Moon, Vasant (compiler) (1990a), *Dr Babasaheb Ambedkar: Writings and Speeches. Vol. I. Mr Russel and the Reconstruction of Society.* Bombay: Education Department, Government of Maharashtra.

Moon, Vasant (compiler) (1990c), *Dr Babasaheb Ambedkar: Writings and Speeches. Vol. 6. The Problem of the Rupee and the Evolution of Provincial Finance in British India.* Bombay: Education Department, Government of Maharashtra.

Omvedt, Gail (1997), "Dalits and Economic Policy: Contributions of Dr B.R. Ambedkar". *Fourth World* 4 (I): 22-26.

Teltumbde, Anand (1997), 'Impact of New Economic Policy on Dalits in India'. Occasional Paper Series 1, Pune: Department of Sociology, University of Pune.

Thorat, Sukhdeo (1997), 'New Economic Policy and Its Impact on Employment and Poverty of the Scheduled Castes'. Occasional Paper Series 2, Pune: Department of Sociology, University of Pune.

4

Dalit Movement: A Sociological Analysis

Among sociologists it is possible to discern a dominant ideological current that has bearings on the study of the Dalit movement.

The study of the Dalit movement has attracted some leading sociologists over the past many decades in India and abroad. Among those notable scholars who fall into this liberal category is M.S.A. Rao who has used similar concepts for understanding the emergence of the protest movement among the backward classes and the Dalits in India (1982: 4). Rao, taking a cue from Merton and Runciman, has argued that social mobility forms the major basis of the theory of relative deprivation (1982: 4). Rao further argues that the relative deprivation is connected with the moment of emulation of a positive reference group (1982: 194). Other scholars too have tried to link the emergence of the Dalit movement with the issue of relative deprivation, reference groups and social mobility (Joshi, 1987; Issac, 1964; Lynch, 1974; Silverberg, 1968; Singer and Cohen, 1968; Sachchidananda, 1978; Bhat, 1971; Ram, 1988; Patwardhan, 1973).

While studying Dalit mobility it has been suggested by some scholars that the process of Sanskritisation could be a model, i.e., certain Dalit groups or individuals try to adopt either ritually or culturally higher groups or individuals in order to achieve a similar social position or to adopt the values that promote the aspirations of an atomised individual in a civil society. According to this view if the Dalits fail in their achievement of this imitation of the Sanskritisation model of upper mobility, they then suffer from relative deprivation because at the social level their attempt to overcome relative deprivation is restricted by the upper-caste group whom they cite as a reference group existing mostly in a pre-civil social situation which is still dominant in some parts of the country. At another level, the articulation of relative deprivation among the educated Dalits might take place when compared to the Westernised high caste. Thus, in the Indian case, as Oommen has pointed out, the deprivation is multi-faceted (1990: 255). However, studies establishing a link between the emergence of the Dalit movement and relative deprivation, social mobility and reference group theory, though inadequate in understanding the Dalit movement, need to be supported on the following theoretical and strategic grounds. Both historically and dialectically, this concept of relative deprivation could capture social reality at a particular historical juncture when Indian society was trying to release itself from the feudal ethos which was facing an ever-increasing threat from the advancing civil society in India.

In this transitional process, the Dalits who were aspiring towards mobility of various kinds but were unable to achieve it due to the restrictions imposed by the feudal as well as colonial vested interests felt deprived, a fact which time and again prompted the Dalit movement, for example in the 1930s in Maharashtra, to challenge feudal values through a process of emulation and Sanskritisation (Omvedt, 1994). This attempt to imitate the upper-caste values particularly in the case of the Mahars of Maharashtra, certainly contributed to the development of a negative consciousness which according to Gramsci may not constitute a mature and fully evolved class consciousness, but certainly is the first glimmer of such consciousness constituting the basic negative, polemical attitude.

Taking a cue from Gramsci, Ranajit Guha tries to understand this consciousness of the insurgent peasantry in colonial India. He says,

> it was only by attacking the material symbols of governmental and landlords authority that the insurgents upset the established order. They did so by undermining its dominant semifeudal culture as well. Insofar as religion constituted the most expressive sign of this culture in many if its essential aspects, the peasants' defiance of the rural elite often involved an attempt to appropriate the dominant religion or to destroy it. To those who were high up in society the emulation of their culture by the lower strata seemed always fraught with danger. There have been occasions when, thanks to the stimuli given to casteism by British colonial policy, Sanskritising movements among the lower castes to upgrade themselves by adopting the rituals and religious idioms of their superiors were resisted by the latter and generated much social tension and even some actual violence (1983: 20).

In the same vein, the Dalit social protest of 1930s, under the leadership of Ambedkar focused its attention on entering the *savarna* temples and tried to improve the status of Dalits through the imitation of Hindu lifestyle by adopting gods and rituals of the upper castes, i.e., through the process of Sanskritisation (Srinivas, 1962). Although the usual tendency is to view Sanskritisation as a cultural process aimed at bringing about changes in the lifestyle of Dalits, it had important structural ramifications in that the protest orientation and counter-mobilisation were necessary attributes of Sanskritisation movements since the Dalits often did so in a spirit of recalcitrance and the upper castes invariably opposed such attempts (Oommen, 1990: 255). Second, studies understanding the Dalit movement in terms of relative deprivation and social mobility helped to reveal the role of castes and inherited status that have for long influenced the monopolising of the available jobs by the upper castes which viewed caste mobility as dangerous and disruptive of the social fabric. It is in this context that studies establishing a connection between the Dalit movement and the above concepts bring out the latent contradictions of a socio-economic and political nature. Moreover, such studies also reveal that relative deprivation leading to socio-economic mobility has after all a democratising impact on the socio-economic, political and bureaucratic structure of India (Shah, 1991:603).

Studies linking relative deprivation and social mobility with the Dalit movement assume importance at least for tactical and strategic reasons especially when the studies of these movements are denied their legitimate place in the academic world and are considered to be deviations from the mainstream and irrelevant in the Indian context (Oommen, 1990: 30). Oommen, while criticising this approach as historical and biased, has argued that an adequate framework for the study of social movements should take into account the historicity, the elements of social structure and the future vision of the society in which they originate and operate and it is the dialectics between these which provides the focal point for the analysis of social movements (Oommen, 1990: 30). However, the present scenario, highlighted by three major developments of the total marginalisation and annihilation of the rural Dalits, Hinduisation of the Dalit masses and the growing crisis of the Indian welfare state seems to be questioning the theoretical validity of relative deprivation both as a conceptualisation and as a form of consciousness.

Concepts of relative deprivation and also social mobility are quite inadequate to capture this reality at the theoretical level. Given the happenings in the rural areas where the upper castes or class forces are committing brutal atrocities on the Dalits, and when the state's response is either callous or repressive, the Dalits do not feel a sense of relative deprivation so much as a total alienation and exclusion and the threat of physical liquidation. What one observes in rural Maharashtra and also in the rest of the country is the complete alienation of the Dalits from resources like land, water and agricultural implements. Thus, the Dalits do not find sufficient access to either the natural and human resources and, therefore, feel totally marginalised in relation to the so-called decentralisation of political power in rural India. Such a situation where the Dalits are collectively and absolutely worse off, questions the validity of the concept of relative deprivation which primarily presupposes the perception of contrasting one's situation, even at the most trivial level, with that of others worse off than oneself (Runciman, 1966:9). Moreover, it is this perception of total exclusion from the developmental processes that forces the Dalits to protest in the most militant way, ranging from radical reaction to physical retaliation in self-defence. This militancy is evident among the Dalits of Bihar, Andhra Pradesh, Maharashtra and Uttar Pradesh.

In the urban setting in Maharashtra, the concept of relative deprivation and social mobility has some relevance to the new educated employed Dalit class that is emerging from among the Mahars and Mangs. It is true that the Mahars do feel relative deprivation at two levels. First, at the vertical level, the Mahars feel relatively deprived both socially and materially in comparison with the upwardly mobile upper castes. To assuage this feeling of deprivation, these Dalits, particularly officers, float some kinds of welfare associations to gain, among other things, more patronage from the system. This is to overcome their relative deprivation by raising the material and social status of the individual up to the level of those who are immediately above them.

At the horizontal level, for the Mahars and for the Mangs the reference group is the emerging Mahar elites. The Mahars and even the Mangs in the urban setting seem to have developed a sense of relative deprivation often reflecting the feeling of hatred, contempt and jealousy towards those Mahars who according to the group under reference are more fortunate in raising their material status. This feeling of relative deprivation among the less fortunate Mahars and Mangs is now being openly articulated—an articulation that can lead to the formation of a subgroup or a social category based on the region-specific identity of these Mahars. The Marathawada Miṭra Mandal (the organisation of the Dalit teachers from Marathawada University) is a case in point. It is alleged that the members of this Mitra Mandal feel relatively deprived in comparison with the Dalits of north Maharashtra and Vidarbha (Jondhale, 1992). It is interesting to note here that this is true of the Dalits of Telangana who feel relatively deprived in comparison with the Dalits of coastal Andhra Pradesh, particularly of the Guntur region, who, according to the former, are far ahead in terms of sccio-economic and educational achievements.

This and social mobility relative deprivation performs a very important function for the stability of the system. First, the feeling of relative deprivation, if assuaged successfully, has an inbuilt atomising tendency which isolates the Dalits under reference from the large Dalitness. Second, the concept of relative deprivation tends to prevent the formation of a critical consciousness which involves the critique of the Indian state and the lopsided economic development. Instead, it fetters itself to the narrow contours of envy, contempt and hatred against persons from the same social situation. For example, the Dalits (Mahars, Buddhists) of Marathawada who, in educational and material terms, are relatively backward as compared with the Dalits of Vidarbha consider this relative advance of their counterparts from Vidarbha as the major cause of their own backwardness. They, however, do not consider their backwardness as being a result of the feudal ethos that dominated the socio-economic life of Marathawada for 500 years which eventually led to the late arrival of these Dalits in the main channels of advancement.

Similarly, the feeling of relative deprivation makes the Mangs (Dalit) overlook the connection between their backwardness and their traditional skilled occupation which had bound them to the feudal agrarian structure. Due to the socio-economic and technological changes in Indian agriculture and state intervention in the condition of the Dalits in general, the Mangs are now being displaced from the agrarian economy and are compelled to take to education and to the subsequent quest for jobs. This compulsion and displacement is a result of the replacement of the old agricultural implements which were made by the Mangs, by the more sophisticated implements manufactured by the Garwares. In this situation, the Mangs are lagging behind the Mahars owing to their late response to the state which, as we will see, seems to have lost the capacity to accommodate these latecomers in its rather obsolete network of patronage. Why do the Mangs not question the capacity of the Indian state and find faults with the market society which underlines and renews the structures of inequality? Why does their feeling of relative deprivation revolve around the relative advance of the microscopic section of Mahar elites? The politics of relative deprivation finds expression among the Mang elites. These elites, though emerging on a very small scale, are now found vocalising the sense of relative deprivation of the common Mangs with the intention of sharing the spoils with the Mahars by forcing a bargain with the power centres. This political expression of relative deprivation aimed at creating a constituency among the ignorant but innocent Mangs surfaced in one of the state-level conferences organised by the Mang elites in Maharashtra at Ichalkaranji in November 1991. It is interesting to note that in this particular conference the feeling of relative deprivation with a negative reference to the Mahars was articulated by the Mangs with the encouragement and patronage of the upper-caste political forces which are alleged to be instrumental in framing hostilities between the two communities for the electoral politics of the former in the state.

This feeling of relative deprivation, suspends, if not

eliminates completely, the possibility of the development of a homogeneous Dalit unity cutting across castes as well as regions. Second, since relative deprivation underlines the quest for social mobility, this mobility syndrome of Dalits has the potential of diffusing the formation of social consciousness by promoting individual consciousness which has atomising dimensions leading to the isolation and independence of the Dalits from their community. Thus, this feeling of deprivation and the element of mobility inherent in it pushes the Dalits away from the centre of collective struggles to the periphery, thus bypassing the assumption of the historical responsibility that Ambedkar had rested on their shoulders for their emancipation and that of the common Dalits from their dehumanising conditions. Therefore, while studying the Dalit movement in terms of relative deprivation or social mobility one should not lose sight of the fact that social mobility has sustained the belief in functionalism which has a stabilising influence on society and polity.

The real serious damage that the concept of relative deprivation can cause to the Dalit movement today is that it represents a negative utopia in two major senses. One, this concept at the theoretical level, attempts to describe 'what is' without linking it with the question 'what can be' and, thus, results in an adequate description of social phenomena. While it denies to sociology a critically subversive character it also denies an emancipatory consciousness to the groups under reference. It impels the Dalit groups to organise their thought and action not in their own authentic terms but in terms of those privileged sections whose hegemonic world-view underlines the structures of domination. The state plays an extremely important role in keeping the sense of relative deprivation vital. This is done systematically and shrewdly by transferring resources from the more privileged sections to the underprivileged sections as a part of its welfaristic strategies. In doing so the state not only weakens the critical consciousness that had begun to articulate itself against the structure of domination but as a corollary also discredits the movement by co-opting the most vocal and assertive elements into the pacification structures built around the welfare state.

In Maharashtra this was exemplified by Dadasaheb Gaikwad in the early 1960s in the Dalit movement. Later, there was an alliance of the Dalit Panthers with the Left and democratic forces. However, this integrating consciousness got dissolved into separating individual consciousness which brought about the fragmentation of the Dalits into at least a dozen small groups of the Republican Party of India (RPI) in Maharashtra. This diffusion was effected through the introduction of the Integrated Rural Development Programme (IRDP) and National Rural Employment Programme (NREP) package and the discrediting was achieved through the co-option of important Dalit leaders, including Gaikwad, by the state.

Ironically, scholars studying the Dalit movement have not focused much attention on such a vital aspect of the movement which involved the subversive role of state. Oommen has tried to fix the state response to the Dalit movement, but he seems to have given a more formal and legalistic explanation of the state response to the Dalit movement or any other movement of the weaker sections of the population (Oommen, 1990: 187). But an emasculation of any movement, particularly the Dalit movement in Maharashtra in the late 1960s and early 1970s, was done by the state not solely because the Dalit Movement had undermined its authority but more because this phase of the Dalit movement which focused only on the question of redistribution of land has seriously threatened the material interests of the rural rich as a result of the Dalit demand for government land and land declared surplus under the ceiling law. Though the concepts of relative deprivation and social mobility play a diffusionist role as they render the formation of an integral Dalit consciousness difficult in the urban setting, they were relevant inasmuch as they could capture the social reality, although fractionally.

However, it seems now that the growing crisis of the Indian welfare state, the systematic attempt by the Hindutva forces to Hinduise the Dalits and the revitalising of Buddhist culture among the Dalits all seem to have rendered the concept of relative deprivation too fragile to lead to new initiatives. The levels of the feeling relating to relative deprivation and social mobility are conditioned by the capacity of the state to intervene in the conditions of the population sections concerned. This can be corroborated by citing Runciman, who observes that in Europe the welfare provisions of the inter-war period helped to keep the level of relative deprivation lower than the actual hardships imposed by the depression might appear to warrant (1966: 70).

In the Indian context, the experience is quite contrary to that stated by Runciman because, in view of the absolute deprivation of the Dalits it was politically imperative for the Indian state to nurture the feeling of relative deprivation among them by shifting resource (this includes various constitutional provisions and different welfare programmes for the Dalits) from the more privileged sections thus reducing the absolute deprivation into relative deprivation. And this tends towards atomisation, thus denying a collectively critical subversive consciousness to the community as a whole.

Of late particularly in the urban setting, developments in Maharashtra in the sphere of state and religion are likely to conduce towards the initiation of the reverse process: a shift from relative to absolute deprivation. This is so because the current fiscal crisis of the Indian state renders it difficult to shift resources from the privileged to the under-privileged. This impels the state to withdraw largely from the social sphere. This withdrawal is evident from two facts. First, according to a rough estimate, the budgetary provision for social welfare is 1 per cent.

In fact, the percentage outlay on the Scheduled Castes had increased only marginally from 0.35 per cent in the First Five Year Plan to 0.84 per cent in the Fifth Five Year Plan. Thus, we find that the Scheduled Castes, who constitute 15 per cent of India's population and a much greater proportion of the poor, have been provided a disproportionately low share of the plan resources. Second, the state's thrust towards privatisation means practically a total marginalisation of the Indian Dalits because the private sectors would hardly be interested in accommodating them. This growing privatisation and the resultant exclusion of the Dalits from the urban settings also is likely to lead towards an articulation of their critical consciousness as a collectivity. At any rate, this is a likely consequence when deprivation tends towards absolutisation under present circumstances. However, as of today, such an articulation of corporate Dalit consciousness has not found any organised expression among the urbanite Dalits.

The sense of relative deprivation which emanated as a reaction to the upper-caste restrictions against the Dalits adopting certain high-caste social norms had led the Dalits in the later 1930s to overcome it through collective mobilisation. But today, the Hindutva forces are taking the initiative in accommodating the Dalits in the *savarna* culture. The notable example of this deceitful elevation of the Dalits was marked by the laying of bricks during the Ram Shilanyas at Ayodhya by two Dalits who were pressed into God Rama's service by the BJP-VHP combine a couple of years ago. In this particular case it was certainly not a genuine desire to overcome the relative deprivation of the Dalits that led to their mobilisation. However, whatever the reasons, this certainly suspends the necessity for the Dalits to initiate movements towards Sanskritisation.

REFERENCES

Bhat, Anil (1971), 'Politics and Social Mobility in India', *Contributions to Indian Sociology*, December: 105.

Guha, Ranajit (1983), *Elementary Aspects of Peasant Insurgence in Colonial India.* London: Oxford.

Issac, Harold (1964), *India's Ex-Untouchables.* Bombay: Asia Publishing House

Jondhale, B.V. (1992), 'A Report on Milind College', *Maharashtra Times*, July 6.

Joshi, Barbara (1987), 'Recent Developments in Inter-Regional Mobilisation of Dalit Protest in India', *South Asian Bulletin* 7: 112-35.

Lynch, Owen (1974), *The Politics of Untouchability.* Delhi: National Publications.

Omvedt, Gail (1994), *Dalits and the Democratic Revolution. Dr. Ambedkar and the Dalit Movement in Colonial India.* Delhi: Sage.

Oommen, T.K. (1990), *Protest and Change: Studies in Social Movements.* Delhi: Sage.

Patwardhan, Sunanda (1973), *Change among India's Harijans.* Delhi: Orient Longman.

Ram, Nandu (1988), *The Mobile Scheduled Castes: Rise of a New Middle Class.* Delhi: Hindustan Publishing Corporation.

Rao, M.S.A. (1982), *Social Movements in India* (Vol. 1). Delhi: Manohar Publications.

Runciman, W. (1966), *Relative Deprivation.* London: Routledge and Kegan Paul.

Sachchidananda, S. (1978), *Harijan Elite.* Faridabad: Thomson Press.

Shah, Ghanshyam (1991), 'Social Backwardness and Politics of Reservation', *Economic and Political Weekly*, Annual Number, March: 603.

Silverberg, James (ed.). (1968), *Social Mobility in the Caste System in India.* Mouten: The Hague.

Srinivas, M.N. (1962), 'A Note on Sanskritisation and Westernisation', in M.N. Srinivas, *Caste in Modern India and Other Essays.* London: Asia Publishing House.

5

Process of Dalitisation

Sanskritisation, Islamisation, Westernisation and Modernisation are the major cultural processes which have been recognised and researched by sociologists and anthropologists. Another major process which has unfortunately never caught the eye of any sociologists or other scholars is that Dalitisation (Asprashyeekaran).

The phenomenon of conversion from higher castes to the lower Untouchable castes and the change of the caste identity provides an important field of research so far unexplored by sociologists, anthropologists or ethnographers.

This happened due to foreign invasions, local conquests, famines, epidemics, floods in different periods of Indian history. The examples of Maru Bhambhis, Jata Bhambhis and Chamia Bhambhis of Rajasthan were cited in this connection in the article. They were originally Rajputs, Brahmins, Jats and Charans but had been incorporated into the Chamar caste fold. The Pariahs of South India (1816) and Jatava/Chamars of Uttar Pradesh (1920), the Mal Paharias of Rajmahal hills in Bihar (1901), the Kadars of West Bengal and Koragas of South Kanara in Karnataka (1992), all originally tribals, were reduced to the status of Untouchables because of their poor economic condition, landlessness and dependence on others for their livelihood.

Indian sociologists and anthropologists today evince much interest in studies on family, on religion and perhaps also on caste politics, but they do not seem to take interest in the process of *asprashyeekaran* (or Dalitisation). The following observation of Mukherjee on Untouchables may be noted:

> It is only from the beginning of the twentieth century that serious attempts were made to study scientifically the position of untouchables. While some readily came forward to study their contemporary position (to name only a few like Bailey, Bose, Briggs, Cohn, Freedman, Fuchs, Lynch, Mencher, Moffatt etc.), nevertheless there appears to be some hesitation and reluctance to study the past history of the untouchables by Indologists and historians. (Mukherjee 1988: 12).

Caste System and Dalitisation

According to Prabhati Mukherjee (1988: 14) the primary attributes of the Untouchables are: (i) Their (Untouchables) being *asprashyas* to the caste-Hindus, (ii) their segregation into distinct hamlets, non-commensality and non-connubiality with the caste-Hindus. The term 'untouchability' however is somewhat confusing as it may be temporary or permanent For the present study, untouchability has been treated as a permanent phenomenon.

The socio-historical genesis and development of untouchability in India has been studied by Prabhati Mukherjee. Mukherjee has given a very authentic description of the degradation of the *dwijas* and her study is based on the material collected mainly from Brahminical sources, covering a period of about 2,500 years. In addition to those texts which are primarily sacred in character, greater reliance was placed on the secondary evidences obtained from lexicons, Niruktas, grammars of Panini and Patanjali, the *Arthasastra* of Kautilya, accounts of Greek travellers and epigraphical materials (Mukherjee, 1988:14). Besides the Brahminical sources, Mukherjee has also made use of the Jaina and Buddhist sources. The Buddhist ideology was a serious challenge and posed a greater threat than Jain ideology to the Brahminical viewpoint. Regarding the Brahminical literature, one has to ask the question: 'Who writes for whom?' Furthermore, it is always uncertain whether the texts portrayed the 'ideal' or the 'real' situation existing in society (Mukherjee, 1988: 15). While dealing with these issues, Mukherjee concludes that 'Nevertheless, one can probably draw a valid inference regarding the real situation by accepting the "ideal" situation as maximising the trend of a particular phenomenon. The limit thus indicated may refer to the positive or the negative aspect of the phenomenon.' (Mukherjee, 1988: 15). What, however, is not easy while studying the degradation of *dwijas* for describing the process of *asprashyeekaran* is to arrange the available information under well-demarcated phases.

Instances of degradation of the higher castes during the ancient period have been many. Mukherjee reports such cases. She writes: '...not only with regard to the candalas, but some other groups also, which enjoyed a better position previously, there was a general downward movement in the social hierarchy' (Mukherjee, 1988: 41). She further adds, 'for instance, the *nisadas* were regarded by some as belonging to the Vaisya varna... and the *rathakaras* (or *ugra)* were *Dwijas,* i.e. they belonged to the cluster of the first three *varnas....* Eventually the two groups went even lower down in the *Varna* hierarchy' (Mukherjee, 1988: 41-42).

Referring to the castes in this context Mukherjee says:

> What, however, is not clear is why Sutas, Magadhas, Vaidehakas and Ayogavas lost their erstwhile prestigious and independent status in society. A suta while following almost similar occupations like those of ksattr was downgraded as a candala. In some respects, Suta enjoyed a better position in the sense that he was closely linked up with the court that also had the reputation of being a brave warrior. Similarly, from being traders, the magadhas and vaidehakas now became the same as candalas. One may probably explain their downward movement in the social hierarchy from the antipathy to the traders from the time of the Rgveda. And possibly the other job of a vaidehaka as a harem-attendant was not a very honourable one either. For the ayogavas, again, it is hard to account for

> their degradation... In any case, now all of them were reduced to the category of candalas (Mukherjee, 1988: 62).

Thus, we find from the foregoing literature that the number of 'degraded persons' mingling into the Untouchables category increased gradually.

According to the varna model, the Untouchables are outside the caste system and contact with them pollutes members of the other four varnas. Under Manu's code, these people must eat the half-chewed food of the caste-Hindus (Borale, 1968:212). The higher-caste Hindus are prohibited from taking food with the people affected by the institution of untouchability. One can easily understand, then, how cases of breach of socio-religious norms by upper-caste persons were punished. Mukherjee has rightly stated:

> The Vindhya forest is mentioned as the dwelling place for the Kiratas, Sabaras, Pulindas, Candalas and Matangas. Once upon a time the people living there were referred to as kiratas only. The name of the son of a pulinda was Matanga who seems to have been their leader. The same source also reveals the presence of several Brahmanas among them, because they accepted cooked rice from the Pulindas which probably degraded them to the same status. These Brahmanas gave up the study of the Vedas, pious and upright life befitting a Brahmana, and took the life of the kiratas instead. Therefore, in that secluded, fearful and dense forest infested with wild beasts lived the kiratas and those *'fallen Brahmanas'*. Matangas, their leader, roamed the forest, cruel and arrogant (Mukherjee 1988: 67).

Thus, degradation of Brahmins, as described in *Dasa-Kumara-Charita* and the Jatakas, supplies some information about the location of where different categories of degraded people lived and what factors were responsible for their degradation. In this way we may be able to find out who degraded Untouchables were and where they lived. The Buddhist birth stories called Jatakas, written in Pali, may be taken to reflect mainly the degradation of the Brahmins to Mlechha (i.e., low Untouchable caste). Mukherjee narrates an incident from the Jatakas in which '16,000 Brahmans had to leave their own country and go to medya desa (Madhya or Mlechha desa), because they took left-over food from the candalas' (Mukherjee, 1988: 67). Not only the Brahmins but also Kshatriyas were reduced to the status of the Untouchables (Borale, 1968: 37). And therefore, we can safely draw the conclusion that many historically known Untouchables were at one time Brahmins and Kshatriyas.

In order to support the above conclusion from the Brahminical and Buddhist sources, we can in addition examine other evidence also. In his book, *India from Primitive Communism to Slavery* (1949), S.A. Dange has mentioned that the Brahmins were reduced to the status of Untouchables under the following circumstances:

> In places where there was famine and drought, the proud ruling class Brahmins turned to the hated chandalas in their forest retreat to ask for food, and it had become the privilege of conquered enslaved chandalas, to preach morality to the holy vishwamitra of the conquering Aryas not to resort to eating the carcass of a dead dog to preserve his own life (quoted by Borale, 1968: 61).

Other studies (Borale, 1968; Fuchs, 1981; Tripathy, 1994) have also revealed that degradation is not just a recent phenomenon in India but was also present in ancient times. The predominance of the ritual pollution and purity in social and religious life, which were characteristics of the traditional society, introduced an element of degradation. Of this system, Tripathy writes:

> Gradually as the Hindu varna system grew fashionable, strong strict measures were adopted to enforce it. Social inter-course and intermarriage were prohibited. Society became strictly endogamous and was devided into water tight compartments. Those who violated the law of endogamy were excommunicated and were forced to live outside the community. In consequence they had no option other than the low and degrading occupations (Tripathy, 1994: 7).

To the question why upper-caste people were degraded in traditional society, Tripathy answers: 'In puranic period, i.e., 3rd century A.D. to 1000 A.D., due to certain economic forces the people belonging to the higher castes indulged in lower occupations and naturally they were declared as outcastes and once they lost their position it was not possible for them to regain it' (Tripathy, 1994: 4).

Thus, it is evident that there are several factors to explain why these groups of people became Untouchables. One of the most important factors was ritual purity and pollution. This has been supported by Haimendorf when he says: 'The reasons put forward as to why these particular upper castes become untouchables, is usually that of ritual purity and pollution. The untouchables are ritually impure because they follow an unclean profession or vice-versa' (quoted by Mukherjee, 1988: 13). It is clear that such changes have been taking place right from the Vedic times; the process known as *asprashyeekaran* in the contemporary socioreligious realities existed in traditional India as well.

The Impact of Muslim Invaders and Rulers of India: Historicity of *Asprashyeekaran*

We have attempted to understand degradation by considering the traditional value system, namely the Brahminical viewpoint. We should probe further than Sanskrit literature alone. We have, therefore, made maximum use of historical findings. In Indian history, foreign invasions, local waves of conquest, famines, epidemics, floods and other natural and manmade calamities added to the number of Untouchables. Due to this, a new era of social degradation began. During the course of centuries, degradation of high-caste Hindus increased all over India. This degradation was fairly common and presents some curious features. There were interesting developments which show that Hindu society had reached the crossroads. It will suffice to quote here some historical instances and authoritative comments in order to show that high-caste persons were reduced to Untouchables at the beginning of the Muslim and British era.

S.V. Ketkar (1909: 108), analysing the caste system and social life of the people in India during the third century, found that a person could not go into a higher caste but could move down from high status. He could lose his caste status and mingle with persons of the lower castes. He further says, there are many castes who suffered in status on account of their mixing with the low castes or neglect of sacred rituals. Ketkar's statement indicates that *asprashyeekaran* is not just a recent phenomenon in India. On the contrary, it was present during all the ages of Indian history.

From the very day when India became a target of Muslim invaders, its people began to be enslaved in droves to be sold in foreign lands or employed in various menial or lowly jobs within the country. Indeed, from the days of Muhammad bin Qasim in the 8th century to those of Ahmad Shah Abdali in the 18th century A.D., enslavement, distribution and sale of Hindu prisoners was systematically practised by Muslim invaders and rulers of India. In these years and centuries of oppression, such prisoners were reduced to the position of Untouchable castes. We get the following account of the degradation of Rajputs, Zamindars, peasants, etc., during the medieval era in *Muslim Slave System in Medieval India:*

> To be brief, many Zamindars and peasants escaped into the forests because of fear of defeat and enslavement, but in course of time they were reduced to the position of Scheduled Castes, Scheduled Tribes and Backward Classes. For example, many Parihars and Parmars, once belonged to the proud Rajput castes, are now included in the lower castes. So are the 'Rajputs' counted as Backward classes in South India. Take the case of the Thaaru women in the Tarai region as described by Hugh and Colleen Gantzer (Lal, 1968: 64).

To the question, how the Untouchable population increased all over India, Lal answers:

> One has to travel through the country like Hugh and Colleen Gantzer to meet such types, almost everywhere. Today, the SC/ST and OBC (Other Backward classes) account for 50 per cent of the population of India. This staggering high figure has been reached because of the historical forces operating in the medieval times. Muslim rule spread all over the country and resistance to it by Hindus also remained widespread. Jungles abounded throughout the vast land from Gujarat to Bengal and Kashmir to Kanyakumari and flight into them was the safeguard. That is how SC/ST people are found in every state in large numbers (Lal, 1968: 66).

A review of the position of slaves in neighbouring countries—Nepal and Bhutan for instance —from a historical perspective reveals that they are counted among the Untouchables. Das writes; 'Slaves doing impure work gradually merged in the chandalas. Descendants of slaves in Nepal and Bhutan are counted among the untouchables' (Bhagwan Das, 1995: 78).

Thus, a potent source of degradation in pre-British India was demotion of the defeated warrior castes into low Untouchable castes. Such a situation was not limited to any particular part of India, but characterised the system everywhere. In order to humiliate the captives, they were employed in despised occupations like sweeping, latrine cleaning, tanning, shoemaking, weaving, washing clothes, etc. Once they accepted these unclean occupations, they were no longer accepted by their castemen. The captive groups then had to socialise their ritual and style of life and be known as Untouchable castes.

A few studies and reports which have been undertaken to study this process tend to substantiate this trend of *asprashyeekaran*. The origin of the Bhangi caste is described by Pathak as follows:

> The Muslims had brought with them some women who used the Burqua (veil) to cover their faces and they did not like to defecate in the open. The bucket privies were, therefore, designed

> and constructed for their defecation in Purdah. Those made captives were forced to clean latrines like bucket privies. After those captives were released, they were not accepted by their castemen and, hence, they formed a separate caste of Bhangis who were renamed as Mehtar by Emperor Akbar (Pathak, 1991:38).

Similarly, according to Chaturvedi (1990: 9), Kshatriyas and Bhangis have descended from the same source. For, he says, one notices a marked similarity between them.

A type of Sanskritisation started with the census operations in the last quarter of the 19th century. In some sections, the census was considered to be an excellent opportunity for improvement of a caste's social standing. On the other hand, Mead and Macgregor, O'Malley (Pathak, 1991: 38), Desai (1911) and others have referred to the process of *asprashye-ekaran* in census reports. It was natural for an ICS ethnographer to be struck by this peculiar social phenomenon. There was a separate account of degradation in the census reports. The merger of upper castes into lower castes was termed 'degradation' or 'admission of outsiders into lower castes'.

Some idea of social degradation, change of identity and admission of higher castes into lower castes may be obtained from the following statement given by O'Malley in the Census of India (1911; Bengal, Bihar, Orissa and Sikkim) about the Bhangi caste of India. LSS O'Malley writes: 'Obviously, the castes engaged in the disposal of human excreta were not at all divergent of a single caste' (quoted by Pathak, 1991: 38). Regarding the same problem Stanley Rice writes: 'Therefore, not only Kshatriyas, but also those who were engaged in cleaning night soil since ancient time ... and also those who were made captives in wars... in India... are Bhangis and Mehtars of today'.

This has also been realised by Malkani, who writes: 'The Bhangis of today are those people who were warriors made captives after they fell to the enemy'(1961: 27).

If these views of scholars are accepted, we can draw the conclusion that the Bhangis were at one time Kshatriyas.

Processes identical to those mentioned above have also been pointed out by Ghanshyam Shah, Jwala Prasad Misra and Kesington. A reference to social degradation of Rajputs in Gujarat in the 16th and 18th centuries during the Mughal period quoted from the *Gazetteer of the Bombay Presidency*, 1879, by Ghanshyam Shah says: '...during the Mughal period, Bhils gave asylum to some defeated Rajput rulers. During their stay, the guests married their host's daughters. Therefore, their generation, a mixture of Bhils and Rajputs, is considered as half caste called Kolis' (1971: 10).

Misra reports a similar case of degradation of Rajputs to a low Untouchable caste in Orissa. He writes:

> In 1272 during the Thirteenth century (Samvat 1284) Mohd. Gaznavi attacked on 'Anhalwada' Gujarat. Chandra Rao was the ruler, Chandra Rao was badly defeated by Gaznavi. Even then, Gaznavi continued his attacks. Under these socio-political conditions the defeated Solankis had to move to some other places. In Orissa they were settled down permanently near the historical temple - Jagannath. The Jagannath area of the Orissa was known for its making of cotton cloth. The stranded people were forced to take to weaving occupation as a means of earning their livelihood. In course of time, 'Solanki Rajputs assumed a new low caste designation 'weaver' (an untouchable caste) and the original caste name 'Rajput' disappeared in practice (Misra, 1839: 200).

We get the following account of the degradation of Rajputs in the Hoshiarpur district, Punjab, in a report by Kesington, published under the authority of the Punjab government, 1883: 'Ethnologically the most interesting of the people are the Mahtons, who were originally Rajputs, but have long since degraded in social scale owing to their customs of making Karewa marriages with widows' (*Gazetteer of Hoshiarpur District*, 1883-84: 60).

Many similar instances could be produced from the studies of sociologists, historians and ethnographers published on various aspects of caste; these studies substantiate the process of *asprashyeekaran*.

Breach of Traditional Norms and *Asprashyeekaran*

Various ways in which higher-caste Hindus were degraded to low Untouchable castes of traditional Indian society are highlighted here. The point is given emphasis that within the traditional system there was an increase in the Untouchable population.

The laws framed by Brahmin law givers like Manu, Narada, Vasistha, Yajnavalkya were strictly enforced by Hindu rulers who ruled through caste and village heads. Even persons who had taken water from the hands of certain discarded persons lost caste status. Ghanshyam Shah quoting from the *Gazetteer of the Bombay Presidency*. 1879, refers to such an instances of *asprashyeekaran* in the Bombay Presidency. He writes: 'those Rajputs who had taken water from the hands of Bhil women in Gujarat, had been out caste and lost caste status'.

Even the touch of an Untouchable caste person caused degradation. Quoting Barbosa on this point, Hutton writes: '...a woman touched by a pulayan, i.e. of the lowest untouchable caste, was out caste for life and had to leave her house, for fear otherwise of polluting her family' (Hutton, 1951: 78). Such instances are quite common in Indian society, and it is presumed that no caste would be an exception to this rule.

The association of higher-caste Hindus with Muslims lowered their prestige, position and caste status. In some cases it also led to their being outcaste and eventually merging with Untouchable groups. Throughout the Muslim regime, Hindus continued to suffer from the disabilities and difficulties imposed in the name of the dharmic law (religious law). These practices of the upper-caste Hindus led to an increase in the Untouchable population all over India. Bhagwan Das summarises the causes for this rapid growth as follows:

> After the fall of Buddhism, those who continued to follow their religion were also treated as untouchables. Any Hindu associating freely with Muslims was also considered an outcaste and joined the ranks of lower castes and untouchables. Wars, famines, epidemics, floods and other natural and man-made calamities added to the number of untouchables (Das, 1995:46).

We learn from Chhote Lal Sharma's book, *Jati Anvensan* (1971 [1914]) that when the Brahmins of central India breached the sacred rituals, rites and deeds, their actions roused the wrath of the entire Brahmin community. In Madhya Pradesh and Maharashtra, for instance, the Brahmins breached the code of Manu which resulted in outcasting. The outcaste Brahmins were known as 'Kalanki Brahmins' (Sharma, 1971: 156). They had no connection with the parent caste and formed a new separate lower caste of their own. In this connection, one scholar has described eight possible reasons for degradation. The eight reasons are as follows:

1. Mingled with untouchable castes.
2. Received offering made at public places of all castes—high and low.
3. Took alms from prohibited castes.
4. On the suspicion that a new-born child was the result of illicit relation with a Muslim.
5. Engaged in degraded low occupations (Sharma, 1971: 156-7).
6. On committing heinous crime.
7. On suspicion about the caste origin of new born child or born by rape.
8. Solely engaged in the cultivation of heinous agriculture product and plantation.

These instances support the view that degradation to lower castes was caused by the cultural rigidity of the caste system. A major cause behind degradation, therefore, might have been the violation of social and religious norms, though there might also be other factors like economic constraints and crisis, etc. However, the groups degraded were from upper castes for whom the psychological appeal of belonging to the upper strata of society must have been very strong. The main structural deprivations here were those of the rights and liberties against the dharmic law (religious law). In all traditional societies where the system of social stratification is closed and there are legitimate structural means to move down in the social hierarchy, the breach of norms or of customs and rituals could lead to such a move downwards.

With some variation, the process of *asprashyeekaran* continued during the British rule. Even today we may observe the process in Indian society. In Gujarat, Audhich and Nagar Brahmins are cases of *asprashyeekaran*. Govind Bhai H. Desai (1911: 245), the then Superintendent of Census Operations, Baroda, observed that Parajia Brahmins were originally Audhich Brahmins and were living in a village known as Ismaliya. Later on they moved to another village, namely, Paroj near Junagarh. Here they became the priests of Ahirs and Charans. Not only this, they started eating with them, which was totally antithetical to their own group. As a result, the Parajia Audhich Brahmins were degraded. In course of time they became a distinct 'endogamous group'.

Of the Nagar Brahmins, Desai (1911: 245) writes that they accepted low-caste occupations like acting as fiddlers of female singers. The norms of not allowing the Brahmins to do polluted and degrading work resulted in the lowering of high social position of Nagar Brahmins. They were reduced to the status of musicians (Untouchables) and segregated from the Nagar caste. In this connection the observation of M.N. Srinivas may be noted: '...throughout history of caste new caste groups arose as a result of such fission from the parent group body' (1977: 30).

Sharma's and Desai's studies illustrate the degradation which occurred in the social position of the Brahmins when they breached the mores, rituals and beliefs of their own groups. Socio-religious factors were responsible for the degradation of a large number of Brahmins in Madhya Pradesh, Maharashtra and Gujarat to Untouchable castes—as had happened among Bhangis, Balahis, Meghwals, Bairwas and so on.

Historically, socio-culturally and nominalistically a caste has its own image and identity on the basis of which it considers itself distinct from other castes. It tenaciously sticks to and justifies this identity in spite of various changes taking place. It is this sense of identity which is the basis for survival of the caste. However, during times of hardship, distress and economic crisis, caste members may be forced to do unpleasant work. The Rajasthani Gancha from Nagpur, Didwana, Ajmer and Pushkar (all in Rajasthan), for instance, are another case of Bhangiisation. As degraded Bhangis (Untouchables), they offer a unique example in Rajasthan. In this connection, when we talked to some of the old Gancha Bhangi informants about their conversion, they narrated that nearly four or five centuries ago their forefathers converted themselves to the Bhangi caste. They were originally Gancha by caste and their main traditional occupation was to prepare baskets and other domestic articles from bamboo. Among the major problems of the Gancha, special mention may be made of their poor earning from the traditional occupation which seems to be too small to maintain a family of five or six persons. This was one of the most serious problems which their forefathers faced. Thus, they were forced by economic constraints to do dirty, unpleasant, polluted and degrading work like scavenging. As a result of this, they were reduced to the status of Bhangis. In course of time, they became a distinct endogamous caste group. At present, along with Bhangis, the Gancha Bhangis, both men and women, are employed in various Nagar Palikas of Rajasthan state. They are engaged to sweep and clean roads and drainages. They are also engaged privately to remove garbage and to clean latrines.

Gancha Bhangis are not found at all in many towns and are very few in other towns such as Nagaur, Didwana, Ajmer and Pushkar (all in Rajasthan). According to the 1971 Census (No.36: 2), the population of Gancha Bhangis in Rajasthan was 2,076. The Gancha Bhangis and their family members are treated as Bhangis by caste-Hindus and non-Hindus. They are not allowed to sit, dine or mix with clean caste or occupational groups. The Gancha Bhangis do not have social interaction with their Bhangi counterparts except at the job site. They do not invite the Bhangis on the occasion of marriage, festivals, etc., nor are they invited on such occasions by Bhangis. The Gancha Bhangis do not eat from the hands of the Bhangis but the Bhangis eat from their hands. Nor have the Gancha Bhangis developed any socially recognised commensal relation with Bhangis. This situation has led to occasional quarrels among them. We have heard and also observed such situations minutely and have found that Gancha Bhangis demonstrate a sense of superiority although they are in a minority. We think this prevailing situation of conflict among the Bhangis and Gancha Bhangis is unique and needs a detailed scientific study for a full picture of their cultural complexities. Not only the Gancha caste, but even tribals have engaged in sweeping roads, etc. The tribes were formerly not connected at all with cleaning the roads and drainage, as the description of tribals in anthropological literature shows. Jha (1994: 3-9) supplies some important information about the 'tribal scavengers' in Bihar, where different categories of tribal groups sweep and clean the roads. From that we may be able to find out why they accepted this lowest work. The city of Ranchi was a small tribal village before 1834. After the establishment of the British administration, Christian missionaries came to India; in 1845, they arrived in Ranchi and in less than 50 years turned it into the Cathedral

Headquarters of Christian churches. The history of Ranchi city took a new turn when the Ranchi municipality was established in 1869. It is important to mention here that the forefathers of the Bhangis of Ranchi came from Rajasthan along with their masters and settled down here along with them. They had been brought by their masters to serve at their houses, clean the night-soil and remove the garbage from the streets and courtyards. This is why when the Ranchi municipality was established in 1869, there was not a single Bhangi in the municipality. In 1883, some of the migrated Rajasthani Bhangis were employed as scavengers to carry the night-soil and to clean service latrines. In the meantime, the government agencies wanted to appoint tribal men and women to work as scavengers in the government offices as well as in Ranchi municipality, but the tribals refused to serve as Bhangis or Mehtars to carry night-soil. Thus adivasis maintained a social distance from Rajasthani Bhangis and considered themselves above them. But, the situation took a new rum after India's Independence when some adivasis were appointed by the Ranchi Municipal Corporation to clean drainage and roads. Jha, describing the Ranchi municipality and the problems of the Bhangis in Ranchi, Chotanagpur found that: 'It is very interesting to note that being a tribal city, located in the midst of tribal population of Chotanagpur the strength of the tribal scavengers is Kanchi Municipal Corporation presently is only 227 out of 661 scavengers' (Lal and Sinha, 1995).

Unemployment among both educated and uneducated Indian youth, overgrowth of population, economic crisis, hardships and constraints, the limited number of job opportunities in government sectors, are all significant factors in contribution to a decline in the prestige of purely traditional occupations. Similar conditions exist in other developing countries but what is unique to the Indian situation is that all those higher caste/tribes, who have accepted scavenging jobs as the primary source of their income, for instance, adivasis of Bihar, are poor and their condition is hardly better than that of the Bhangis. A scavenging job provides not only a source of livelihood but economic security also. It would be significant to add here that in sweeping work particularly, no skill is required and this appears to have attracted the tribals, other backward classes and higher-caste Hindus to accept this work in Nagar Palikas, railways and some other government organisations (Lal, 1992a: 273-83).

From the above instances the picture that emerges is that *asprashyeekaran* has been a major process of social change in Indian history and it has occurred in every part of the Indian subcontinent. It may have been more active at some periods than at others and some castes are more affected than others, but there is no doubt that the process has been universal.

REFERENCES

Census of India (1911), *Bengal Volume III, part 2; Bihar Volume III, part 3: Orissa Volume III, part 15. Sikkim Volume III. part 18.* Calcutta: Manager of Publications. Government Press.

Census of India (1971), *Rajasthan Series No. 18. Rajasthan Part V. Special Tables and Notes on Scheduled Castes and Tribes.* No. 36. New Delhi: Government of India.

Chaturvedi, D.D. (1990), *Ancient India: An Introductory Outline*, New Delhi: Manohar.

Dange, S.A. (1949), *India from Primitive Communism to Slavery.* Bombay: Asia Publishing House.

Das, Bhagwan (1995), 'Socio-economic Problems of Dalits', in Bhagwan Das and James Massey (eds), *Dalit Solidarity.* Delhi: ISPCK.

Desai, Govind Bhai H. (1911), *Census of India.* Vol. XVI, *Baroda, Part I. Report.* Bombay: Bombay Presidency.

Fuchs, Stephen (1981), *At the Bottom of Indian Society.* New Delhi: Munshiram Manoharlal.

Gazetteer of Hoshiarpur District 1883-84. *Tribes and Castes.* Compiled and published under the Authority of Punjab Government, Lahore. The Civil and Military Gazetteers Press. Chapter III. by D. Mahtons.

Hutton, J.H. (1951), *Caste in India* (Second edition). London: Oxford University Press.

Jha, M. (1994), 'Problems of Scavengers in a Tribal City: A Case study of Ranchi, Chotanagpur', *Man in Asia* 2: 3-9.

Ketkar, S.V. (1909), *The History of Caste in India.* Vol. I. Ithaca: Messers Taylor and Carpentar.

Lal, A.K. and A.N. Sinha (1995), *Letter to Shyam Lal from A.K. Lal and A.N. Sinha.* Patna: Institute Studies.

Lal, K.S. (1968), *Muslim Slave System in Medieval India.* New Delhi: Aditya Prakashan.

Lal, Shyam (1991), 'Origin of the Bhangis: A Hypothesis', *Eastern Anthropologist* (2): 83-98.

Malkani, N.R. (1961), *Report of the Scavenging Conditions Enquiry Committee.* Delhi: Ministry of Home Affairs, Government of India.

Mukherjee, Prabhati (1988), *Beyond the Four Varna: The Untouchables in India.* Delhi: Motilal Banarsidass.

Nagar, Amritlal (1990), *Nachyo Bahut Gopal.* Delhi: Rajpal and Sons.

Pathak, Bindeshwar (1991), *Road to freedom. A Sociological Study on the Abolition of Scavenging in India.* New Delhi: Motilal Banarsidass.

Shah, Ghanshyam (1971), *Caste Association and Political Process in Gujarat.* Bombay Popular Prakashan.

Sharma, Srotriya C.L. (1971), *Jati Anvensan.* Part I. Phulera: H.D.V.V. Mandal, Samvat.

Srinivas, M.N. (1977), *Social Change in Modern India.* New Delhi: Orient Longman.

Tripathy, R.B. (1994), *Dalits: A Sub-Hitman Society.* New Delhi: Ashish Publishing House.

[This chapter is based on the article of Shri Shyam Lal. We owe gratitude to him.—Ed.]

6

Harijan Sevak Sangh

Gandhi's constructive programme was devoted to social reform and development of the backward communities. His aim was to regenerate a new spirit, a new thinking and self-reliance amongst the Harijans. This kind of feeling, he believed, would greatly enhance their prestige and self-respect. They could raise their heads by becoming economically stronger by hard work and incessant labour.

It was made clear at numerous meetings and through his writings that untouchability was a cruel and inhuman institution. It always violated human dignity by compelling untouchables to do work which was unclean and degrading. It was opined that untouchability was against the spirit of democracy which made no distinction among citizens of a free country. It also raises economic problems. The untouchables were the poorest section of Indian society. Their avenues of employment were strictly limited. They lived apart, in unhygienic surroundings, on the outskirts of villages and cities. Though they were Hindus and believed in and worshipped Hindu gods and godesses, they were not allowed to enter Hindu temples. Public institutions like schools, hostels, etc., were closed to them.

To boost up the work for the upliftment of Harijans, Gandhi laid the foundation of the Harijan Sevak Sangh. Its main function was the removal of all such disabilities which hampered the progress and development of Harijans. As it consisted of dedicated workers it did remarkable work. So far so, Gandhi brought a Harijan family in the Ashram and he adopted their daughter as his own. He also offered his blessings on the eve of marriages which were celebrated between Harijans and Caste Hindus. A few such marriages were celebrated in his own Ashram.

In an article on 'Task before Harijan Sevaks', Gandhi stated that the growing number of reformers should be active in the execution of various programmes and should not sit still. Rather they should demonstrate that change by their visible conduct. He was sure that the change to full self-reliance would never come unless all the workers realised that this was essentially a religious movement. He opined that propaganda among Caste Hindus could only be successfully carried out by influential persons with a remarkable capacity in them.

Though I have concurred in the policy of centralisation I have always desired, as I have no doubt the Board too has desired, decentralisation at the first opportunity. But that could only be done when the Provincial Boards were ready and able to raise their own funds, I would love nothing so much as that every village had its Harijan Board and was able to find its own funds. When that day comes, it will also be one of complete abolition of untouchability in every shape and form. For the present it has to be unfortunately admitted that the cause is still led by a handful of earnest reformers scattered all over the country. Not all of them are able to raise funds locally nor are they all sure of the policy to be followed. I use the word policy deliberately. For while everyone knows the goal, even-one does not know the grave limitations under which the reformer labours. The slightest error of judgment, a hasty action or a hasty word may put back the hands of the clock of progress. Policies have, therefore, to be cautiously evolved in the light of experiences daily gained by the few who have no other thought but that of serving Harijans and riding Hinduism of its greatest blot.

Ever since the inauguration of the Harijan Sevak Sangh, the central organisation has been feeling, every properly, the provincial branches. But the time has certainly arrived for the branches to stand on their own and be self-sustained even though it may be at the sacrifice of a part of their programme. The work in each province, and for that matter in each district or taluka, should be an unequivocal demonstration of active Savarna support. For the chief mission of the Sangh is to touch the Savarna heart and change it. Supposing the central organisation had collected from two or three reformers a crore of rupees, and with it established branches all over India to cover it with schools and hostels for Harijan boys and girls, it would not have hastened the day of the doom of untouchability. For the Savarna heart would remain as stony as ever. Supposing conversely that without cost of a single pice, by some stroke, of good fortune, the Savarna heart was changed and untouchability became a thing of the past, the whole object the Sangh would be fulfilled. For in that case every public school, place of worship and other institutions would be open to Harijans precisely on the same terms as to Caste Hindus. That day may be far off or much nearer than many people expect. Anyway that is the goal of the Harijan Sevak Sangh, and never the opening of separate schools, wells, temples and the like for Harijans and consequent perpetuation of untouchability. At present these things are undoubtedly done, but they are done only as a means to the end. They have become necessary because the Savarna heart is slow to change.

The growing number of reformers must not sit still and make protestations of removal of untouchability from themselves. They must demonstrate that change by their visible conduct. The spending of their purse for the Harijan cause is a tangible proof of the change and, therefore, an essential part of the programme. But immediately it becomes a corner confined to a few individuals who salve their conscience by liberal donations, it ceases to be a token in the manner indicated by me. Hence it becomes a matter of duty for the Central Board to invite the attention of the branches to this fundamental part of the programme and for the branches to appreciate it and prepare the way to becoming wholly self-reliant. Indeed the burden has been progressively thrown on provincial boards of financing their own institutions. But the time has come for definite and decisive action in the direction.

This change to full self-reliance will never come unless all the workers realise that this is essentially a religious movement. We are a nation spending lavishly for causes which the masses believe to be religious. One has only to go the places of pilgrimage to have an ocular demonstration of the fact. A study of the history of religious endowments will reveal the tragic story of fortunes being entrusted to them by credulous millions without ever caring to know-how they were spent. It is enough for people to believe that they pay their mite to a cause which in their opinion is religious. Harijan workers have a cause that is wholly religious in the best sense of the term. If they have a living faith in it, if they do not move mountains, they will at least get from their surroundings enough for the institutions in their charge.

The Harijan Sevak Sangh is looked upon as a part of the Congress. But very few Congressmen are Harijan workers. Why?

Ans. The Sangh is not a part of the Congress. It was the outcome of the fast I undertook in 1932 when I was in jail. The meeting of Hindus drawn from every class, which was held under the Presidentship of Pandit Malaviyaji and which gave birth to the Sangh, deliberately decided to keep the organisation separate from the Congress and non-political. It was this quality of the Sangh that enabled Seth G.D. Birla to become its President and Shri Thakkar Bapa its Secretary. Nevertheless there are ought to be many Congressmen in the Sangh, because practically all reformers are drawn into the Congress fold. But it is true that there are plenty of non-

Congress persons in the Sangh. It is also true that those Congressmen who are only interested in politics do not come into it. It is, therefore, sometimes wrongly thought that Congressmen do not take an interest in the Sangh. It is the duty of every Congressman to remove untouchability, root and branch, from his life.

Harijan service has really developed into mere Harijan uplift. Practically no work is done among Caste Hindus for the removal of untouchability. What is the remedy for this?

Ans. Experience shows that propaganda among Caste Hindus can only be successfully carried out by influential persons whose words carries weight with the general public. Such persons are hard to find. But it is within the capacity of every Harijan worker to carry on mute propaganda. Our Caste Hindu workers are often satisfied with mere uplift work among the Harijans, which is not sufficient. Many workers, while they do not observe untouchability themselves, are unable even to convert their own families. How then can they influence the outside world? Moreover it is my confirmed opinion that every Harijan worker has to make a point to beg for even one pice for Harijans from those Caste Hindus with whom he comes in contact. If all devoted themselves, heart and soul, to this task, very good results would ensue.

Should not the Sangh take upon itself the service of those Harijans who have been converted to Christianity or Islam and are yet treated as untouchables? Are we not out to remove untouchability root and branch and, therefore, help all who come under its sway?

Ans. This question has already been answered in the columns of *Harijan* but must bear repetition so long as it is raised. The moment untouchability is utterly banished from Hindu society it will, *ipso facto,* disappear from elsewhere too. Whatever the merits or demerits of the case, it is clear that our interference with converts will be the cause of strife with Muslims and Christians. Such converts have either broken off all contacts with, or they have been in their turn boycotted by Hindus. They have thrown in their lot with other sects whose leaders will not allow them to maintain their old contacts. Hence the Harijan Sevak Sangh quite rightly decided from its inception to confine its area of work to Harijans who had not left the Hindu fold. A convert, having left his original fold, is no longer guided or controlled by it.

What should be the attitude of the Sangh, if Harijan boys wish to enlist in the army?

Ans. They should be allowed to do so. They may not be controlled by the Congress policy or Ahimsa. They must be given absolute freedom of choice.

Harijans are of opinion that Caste Hindus who are sympathetic to their cause should not use those temples where they are not allowed entry.

Ans. They are right. It is the bounden duty of Harijan workers not to go where Harijans are not allowed and likewise to dissuade Caste Hindus.

Harijans are legally entitled to send their children to many educational institutions as also to draw water from public wells. But public sentiment still militates against this being put into practice. Should Harijans resort to the law courts for justice in these matters or wait patiently until the Caste Hindus are converted?

Ans. Where there is no danger of violence being done to them, the Harijans should exercise their legal right and where necessary, resort to law courts. Harijan workers must continue agitation among Caste Hindus and not rest content with mere legal rights.

Is it not essential to reform the insanitary methods employed by sweepers for cleaning latrines and scavenging?

Ans. It is not necessary. What is more, until this is done the condition of sweepers will remain pitiable. To this end it is the duty of Harijan workers and Caste Hindus to do sweepers' work themselves. No Caste Hindu will employ the methods used by sweepers. He will do the work scientifically. For example, he will never remove excreta in a basket or carry it on his head; he will cover excreta with dry earth and remove it in a metal vessel. He will avoid touching dirt with his hands as far as possible; he will clean the vessel with water and a rod; he will bathe immediately after doing the work; he will wear special clothes when scavenging. These reforms do not cost much. They require intelligence, hard work, and love of an ideal. We may not relegate sweepers' work to one particular class. Therefore, all should learn it the same way as cooking. Each person should be his own sweeper. If this ideal were to be put into practice in society, the miserable condition of sweepers would at once be rectified.

The Harijan Sevak Sangh was mainly concerned with the welfare work. The members were also advised to organise unions or even induce hartals, not from political motives or for such purposes, but for bettering the social or economic position of Harijans. 'The Harijan Sevak Sangh, however, being a non-political organisation should never put expediency before its primary duty towards the Harijans.'

The Communist Party as successfully organised sweepers' unions and helped them to secure their rights through hartals, etc. But the Harijan Sevak Sangh's activities are confined mostly two welfare work. It cannot, therefore, successfully compete with the Communists for popularity among the Harijans. Don't you think that in view of this, the Harijan Sevak Sangh ought to alter its policy and method of work?

Ans. We must be guided in our policy by our sense of right, not by the lure of winning cheap popularity. If the Harijan Sevak Sangh is convinced that it is working on the right line, it will keep on to it, regardless of what others might or might not do. 'Thus we may organise unions or even induce *hartals,* not from political motives or for such purposes, but for bettering the social or economic position of Harijans.

The feeling is gaining ground among the Harijans that the Congress is showing more solicitude for Muslim demands than for the just rights of the Harijans. What have you to say to it?

Ans. The Congress being a political organisation is likely to be more susceptible to political pressure, which the Muslims are in a far stronger position to exert than the Harijans. If it succumbs to that pressure, it will pay the price for it. The Harijan Sevak Sangh, however, being a non-political organisation should never put expediency before its primary duty towards the Harijans.

Would you advise the so-called Savarna Hindus to start, even under the present circumstances an agitation in selected places for securing elementary civic and social rights for the Harijans? Would you for this purpose advise the Harijan Sevak Sangh to organise Satyagraha against the Savarna Hindus if necessary?

Ans. I would not advise the Sangh as an organisation to offer Satyagraha against the Savarna Hindus, but I would certainly not only advise but expect members of the Sangh in their individual capacity to organise such Satyagraha in their respective places. I shall certainly support any such move on their part if it is undertaken in the proper spirit. It is their duty.

Would you, in the absence of popular Governments in the provinces, advise the Sangh to carry on a vigorous and energetic programme of temple entry for Harijans?

Ans. I could. I understand it is being done even at present but at a rather slow pace. I would certainly like its tempo to be stepped up.

Should not the Harijan Sevak Sangh try to secure for the Harijans political power by demanding due representation for them on Grama Panchayats, municipalities and Legislatures?

Ans. Certainly it ought to. No effort can be too great for it.

Should not the Sangh give instructions in the essentials of Hindu religion in the Harijan hostels and in Harijan gatherings of adults?

Ans. It ought to be the primary duty of the Sangh to give to Harijan children and adults a grounding in the essentials of Hindu religion. If they were brought up in ignorance of these, they would not continue to remain in the Hindu fold, and the responsibility for it would rest on those who had failed to give them the necessary instructions.

Shri Sitaram Shastri of Vinaya Ashram, Guntur, asked whether the Sangh ought not to specially train a body of missionaries to carry on propaganda work among the Savarna Hindus. He was prepared to start a training centre for that purpose in his Ashram if he were given adequate help.

Gandhiji, however, had grave doubts as to the practicability of the suggestion. In fact the question had actually been raised by Shri Ghanashyamdas Birla several years ago and dropped after full discussion. He would be quite satisfied if at least the members of the Sangh would fully come up to the ideal.

Gandhiji was next asked: "Ought not we to set up a precedent for having Harijan representatives in the Sangh or at least one member in the Executive Committee of the Sangh?" In reply he referred to the history of the birth of the Harijan Sevak Sangh at the conclusion of the Poona Pact, which resulted in the modification of the decision of the MacDonald Government, on the question of the representation of the minorities. 'It was felt that if the rot was to be effectively stopped Hinduism ought to be completely rid of the curse of untouchability. This called for a real change of heart and repentance for its past sins on the part of Hindu society. It was to that end that the Harijan Sevak Sangh was formed.

"I am, therefore, opposed to both the propositions," proceeded Gandhiji. "I know that under the present arrangement some Harijans are included in the Board of the Sangh. But this was a concession to Thakkar Bapa's weakness. I have described the Harijan Sevak Sangh as an organisation of penitent sinners. Its object is to call upon the so-called Savarna Hindus to do expiation for having harboured untouchability. The inclusion of a Harijan in the Sangh would be mere eye-wash and make-believe, as his would be a mere voice in the wilderness. Before long, he would himself heartily wish to be out of it. I say this from my personal experience of the way in which committees function. I know the Sangh cannot always keep up to the mark. It is, of course, open to the Sangh to alter its scope and give Harijans a majority in its Executive Committee or appoint a competent body of representative Harijans to act as a Board of Advisors and Supervisors and keep the Sangh on the alert and on the right track."

Gandhiji was next asked to give his opinion on the recent work in the Gwalior State to enlist the services of the Sadhu community in the cause of Harijan uplift. Gandhiji replying said he had grave doubts to the correctness or advisability of the step. It seemed to him to smack of politics. He would welcome the assistance of true Sadhus, if it was available. But he confessed, he looked in vain in the country for Sadhus of his conception. Such Sadhus as he saw disappointed him. There might be here and there honourable exceptions and their help would be welcome. But he was frankly sceptical of the possibility of utilising Sadhus as a body for their work. Even if they tried the experiment, he was afraid they would come to the parting of the ways before long.

Another friend asked whether a portion of the Kasturba Memorial Trust Fund ought not to be earmarked for Harijan sisters. Gandhiji's reply was that they could have the whole of it if they could show the capacity to utilise it. No special earmarking of a part was, therefore, necessary.

The questions and answers finished, Gandhiji addressed a few general remarks to those assembled to give his diagnosis of the relative sluggishness of the Harijan Sevak Sangh's activities and his remedy for the same. "I am responsible for the policy of conducting Harijan uplift work through the agency of the Savarna Hindus. They had to do expiation. All of them, I argued to myself, could help with money even if they could not, owing to lack of necessary qualifications, render direct service. For instance, they might not be able themselves to do teaching work, but they could engage a competent teacher to give education to Harijan children. That would be one way of doing expiation. They would be able to penetrate Harijan society and help in its progress." He knew there were sceptical critics, who questioned whether this kind of work could lead to the eradication of untouchability. He himself was at one time among the doubters. But he had since realised his mistake. He owed a debt of gratitude in this respect to the late Shri Devdhar, at whose activity he had at one time looked askance and which he had even criticised. A year's experience, however, had cured him of his conceit and taught him humility. He realised that if he confined himself exclusively to doing propaganda among the Savarna Hindus with a view to their conversion, he might have to wait till the Greek Kalends and in the meantime the actual uplift work among the Harijans would remain hopelessly bogged. His own experience has since convinced him that if they could only have sufficient workers with the requisite purity and devotion and spirit of sacrifice to work among Harijans, untouchability would become a thing of the past, even if the Savarna Hindus were left severely alone. But that would mean that they must become Harijans at heart and live and labour among the Harijans as Harijans. "But can the members of the Harijan Sevak Sangh truthfully claim to have eradicated the last trace of untouchability from their own hearts? Are their professions altogether on a par with their practice?" he asked.

A member asked as to what his criterion was in that respect. "Are you married?" questioned Gandhiji in return. "I happen to be", replied the puzzled interlocutor. "Then have you an unmarried daughter?" resumed Gandhiji. "If you have, get for her a Harijan bridegroom not to satisfy her lust but in a purely religious spirit and I shall send you a wire of congratulations at my expense."

"You will now realise," continued Gandhiji, " why the Harijan Sevaks are unable to move the hearts of the Savarna Hindus. The reason is that they have not that fire of faith in their hearts, impatient hunger for service which is the first essential for an effective appeal. Let but a handful of Savarna Hindus go forth in that true missionary spirit and they will leaven the entire Hindu mass. But not even a whole army of missionaries so-called will produce any effect upon them." It needed a Malaviyaji to make such a missionary. He (Gandhiji) could not convert his own sister. And if he could not, argued he, how could he blame others? That would show how hard and thorny was that path. It was, however, open to them if they felt that they had the necessary qualification, to try the experiment for themselves in their locality.

The reason for this partial failure, Gandhiji proceeded to explain, was also that the approach of most of the members of the Harijan Sevak Sangh to their mission was not unmixed with political motives. If they really wanted to penetrate the hearts of Savarna Hindus, they ought to be filled with a purely religious spirit. Mere dialectics was a poor weapon for this kind of work. As it was, they were too much weighed down by inertia, heedlessness and woodenness of mind.

"The other method is more fierce and not altogether free from danger," continued Gandhiji. "It is the method of fasting." He himself had before condemned fasting when it seemed to him to be wrong or morally unjustified. But to shirk a fast when there was a clear moral indication was a dereliction from duty. Such a fast had to be based on unadulterated Truth and Ahimsa.

The creation of Harijan Boards was suggested and the qualifications of members were laid down. Only those who were to show sincerity, deep interest and honesty of purpose were to be enrolled as members. The member should have firm belief for the removal of untouchability from its roots. He should serve the Harijans in numerous ways.

What should be the qualifications of members of Harijan Boards and what should be the number constituting them are the questions often asked. Only those will be included who are eager to serve the cause and whose presence will promote the usefulness of the Board to which they belong and whose capacity for service will be increased by their being members of a Board.

No one should allow himself or herself to be a member of a Board unless he or she:

1. believes in the uttermost removal of untouchability;
2. pays something to the Board according to his or her capacity;
3. does some definite Harijan service, e.g., having a Harijan in his or her home as a member of the family, or at least as a domestic servant, or his teaching a Harijan or Harijans, or paying a regular visit to Harijan quarters and cleaning them, or, if he or she is a doctor, treating Harijan patients free of charge, etc.;
4. sends to the Board a diary containing a record of his or her service from month to month.

If some such conditions are observed, there need be no restriction on the number of members. The more, the merrier. Such Boards will meet to take notes, exchange experiences and solve mutual difficulties. They will never waste time in fruitless discussions.

There may be Advisory Committees attached to the Boards. These will lay down for themselves some minimum qualifications. Naturally the qualifications of Advisors will be less stringent than those of members of regular Boards.

What if members with the qualifications I have described cannot be found is the natural question arising from the bare mention of them. I must repeat the answer I have given often enough before now. The persons invited by the Central Board to form Sanghs in their own provinces will, in the absence of members having the necessary qualifications, perform the service through agents. "Act True" must be the motto of every Harijan Board, and there should never be any departure from the wholesome maxim.

The sense of unanimity should prevail among the members of the Advisory Committee of Harijans. The factions and divisions should be avoided and 'Let there be no quarrels among you'.

Gandhiji had suggested the formation of Advisory Committees of Harijans to assist Harijan Sevak Sangh Boards consisting of Caste Hindus. When asked for guidance in this matter by a Harijan correspondent, Gandhiji replied:

'I should suggest the formation of compact, small representative Committees who would truly represent the opinion of local Harijans. They would frame rules for the conduct of their proceedings and formulate their expectations of Savarna Hindus and generally watch the proceedings of Harijan Boards. These Advisory Committees, wherever they are formed, would advise Harijan Boards of their existence and show their preparedness to help the latter. If the Boards are sincere in their desire to discharge their debt, that is, to serve Harijans, they will establish the friendliest contact with the Advisory Committees, and perfect co-operation and harmony will prevail. There may be friction in the beginning because of mutual suspicion. Harijan Boards, being naturally better organised and better off in every respect, will have to exercise tact in handling what may appear to be extravagant demands. Advisory Committees would endeavour to be considerate. The more considerate they are, the better able they will be to help themselves. From their ability to conduct themselves in a dignified manner, they will learn the art of asserting themselves if the occasion ever arises. For they should know that Savarna Hindus will never be able to discharge their debt except with the co-operation of Harijans. But the question of asserting themselves does not arise just yet, because the vast mass of Harijans have been rendered so completely helpless that they have no power of resisting injustice, even if they wanted to. Let me explain what I mean. Harijan Boards have three functions, to raise the economic, social and religious status of Harijans, or to put it in another way, to remove the difficulties that Savarna Hindus have for centuries put in the way of Harijans raising their heads in any department of life. Thus the Harijan Boards have to provide wells, scholarships, boarding houses, schools and social amenities, wherever the need arises. In all these, the general body of Harijans simply take the help wherever it is offered. Advisory Committees can, therefore, help the cause and themselves by making useful suggestions to the Boards and also rendering such help as they themselves can to those whom they represent. Thus only will they acquire the power of asserting themselves. In short, Advisory Committees will best help the cause by taking up internal reform and causing an awakening among the Harijan masses, so that they may begin to realise that they are men and women entitled to the same rights as are enjoyed by the other members of the society to which they belong.'

At Rajahmundry a deputation of Harijans met Gandhiji and had a long talk with him. They agreed, among other things, that, as they had sufficient men among them who were enlightened and efficient, they should be entrusted with the reins of the Harijan Sevak Sangh. Caste Hindus, they said, might help in the work, but the office bearers should be all Harijans. Gandhiji gave them the following reply:

> One important question that you have raised is that the Harijan Sevak Sangh should be principally manned and

> managed by you. That shows that you have not followed the pages of the *Harijan.* That show's also that you have not understood the origin of the Board. The Board has been formed to enable Savarna Hindus to do repentance and reparation to you. It is thus a Board of Debtors, and yon are the creditors. You owe nothing to the debtors, and therefore, so far as this Board is concerned, the initiative has to come from the debtors. You have to certify whether the debtors discharge their obligation or not. What you have to do is to enable and help them to discharge their obligation; that is to say, you can tell them how they can discharge their obligation you can tell them what, in your opinion, will satisfy the great body of Harijans. They may or may not accept your advice. If they do not, naturally they run the risk of incurring your displeasure. A debtor may go to a creditor and say to him, 'I have brought so much money, will you take it?" The creditor may say, 'Off you go; I want full payment or none.' Or the creditor may say, 'What you have brought is not part payment, but worse.' All these things you, creditors, can do. And so, when this Board was. established and some. Harijan friends wrote to me, I told them that Harijans should form themselves into Advisory Boards or Boards of Inspection. I want you to understand this distinction thoroughly. You will please see that there is no desire not to accept your advice or co-operation or help. I am only putting before you the true and logical position. This is a period of grace that God has given to Caste Hindus, and it is during this period of grace that they have to prove their sincerity. And I am moving heaven and earth and am going about from place to place, simply in order that this obligation on the part of Savarna Hindus may be fully discharged.

A member of the deputation then suggested that the Board should appoint Advisory Committees of Harijans of its own selection. Gandhiji, 'as a fellow Harijan by choice', showed them the danger underlying this suggestion and said, "Do not ask the Board to select a Committee of Harijans, but select your own Committee and say to the Board, you have selected these members and it should carry on correspondence with them. There is another danger in the suggestion. There may be factions and divisions among you.

Different committees may be appointed by different factions. The Board may recognise all of them. But that will be unfortunate. Let there be no quarrels among you. Present a united front to the debtors. The debtors may put you against one another, though the Board, if it is worth its name, will not do that, The Congress has been able to present a united front. Today, the Congress is full of simple men like you and me. You should have a body of business-like men who will put down with a strong hand all quarrels among you. Then you will dominate the Board without being on it. Do not be easily satisfied. Tell the debtors you are not going to be satisfied with 5 shillings in the pound but that you must have 20 shillings in the pound. This is not a matter for bargaining".

The Mahatma recommended a 'Harijan Day' to be fixed under the auspices of the Harijan Sevak Sangh. It should be a day of sanitation and cleanliness. The poorest could do this by denying themselves a meal or a portion thereof. House to house collection was to be made by the members. The literature should be sold or given away as the exigency of the time might require.

The fixing of a special day can only be warranted by extraordinary effort. In a sacred cause like the Harijan cause, a special day should be one of greater dedication, prayer and intensive work. I should divide the day somewhat after this style:

1. I should begin the day from 5 A.M. with prayer and set apart for the cause some money or cloth or grain according to my means. The poorest can do this by denying themselves a meal or meals or a portion thereof without feeling the slightest deprivation. Preferably donations in kind should be converted into cash. Where this is not possible, they should be given to the most deserving and needy Harijans.
2. The work of the family Bhangi, if there is any, should be wholly done by the family or at least shared with him. This will enable one to understand the nature of the service

that the Bhangi performs and may also lead to an improved method of performing such services. Not many persons have any consideration for the 'knight of the broom' at the time of using the sanitary conveniences. If we had no untouchability in us and if we even occasionally shared the work with the Bhangis, we would have a different method of working the home sanitary system.

3. Having done these two things, we are ready for corporate effort for the day, which should open with house to house collection of donations in cash or kind. This work should be finished by a given hour. The donations should be handed to the local committee, which will in its turn, hand the collection to the superior committee till it reaches the headquarters of the province. Collectors should take with them a judicious section of literature including leaflets, pamphlets books and even copies of *Harijan,* English or vernacular edition as may be required. The literature should be sold or given away as the exigency of the moment may require. But each committee should bear the cost of the literature ordered by it. If extra copies of the *Harijan* required, previous advice should be given to the publishers so as to enable them to print extra copies.

4. Harijan quarters should be visited in each place and they should be cleaned wherever necessary. Meetings of Harijan should be held and their wants noted. They should be advised as to the part they have to play in the removal of untouchability. Dr. Deshmukh's authoritative opinion should be used in support of the plea for the giving up of carrioneating. Children can arrange meetings and excursions for Harijan children. Possibilities of inauguration of improved methods of sanitation should be explored. It is neither difficult nor expensive if the people will shoulder the burden willingly. In the end it means a visible addition to the health and wealth of the community.

5. The day should be wound-up by a general meeting of both Savarnas and Harijans to pass resolutions, pledging the meeting to the removal of untouchability and emphasising the desirability of permissive legislation regarding temple entry.

6. Where public opinion is favourable, public wells and private temples should be opened to Harijans.

An accurate report of the work done should be sent to the Central Committee.

Hardly has the great central organisation of the Servants of Untouchables Society made the commencement, when complaints against it and the provincial organisations have cropped up. They come chiefly and naturally from Harijans. One of these correspondents sent to me some time ago an able letter, undertaking to give details if I desired. I took him at his word and asked him to give me details; and the letter he has sent me in reply is abler than the first. It will compete with any well written report of an inspector. It contains a summary of reports of every organisation claiming to work in the writer's province for the uplift of Harijans, and after giving me sufficient details, his one conclusion about all the organisations practically without exception is:

> "They are run principally by Caste men who have their own axes to grind or who are in need of some occupation that would maintain them decently. The utmost that some of these have done is to fling a few scholarships at Harijan boys. Some others have been great at delivering lectures. All have come to us as patrons. Hardly has anyone come as a friend and equal, let alone as a servant. Your provincial organisation is no exception. It is difficult for a Harijan to approach its chief man without fear and trembling. He is always in danger of being met with a frown."

My correspondent is also not without suggestions, which may be summarised thus:

> "If you are to take advantage of the great awakening that has taken place, you must concentrate upon primary education on a mass scale. You will not drive out the ignorance of ages without spreading that education. We shall certainly help, but seeing that Caste Hindus want to remove untouchability and make us one with them, there is no better way of employing their money and their labour than in imparting this education."

It is necessary to know the Harijan mind in any programme of work that may be taken up. Caste Hindus, for whom removal of untouchability is a matter of penance and purification, have undoubtedly to do much more than open schools everywhere. I have discussed elsewhere where such schools may be opened. The conduct of Caste Hindus would be generally tested by its reaction upon the mass mind of the Harijans. If we have really changed towards them, they will feel the change in a thousand ways. Our activity, I mean that of Caste Hindus, will affect every department of their lives. Even in the remotest village we are interdependent, so much so that this interdependence cannot be dissolved all at once, even if we desired it, without resulting in the greatest harm to the nation in general; and this interdependence, which is today that of slave and master, will never be corrected unless there is absolute religious equality. It is a tremendous task, but as we progress towards the goal, the truth must dawn upon every Caste Hindu that there is no halfway house between abject slavery and perfect religious equality. Hence my bumble insistence upon temple entry without losing sight of the other things we must do.

My correspondent is bitter in discussing what he considers to be the extravagant management of the different organisations that have come under his lash. As an expert organiser that I may claim to be, I have been generally guided by the rule that the cost of administration, that is, overhead charges, should never exceed 10 per cent of the receipts—5 per cent being the ideal—the balance going to the cause which brought the organisation into being. I suggest this test to the Central Board and the Provincial Boards and all other independent Harijan organisations run by Caste Hindus. Let it not be said of us that we spend more on running the organisations than upon Harijans themselves. Let us see to it that, out of every Rs. 100 received as donation for the Harijan cause, Rs. 90 go straight into the pockets of Harijans. Therefore, our officials should be largely volunteers, never highly paid wherever paid service is required. Wherever it is possible, we should get Harijans. We should select candidates and train them. The correspondent says that peons in the organisations inspected by him are not drawn from the Harijan ranks.

Let every organisation for the service of Harijans introspect itself in the light of the criticism I have condensed and the suggestions I have made.

'I have repeatedly said that this work can be done only by those who sincerely believe untouchability to be a stain on Hinduism. This is a movement requiring the change of heart of millions. It cannot be led to success by any political manoeuvres. It can be done only through self-purification. This is a great sacrificial fire in which we have to burn our load of sins and come out purified. Those who do not take to this work with faith and spirit will fail to move the hearts of millions. We shall be nowhere if we deceive ourselves or the Harijans. The success or failure of this movement depends on our getting the right type of workers. We are on our trial today. If we miss today the opportunity that God has given us, we may never hope to get the opportunity again in this generation. What we refuse to do voluntarily today we shall have to do in future perforce, and we shall repent for having lost this opportunity. I pray to God that we may come out successful from this trial and save Hinduism and ourselves from destruction.

Injustice is being done all the word over, but we have given to it the sanction of religion. These distinctions have not been created by God. The Harijans are on the lowest rung of the ladder not because of any inherent defects but only because they have been kept down by the so-called higher castes. God had bestowed on them the same talents that He had given us, but we deny them the opportunities for using them. They should surely have the same rights and privileges and the same opportunities of growth that we enjoy.

We are now awake to the wrong we have done to them, and the least we can do by way of penance now is to contribute money for their uplift and to share with them all the amenities of life that we have created for ourselves. We are all creatures of the same God and, therefore, equal in His eyes.

From the money that you give for this cause, you will reap a hundred-fold, for it is like grain sown in good, manured soil. The money spent after luxury and lust is, on the other hand, wasted like grain sown in barren soil.

I am told you have suffered heavily. But you should know that no nation has ever come to its own without having passed through the severest fire of suffering. Voluntary suffering only adds of our strength. I, therefore, congratulate you for having suffered. But I should also like to remind you that one of the causes that add to our sufferings is this curse of untouchability. We have oppressed the weak. We reap as we have sown. It is for us now to undo the wrong we have done to the Harijans and remove the yoke of serfdom from their shoulders.

Caste Hindus must first ask you to forgive the wrongs they have done to you. But I should also tell you, as a Harijan by choice, that you should give up your evil habits, especially carrion and beef-eating. The whole world looks upon carrion with abhorrence. And beef-eating should be given up because that is a *sine qua non* for a Hindu. The cow is the giver of plenty, and by killing her we kill ourselves. Then, I would urge you not to accept leavings. And above all, you should abolish the distinctions of high and low that have crept in among yourselves. And these things you should do, not in a bargaining spirit but because they are good in themselves. I would, therefore, ask you also to give up drink, irrespective of the fact that many other Hindus drink.

A friend writes:

"I observe that there are some people in the Harijan service organisations not working in the spirit in which you want

> them to, that is, merely for the sake of serving Harijans. They are seeking its shelter in order to satisfy other ambitions .... I know that you do not desire civil resistance to be mixed up with Harijan service organisations. If you propose to make any public use of the letter you may emphasise this last point and make it clearer .. . . "

I am thankful to the friend for giving mo the benefit of his experience. It is a most difficult task to keep a big organisation like the Servants of Untouchables Society with branches all over India free of all self-seekers and time-servers. I have discussed the subject fully with Seth Ghanshyamdas and Thakkar Bapa. I know that they are both anxious to keep the organisation as pure as possible. Personally I can do no more. It was because of my utter helplessness that I undertook the fast of 21 days. On discovering impurities amongst Harijan servants, I saw that it was no use merely writing about impurities. I was searching for a way out of the difficulty. The reader should believe me when I tell him that the fast was the last thing in the world that I was thinking of, but as I have described in these pages, it came to me all of a sudden and gave me great relief. I know that it did much good. But, how far could the fast of a single mortal go? Hence it was that I developed the idea of a chain of such purificatory fasts. The idea has by no means been dropped. It comes to me again and again, But it does not admit of a mechanical organisation. Several co-workers are ready to inaugurate or take part in the chain after it is inaugurated, but I have not yet found the way to begin it. The proper way will have to come to me or to the co-workers before the chain can be begun. Meanwhile I can only reiterate my conviction that untouchability will not be removed root and branch except through the service of men and women who take it up for its own sake and in a religious spirit. Unless we have a fair number of such servants throughout the length and breadth of India, we will never succeed in changing the hearts of millions of human beings. The *Savarna* Hindus are at one end, Harijans at the other, and the evil custom of ages, which has assumed the dignity of religious tenet, will not be uprooted without penance and purification. Whilst it gladdens my heart that thousands of people flock to the meetings that are being held in towns and villages and that they willingly give their pices as a token of their approval of the movement, I am painfully conscious of the fact that, if the thousands were suddenly called upon to enforce in their own lives what they seem to approve by their attendance at these meetings, they would fail to respond. not from want of will, but from sheer inability. I have discovered this again and again amongst my closest associates who have frankly confessed their inability to enforce immediately in their conduct what they knew was the right thing and what they knew had to be done immediately. They had to put up a brave fight against their traditional repugnance. The mere intellectual grasp that untouchability is an evil, corroding Hinduism, and that belief in it is tantamount to disbelief in God, His goodness and His Fatherhood, is not enough to destroy the monster. The vicarious penance of the comparatively pure is needed to bring about a change in the hearts of both *Savarnas* and Harijans.

A movement, so grand and so pure, so religious and so humanitarian, must not be exploited by anybody for his own end. Certainly, not for its political consequences. It will be discovered, as the movement progresses, that the political approach can only end in accentuating the strife. It can only add to the confusion already existing and add one more, if not many more warring parties, to the existing ones. May God save us and save the movement from such a calamity!

So far as the connection of civil resistance with the movement is concerned, I am as emphatic as ever that Congressmen who desire to offer active civil resistance should not accept office in the various organisations, and much less can they be used for serving the purpose of civil resistance. Civil resistance is a unique weapon, it does not admit of alloy. It is a weapon of the fearless and, therefore, needs no shelter; but it has to be wielded in the open daylight. 'Therefore, whilst Congressmen who are also civil registers on active service may do, as they are bound to do, such service to the cause as they can, they may not belong to the Servants of Untouchables Society or any of its branches. By holding office in the organisations they will harm both civil resistance and the Harijan cause. It would be like a man going to a temple to pray and using the act of worship for advancing civil resistance. Neither God nor man will be cheated in that manner and, as I have said often enough in these columns, the great reformation of Hinduism will not be brought about, if it is to depend purely upon Congressmen. For, much as I would like to think that every Indian is a Congressman, I know that such is not the case. Nor is every Hindu a Congressman, if only because every Harijan is not a Congressman. Therefore, a Harijan organisation must in the very nature of things be strictly non-political and non-party and should contain in it both Congressmen and non-Congressmen, office-holding being restricted to those who are not active civil resistors and who will not exploit the office secretly or openly to advance the cause of civil resistance.

A correspondent sends me the following questions for answering:

1. In the propaganda against untouchability, should a worker make use of the Hindu Shastras and religious texts to show that Hinduism does not sanction untouchability as we practise it today?
2. Should a Harijan sevak, even in his private capacity, take part in inter-dining functions?
3. Should a Harijan who is employed as a domestic servant sit at meals alongside all the members of the family?

These three questions, the correspondent says, have been seriously discussed in the columns of a newspaper and the readers have been advised that Harijan workers should serve with all seriousness, I, therefore, beseech you, to purify your hearts of the sin of untouchability, to treat Harijan boys and girls as if they are your own children, brothers and sisters. We have for long ages suppressed Harijans and today if we sacrifice our all for their sake we shall be only making some slight and tardy reparation for all the wrongs inflicted upon them in the name of religion. Therefore, whatever you give, whether it is a trinket or heavy piece of jewellery or silver, I want you to give as merely a token of your determination to rid yourselves of this taint of untouchability, the idea that you are high and somebody else is low. May God give you wisdom to see this very simple truth and enforce it in your life. Now you can give the things, whether jewellery, or silver or paper, whatever you want to give.

In an address presented to him at a public meeting held at Calicut on 13 January, 1934, Gandhi replied:

'I am much obliged to you for these addresses that have been presented to me this evening and I thank you for the self-restraint you have imposed upon yourselves by not desiring to read those addresses to me. Only you have thereby appreciated the fact that I have been going from one place to another from day to day, now for over two months, and at the end of the day I am, therefore, fatigued. You, wise men that you are, have appreciated this fact and absolved me from the duty of having to listen to these addresses. You having exercised this self-restraint, naturally it was up to me to read those addresses and be prepared. But I must say to you that I had no notion whatsoever that I was to have all these addresses nor have I been given copies of these addresses. Had I been given copies I would certainly have read them. However I have no doubt whatsoever that these addresses contain nothing more than what I have noticed in the numerous addresses that I have been receiving throughout these two months or more. Almost without exception they have expressed to me great joy, not only their sympathy with the cause that I am espousing for the time being but they have in these addresses signified their intention, nay their determination, of doing everything that these various bodies of gentlemen or ladies could possibly do in their own sphere to advance the Harijans' cause.

It has given me a great deal of satisfaction and joy to discover that there is consensus of opinion on the part of the intelligentsia. I would have been painfully surprised if it had been otherwise. Not only has it been so with reference to the intelligentsia but as far as mere assent goes, I have found to my great delight the masses also are equally with this movement. I am not easily self-deluded. I have no doubt that I have, must have, my due share of self-delusion or else life perhaps would be a positive burden to most of us if not to all of us. But due allowance having been made for self-delusion I can say that all these scenes that I witness every day cannot possibly be a matter of masses or classes coming to me to signify their praise or their satisfaction for services that I might have performed in a previous life or in days gone by. This life has rushed and with me it has rushed with such rapidity that it is impossible for me to have a photography of the events that have happened and, that being the case, I should be intensely surprised and also disappointed that these classes and masses had signified not only their satisfaction and their sympathy by their presence at these meetings but also give me donations more or less and had done certain acts also as a consideration for those services. I would let that pass by. I am assuming that all your addresses contain a serious and solemn pledge that you are determined to do everything that is humanly possible for you to do to render the reparation that is overdue to the Harijans. Malabar, if one were to draw the untouchability map of the whole of India, I suppose will easily wear the black crown and Malabar would be the blackest spot so far as untouchability is concerned. It is a matter of regret but it is no use ignoring the fact. I would turn this blackness to good account and I would invite you to gird up your loins and make such Herculean effort that at the end of the struggle it may be possible to say of Malabar that Malabar had been in the vanguard of progress in this battle against the monster of untouchability. Let it be said of Malabar that Malabar counted no sacrifices too great for removing this evil of untouchability. And what could be a better and more sacred reminder for this meeting than the portrait of Mr. K. Madhavan Nair?

I had the pleasure of knowing him long ago. When I first visited Calicut I had the honour of being introduced to him but I must confess that I did not know him so intimately as I came to know him when he paid me a visit at Yeravda. I came into very intimate touch with him, and when Mr. C. Rajagopalacharia was here and the Guruvayur referendum was going on, naturally I was corresponding with him as with other friends almost from day to day. Then Smt. Urmila Devi and my wife came, into close contact with Mr. K. Madhavan Nair. My wife is a simple woman. She knows nothing, she does not know the English language, certainly she does not know Malayalam, but she was able to tell me in her very simple language that she was very much struck by the simplicity of his character. She merely strengthened the impression that Mr. Madhavan had left on my mind and that impression is still indelible. I have the most vivid recollection of my contact with him and what struck me most was his transparent humility. This is his faithful picture and I congratulate the artist on presenting the citizens of Calicut with this picture. I think there you can easily see humility written in his features. I don't think that the artist has enhanced the transparence of his humility. I think the artist is incapable of doing that. To look at Mr. Madhavan Nair and look at the living eye would give you a better illustration of that humility. The whole of his behaviour is on the picture. Mr. Madhavan Nair is in front of me today as I saw him in Yeravda. He stands vividly before me and this is the one peculiar impression that he left on me.

I discovered also that he was a man of very few words. You do not find many people who are economical in the use of language or their words. In his contact with me Mr. Madhavan Nair showed this quality in a supreme degree. His letters were compact, nice, neat and the briefest possible. Whatever he had to say he expressed in a few words and he had finished. That was the man. If you were to recall the men who had died in body but are even now still living, you will discover that they are living not because of their intellectual gifts but because of virtues which you and I and every one of us can cultivate if we have the will and if we will make the necessary effort in order to cultivate them. Therefore, I would say you will be doing wrong to the memory of the man whom I have described as I have known him, if you think that you have performed your duty by calling upon me to unveil his portrait and for having witnessed this ceremony and having heard a few words in praise of his memory; nay, you will be doing wrong. But you will be doing the right thing if you will treasure this as a perpetual reminder to you that you also would like to be if not wholly at least somewhat like Mr. Madhavan Nair. At the end, to put a finishing touch, Mr. Madhavan Nair died in harness so far as the Harijan cause is concerned. He was a true co-worker in the Harijan cause which is. a matter of self-purification, repentance and reparation. I give you my evidence that Mr. Madhavan Nair, when he took up this cause, had the spirit in him, for every act that he did in connection with the Harijan cause was an act of sacrifice, repentance and reparation. There was no meanness about anything that he did. May his memory ever remain in ray heart and in your own hearts.

I thank you once more for having presented me with addresses. Since I think that this is not the proper time for auctioning these addresses, I hope that tomorrow you will help me to realise some money from these addresses because I know that Calicut will not send me away with disappointment."

REFERENCES

1. J.B. Kripalani, *Gandhi: His Life and Thought*, Delhi, 1970, p. 383.
2. *Harijan*, 17 August 1935.
3. *Ibid.*
4. *Harijan*, 10 October 1936.
5. *Harijan*, 10 May 1942.
6. *Harijan*, 28 July 1946.
7. *Harijan*, 9 November 1934.
8. *Harijan*, 20 April 1934.
9. *Ibid.*
10. *Harijan*, 5 January 1934.
11. *Harijan*, 15 April 1933.
12. *Ibid.*
13. *Harijan*, 4 March 1933.
14. *Harijan*, 1 December 1933.
15. *Ibid.*
16. *Harijan*, 24 November 1933.
17. *The Hindu*, 15 January 1934
18. *Ibid.*

7

The Satyashodhak Samaj

The Satyashodhak Samaj was only the first of many efforts of organisation that were to be made by lower caste politicians and ideologues in the last three decades of the 19th century. Different leaders produced their own analyses of the plight of the lower castes, and concentrated on varying areas of organisation and propaganda. Yet they all worked within the same broad set of assumptions about Maharashtra's history and the divisions in her present-day society. These assumptions were of a fundamental division within Maharashtrian society. On one side lay the vast majority of her population, who lived and laboured on the land, who provided for the material support of all other groups, yet who lived in poverty and ignorance. On the other were the small groups of Brahmans and other literate castes, who had added to their existing religious authority a virtual monopoly of English education and of clerical and professional employment in the British administration. The remedy for the plight of the lower castes lay in education, and in schemes of self-help and social reform. Yet their religious and social values, instilled by generations of Brahman preceptors, lay in direct opposition to such schemes.

On the one hand, some writers and activists made these assumptions very clear while others bent on more practical schemes of education, or concerned to avoid the charge of stirring up hatred between Brahmans and other castes, were content to allow them to remain implicit. Yet the Satyashodhak Samaj, with these as its most firmly held beliefs, assumed a vital role as the ideological conscience for all those who identified themselves with the lower castes, whether they belonged to the Samaj or to one of the numerous other groups working for lower caste uplift. Like all consciences, Satyashodhak ideology often seemed to make awkward and uncomfortable demands in its uncompromising radicalism. These demands were often not met even amongst its closest supporters, whilst the Samaj frequently received bitter criticism from those who felt that the same ends could better be served if its demands were couched in terms less obviously hostile to the higher castes. At the same time, however, the Samaj had come to stand, by the end of the nineteenth century, as a symbol of dedication to the cause of the lower castes that was unrivalled by any other group within the broader movement.

1870s: Religious Reform and Indigenous Radical Traditions

Amongst the different religious reform movements of western India in this period, the Prarthana Samaj, or 'Prayer Society', is one of the most familiar. After the dissolution of the Paramahansa Mandali in the early 1860s, some of its members went on to form the Prarthana Samaj in early 1867. They attempted to combine their strongly-held belief in a single father-god with an observance of the basic social rules of Hinduism. The Samaj's main principle was that 'God is one and without form. It is proper and it is our duty to worship him in a spiritual way. Idolatry is an aberration, it is an insult to God, and debases man and leads him to evil practices.' The members of the hoped that this more oblique approach to the social evils of idolatry and caste division would win greater popular acceptance where the more ruthless attack of the Paramahansa Mandali had failed. M.G. Ranade joined the Prarthana Samaj in 1869, quickly became a dominant influence and set about giving coherence to its religious views. Ranade argued that all the religions of the world were in a process of evolution towards a 'Pure Theism', that would eventually transcend all conventional religious confessions. The Prarthana Samaj could claim to be in the forefront of this movement. To this evolutionary view of religion, the Samaj added a growing interest in the work of Maharashtra's devotional poet-saints, especially in the seventeenth-century poet Tukaram, whom the Samaj came to see as a theist of an older kind. The Prarthana Samaj thus led the search amongst Maharashtra's intellectuals for a synthesis that would incorporate all that was best in the Hindu tradition, while taking account of the criticisms of caste and idolatry that were made by Hindu radicals and European observers alike. They found the material for this synthesis in the work of the poet-saints, whose ecstatic love for a personal God was unmistakably Hindu in origin, and who had themselves strongly deprecated the rigid hierarchies of caste, or the undiscriminating reverence for Brahmans, that characterised contemporary Hindu practice.

The Arya Samaj, founded in 1875 in Bombay by Swami Dayananda Sarasvati, turned to the more ancient past to discover a 'pure' Hinduism with which to confront the corruption of Hinduism in the present. Dayananda set out the religious basis for the Arya Samaj in his book *Satyartha Prakash*, published in 1875. Dayananda argued that the Vedas contained Hindu beliefs in their most ancient and pure form, showing God to be an omniscient, omnipotent, merciful, just and infinite Creator, who was distinct from his Creation. The social hierarchies of Vedic society had been based on the merit, ability, and temperament of the individual, rather than on his birth. Dayananda called for the purging of the degenerate practices of Hindus in the present, and for a return to Vedic religion in all its simplicity and purity. The Arya Samaj of Bombay was inaugurated on 10 April 1875. It was from the start dominated by Gujurati business magnates, such as Mulji Thakershi, a wealthy mill-owner, and Lakhmidas Khimji, a Bhatia, who had taken a leading part in the crusade against the Vallabhacharaya Maharajas for their encouragement of corrupt and licentious habits amongst their devotees. The

Arya Samaj laid great emphasis on the reform of religious ritual. The Samaj rejected the idea that the transaction between the believer and his God, carried out in religious ritual, should automatically have to be mediated by a Brahman priest, who would conduct the ritual in a language incomprehensible to the participants. The *Dnyanodaya* newspaper of 6 April 1876 contained an account of a ritual, carried out under the auspices of the Samaj, which stressed the direct and personal relationship between God and the believer, rather than the mediating role of the priest. The ritual was a sacred thread ceremony, carried out for the son of one Harichandra by Dayananda Sarasvati himself. Some aspects of the ceremony were much the same as the conventional Hindu ritual: an auspicious moment was chosen for the occasion, the boy was invested with the sacred thread, and Brahman priests were on hand to assist Dayananda. What was different was the emphasis on the participation and comprehension of the boy himself and the gathered believers. The boy's age was about twelve years rather than the customary six to eight; the Vedic verses that were spoken in Sanskrit were then translated to the boy; and Dayananda gave a final homily to the audience in their own language. In his work on Dayananda Sarasvati, J. T. F. Jordens describes how me members of the Arya Samaj wished for a religious organisation of their own that would be independent of the corruptions of conventional Hinduism. They turned towards what they regarded as the original sources of Hinduism, searching for a pure form of religious practice for which they could feel respect.

This emphasis on a return to the purity of Vedic society would appear at first sight to contrast very strongly with Jotirao Phule's earlier depiction of the ancient Aryans as the source of all religious oppression in present-day India. However, Phule and Dayananda did share in common the belief in one God, and the desire for a form of social organisation that would reflect the merits and aptitudes of the individual, rather than enforcing birth as the basis both for occupation and for religious status. Phule recognised Dayananda's emphasis on Aryan society as a means to an end with much in common with his own. In September 1875, therefore, we find Phule and his friends taking a prominent part in a procession in Pune given in honour of Dayananda. The organisers of the procession, fearing opposition from the conservative Brahman party, asked Phule and his friends for their support. The procession included other reformers, notably M. G. Ranade. The opposition constructed an effigy of Dayananda, put garlands around its neck, sat it on an ass, and followed the main procession, exchanging insults and blows with Dayananda's supporters. The procession carried on regardless, and finished with a gathering at the end of the day to hear speeches on social and religious reform.

Besides these two reform societies, there were also other individuals and small groups in Pune, much less prominent or well organised, who turned to the Hindu past to find material for their criticisms of the present. This is particularly important for our purposes, since a few of these religious radicals were included amongst Phule's friends and colleagues, while others were to join him in the Satyashodhak Samaj. The influence of radicalism drawn from sources within the Hindu tradition is important both for our understanding of the Satyashodhak Samaj, and for our view of the development of Phule's ideas. Phule's own brand of religious radicalism has been traced back to the religious and intellectual upheavals of the 1840s and 1850s. Throughout his career, however, his circle included writers and activists who shared his concerns, and whose ideas owed more to older and indigenous movements of opposition to Brahmanic Hinduism. Phule undoubtedly shared and discussed his theories with men like these. Before we go on to look at the founding of the Satyashodak Samaj, it will be useful to look at the influence of pre-nineteenth-century religious radicalism, to assess its importance in Satyashodhak ideology. This will also help us to appreciate what he came to owe to fellow radicals. From this perspective, his work appears not only as an individual effort of criticism and imagination, but also as the product of a pooling of experience and ideas amongst a number of like-minded men, some of whom brought to these exchanges an older variety of religious radicalism.

The greater religious systems of Hinduism have always been accompanied by individuals or groups who challenged them. The objects of criticism were most frequently the religious authority of Brahmans, the division of society into castes based on birth, and the elaboration of ritual, pilgrimages, and asceticism as means of winning religious merit. Chief amongst these traditions of criticism were the devotional *bhakti* cults, which originated from the tenth century in south India, and flourished in central and northern India between the thirteenth and eighteenth centuries. The *bhakti* sect was characterised by the abandonment of the self in devotion and love for a personal God, and by the deprecation of all man-made social and religious distinctions. One of the earliest of these poet-saints in northern India was Ramanand, who came to Banaras from the south of India in the fourteenth century, wrote in the vernacular instead of Sanskrit, and accepted followers from all castes. The most important of his followers were Nanak, who was active in the late fifteenth and early sixteenth centuries, and Kabir. Nanak, the founder of the Sikh community, was a monotheist and a bitter opponent of the rigid hierarchies of caste. Kabir was originally a Muslim, who abandoned Islam and set out to found a religion in which there would be no man-made barrier between the individual and his God. He directed biting criticism at the pretensions of Brahmans to special religious authority in mediating between man and God. It is significant that, unlike other devotional sects, the extreme anti-Brahman and anti-caste stance of the Sikhs and the followers of Kabir meant that they have remained separated from the larger body of Hindu society. Where, on the other hand, the followers of a devotional sect saw *bhakti* as a supplement to Brahmanic religion that might be more accessible than the rigours of a path to God through knowledge and self-discipline, an accommodation within Hindu society was much easier. This was rather more the character of the Maratha saint-poets, Jnaneshvar, Namadev, Ekanath and, most important, the seventeenth-century poet Tukaram, whom we have already seen adopted by the Prarthana Samaj. Tukaram exhorted his followers to reject the idea of attaining merit and salvation by reading holy books, fulfilling caste obligations, making gifts to Brahmans, or subjecting the body to extremes of asceticism. The love of God was more important than all of these. It was not caste superiority that made a man holy, but simply his love for God. A true Brahman was one who loved God with a pure heart, and such a man might be of any caste, even an untouchable.

Besides the major figures of the *bhakti* movement in Maharashtra and elsewhere in India, there were also available to nineteenth-century reformers and radicals the ideas of a very diverse mixture of critics of Brahmanic religion, whose antecedents are less well documented. One of the most important of these was a fiercely anti-Brahman tract called the *Vajrasuchi,* or *Vajrasuchik-Upanishad.* The religious historian, R. C. Dhere, has estimated that this text goes back to the ninth century or earlier. The identity of its author is uncertain. It was most frequently ascribed to one Ashva Ghosh, who may have been a Buddhist monk, Dhere traces the influence of this work upon the Marathi saint-poets, Bahinabai, a disciple of Tukaram, and Shrirshyamaraj, brother of the poet Gopalanath, who was writing early in the eighteenth century. The influence of the *Vajrasuchi* appears again early in the nineteenth century, in the writing of a Gurav living near Pune, who composed a work called the *Nathalilamarat,* in which he paraphrased parts of the *Vajrasuchi.* In 1829, the British Resident at Kathmandu, Mr. B. M. Hodgson, was presented with a copy by a Buddhist friend. Hodgson was interested by the contents, had a translation made, and read it to the Royal Asiatic Society of Great Britain and Ireland in 1831. During the nineteenth century, the reformers Ram Mohan Roy, Dadoba Pandurang, and Vir Savarakar also found support for their ideas in the work.

A close friend and colleague of Phule's was the Bhandari reformer from Bombay, Tukaram Tatya Padaval. We have already seen how Phule volunteered to publish the second edition of his work, *A Critique of Caste Divisions,* which appeared in Bombay in 1865. Padaval wrote in the introduction to the work that he had modelled some of his arguments upon those used in the *Vajrasuchi,* and because of its usefulness had included a translation of the work at the end of his book.

What was striking about the *Vajrasuchi* was that it used arguments, taken from within the Hindu scriptures, to refute the principles usually advanced to support caste divisions. It led the reader to conclusions very similar to those reached by the religious reformers of the 1840s and 1850s, and was quite compatible with the arguments of Christian missionaries and the anti-clericalism of European religious radicals, from which these reformers had drawn much of their inspiration. The *Vajrasuchi* began by asking what Brahmanhood consisted of: whether it derived from a man's parentage, his wisdom, his actions, or his reading of the Vedas. Brahmanhood could not lie in birth, since there were instances in the Hindu scriptures of people being born even of animals, who later attained to Brahmanhood. It could not be wisdom, because many *Shudras* had also acquired great wisdom. It could not be virtuous conduct, or many *Shudras* would also be Brahmans. It could not be reading the Vedas, for Ravana, the demon King of the *Ramayana,* was deeply versed in the Vedas. The *Vajrasuchi* then turned to attack the doctrine of the division of society into four classes or *Varnas.* It was not true that the *Shudras* were the lowest of the four simply because they were mentioned last. If all the four *Varnas* had proceeded from the body of the god Brahma, as the Hindu scriptures said they did, then they must all be alike. If a father and mother had four sons, they were essentially equal and alike. The similarity of all men's physical and emotional faculties also proclaimed their essential likeness. In fact, the author argued, the division of Hindu society into *Varnas* had been in origin only a division of occupations that had become rigid through the passage of time. It was clear, therefore, that true Brahmanhood resided in the merit and virtue of the individual, and that birth had nothing to do with it.

For a reformer like Padaval, a tract such as the *Vajrasuchi* would have served, as confirmation from another source, to reinforce the radical ideas of religion chat were already in circulation in the 1840s and 1850s. This was also very likely the case with Dadoba Pandurang. R. C. Dhere has pointed out the close parallels with the argument of one of the chapters of Dadoba's work *A Discussion on Religion*, published in 1868. In the sixth chapter, entitled 'The whole of human kind is of one caste', Dadoba asked what caste superiority consisted of, eliminated the various possibilities in the same way as the author of the *Vajrasuchi*, and concluded that men were distinguished from one another by their virtue, not by their birth. For Dadoba as for Padaval, his reading of the *Vajrasuchi* combined to reinforce the radical ideas such as those that he absorbed from the agnostic Henry Green, and from the strategies that the Christian missionaries employed to undermine the principle of a religious hierarchy with Brahmans at its head.

There is no record that Phule and Dadoba Pandurang ever met. Another young radical, who drew his ideas in part from indigenous sources, and who was to play a very important part in the Satyashodhak Samaj, was Krishnarao Bhalekar. Bhalekar (1850-1910) was born in the village of Bhamburade, near Pune. His family, like Phule's, were Malis. They moved to Pune after Bhalekar was born, where his father went to work as a clerk in the District Court. Left an orphan at the age of sixteen, Bhalekar went for his education to one of the mission schools in Pune, and then started work in the English office of the the District Judge's Court in Pune. He was very active in the late 1860s and early 1870s, organising anti-Brahman activities in his native village. He described how his search for religious truth had begun while he had been at the mission school, between 1864 and 1868. In 1866, he began to go regularly to hear the public lectures that were given in his village by a Hindu *sadhu,* Jangali Maharaj. Listening to these lectures, he became convinced that many Hindus had wandered into religious error because of their ignorance, and that it was upon this ignorance that the Brahmans relied to make a living. With a group of his friends, Bhalekar accepted Jangali Maharaj as his *guru, and* accompanied ḥim on a pilgrimage to Alandi, sacred to the memory of Tukaram.

Fortified with his new religious convictions, Bhalekar wrote in 1868 a book of poems attacking the vanity of empty rituals. He then staged a mock *Satyanarayan* ritual in his village and invited the villagers to watch. A crowd of people gathered, and some criticised him for making fun of his own religion, but they watched all the same. Since this was not very popular, Bhalekar devised a performance on another aspect of relations between Brahmans and other castes. This was a play, called *Sir Ignorance, the credulous Deshmukh.* It described how the ignorance of Rajas, landowners, and others in positions of power allowed their ministers to deceive and take advantage of them. Bhalekar and his friends, who included one of the Brahmans of the village, performed this play one night in front of the temple of Vithoba. Bhalekar also established a library for the poor in the temple. Eventually, Phule in Pune heard of Bhalekar's activities, and went to visit him in Bhamburade. The pair discovered that their families were related, and from that time Bhalekar began to make regular visits to Phule's shop in Pune, where he and his friends met for discussions in the period immediately before the founding of the Satyashodhak Samaj.

Gyanoba Krishnaji Sasane, born of a Mali family in the village of Hadapsar, near Pune, in 1851, was another of Phule's circle whose religious radicalism derived in part from indigenous sources. His great-grandfather had been in the army, but the family had settled down as farmers in the village of Hadapsar. Sasane's grandfather, Mhasaji, had been a devoted follower of the anti-Brahmanical and devotional sect founded in north India by Kabir. The once-prosperous family fell into poverty and debt in Sasane's father's time, but this did not stop the young Sasane going to school in Hadapsar, spending the daytime tending cattle and breaking stones, and going to school in the evening. At the age of thirteen he found his mind turning towards questions of religion. He left the village and took up the life of a *Sanyasi*, a wandering religious ascetic. On his travels he fell with a *bairagi*, a religious mendicant, who was a follower of Ramanuja, the great theistic philosopher, active in the eleventh century, who provided the philosophical basis on which many of the later *bhakti* cults were founded. Sasane was drawn towards the path of *bhakti*, and spent much time reading and questioning the holy men and ascetics that he encountered. After three years Sasane tired of the life of a mendicant, threw off his *bairagi's* clothes and returned to his village, where he took a job working as a clerk for a contractor, getting stone for construction works in Pune. Sasane first came into contact with Phule when he was in his early twenties, and searching for a wife. Phule used his influence in the local Mali community to help Sasane and a wife was found in the family of Narayanrao Vithoba Shinde, of Paravati village, near Pune. This was in 1874, the year after the founding of the Satyashodhak Samaj, and Phule persuaded both families to have the marriage conducted according to Satyashodhak principles, without the aid of a Brahman priest. The ceremony passed off successfully, despite fierce opposition, both from within the Mali community in Pune and from the local Brahmans. Sasane kept up his contacts with Phule, joining him as a business partner in the late 1870s in a scheme to transport vegetables from Pune to be sold in the markets of Bombay. Throughout this period, Sasane's interest in religious questions remained undiminished. He showed the same capacity, which we saw in Padaval and Bhalekar, to combine ideas from a very wide range of sources to form his own distinctive understanding of social and religious reform. As well as being a member of the Satyashodhak Samaj, he also became very friendly with two Christian converts in Hadapsar, Ramachandrapant Bhaskar and Kashinathpant Panchandikar. He came into contact with the convert and ordained priest, Baba Padmanji, whose books he read with pleasure. During the 1890s he joined forces with some of the Scottish missionaries from Pune to open a school in Hadapsar, which he ran successfully for many years. To the end of his life he also maintained his interest in the study of *bhakti* texts, journeying to Pandharpur and Alandi to have them elucidated.

We turn now to the period immediately before the founding of the Satyashodhak Samaj, where again we find evidence of the influence of the ideas of Kabir on Phule and his circle. Tukaram Hanamant Pinjan, who later became a member of the Satyashodhak Samaj, described how, a few months before its foundation, Phule's friends and colleagues used to gather every Sunday at his shop in Pune. Amongst those who came was Dnyanagiri Buva, a member of the Kabir *panth*. Dnyanagiri Buva used to read to the assembled gathering from the *Bijak* book written by Kabir, translating it from its original Brij into Marathi. The book contained much information about the selfishness and evil conduct of Brahmans. Phule, Pinjan recalled, had long since been convinced that the non-Brahmans suffered all sorts of difficulties as a result of Brahman attitudes. Having received farther confirmation of this belief in the writings of Kabir, he began to turn over in his mind the practical steps that would improve their position. The gathering agreed to Phule's proposal that they should organise themselves into a definite society and, after much discussion, upon the name, the Satyashodhak Samaj, the 'Truth-Seeking Society', and it was inaugurated on 24 September 1873.

Organisation and Propaganda in the Early Satyashodhak Samaj

The members of the new society lost no time in making known the purpose of their activities. There was certainly none of the secrecy that characterised the Paramahansa Mandali. The *Satyadipika* newspaper of October 1873, then edited by Baba Padmanji, reported that a great revolution was at present going on in Pune, About 700 families from the *kunbi,* Mali, potter, carpenter, and other *Shudra* castes had launched a movement to make themselves independent in religious matters from Brahmans. The present fortnight of the month of Bhadarapad was the time appointed for making offerings to the spirits of male ancestors. These families were refusing to call Brahmans to perform these ceremonies as was customary, and were giving to their own caste-fellows the food which would otherwise have been offered to the priest. The aims of the socicty were clearly set out by its secretary, Narayan Tukaram Nagarakar, in the first report of its activities that was published in 1877:

> Some wise gentlemen founded this Samaj on the 24 September 1873, order to free the Shudra people from slavery to Brahmans, Bhats, Joshis, priests and others. For thousands of years, these people have heedlessly despised and exploited the Shudras, with the aid of their cunningly-devised books. This action was taken, therefore, so that through good advice and the spread of education, the Shudras might be got to understand their real rights, and freed both in religious and more general matters from the false and self-interested books of the Brahmans.

Nagarakar subscribed strongly to the view that British rule represented a unique opportunity for the *Shudras* to acquire the education, self-respect, and independence of judgement that they had always lacked, while their faith in Hindu religion remained unquestioned. Nagarakar finished the report with an exhortation to the members of the society:

> Because of the unprejudiced and altruistic wisdom [of the British government] all castes, great and small, have had a chance to partake of the benefits of education. At present, the ignorant state of the people, and their foolish religious beliefs, has meant that the proportionate spread of education among the Shudras, compared to other people, is very small. So this is the time that we should be carrying out reforms among our people. We must hope that the educated amongst us will look to the reform of the country and of their own people, that they will have no fear of the wiles of cunning people, and will not hesitate to fix their minds firmly on following the truth. If they do hesitate, then our Shudra brothers will never free themselves from the prison of mental slavery.

The society had a clear set of rules, twenty-eight in number, that were drawn up shortly after its inauguration. The first rule stated that the condition of the *Shudra* at present was appalling and that the society had been established to make some amends for the terrible neglect that prevailed concerning the real rights of men, their duties and proper course of action, and the means that must be employed to remedy the miseries of the *Shudras* themselves. The next rule settled the name of the society, and the third stipulated that the rules had been laid down to ensure the smooth running of the society. The fourth rule forbade all discussion of political issues. The fifth and sixth allowed people of other castes and towns to join the society, provided they accepted its rules. The seventh and eighth dealt with details of internal organisation. The ninth, one of the most important, set out the vows that all members of the society were required to take on joining it. These were as follows:

1. I will not worship anything except our Creator.
2. I will not bring into discredit the pure rights that have

been given by our Creator by countenancing either those who, through the arrogant assumptions in their books, behave as though others were inferior, or those who accept such inferiority.

3. I will stop being party to the killing of animals, and will give up alcohol, as far as I can.
4. I will hold firmly to my pride in the truth, will help the old, the lame, and the very young in our society, and will strive to give enough education to all our children that they may understand their rights.

The tenth rule stipulated that each member should give the fruits of one do's work a year for the society's expenses. The next twelve rules dealt with internal organisation: the election of officers and other decisions of the society were to be taken by majority opinion, a managing committee was elected to look after routine business, and a meeting of all members should take place four times a year. The twenty-third rule turned once more to the aims of the society. It contained four clauses. The first was that members should spread truth and right-thinking amongst their people, and the second that they should advise their people, through newspapers and lectures, about men's real rights and dudes in the world. The third clause stipulated that they should make every effort to spread education by teaching women and children, by helping those who wished to go to the University in Bombay, and spreading the knowledge of improved techniques in agriculture. The fourth and final clause was that they should attempt to curb vice and harmful social practices. The remainder of the rules reverted again to details of organisation,

From its inception, the society devoted a very large part of its energy to the proselytisation of the lower caste communities in Pune and the surrounding villages. Members toured, lecturing and distributing tracts, giving *upadesh*, or 'advice'. The society's first report praised the efforts of Krishnarao Bhalekar, Ravaji Sirole, and others of the village of Bhamburade. Having become members themselves, they had established a branch of the society in the village and, with the help of poetry and music, had given advice to the villagers and won over new members. In the village of Hadapsar many had become members, and the business of imparting advice was proceeding very satisfactorily. In the village of Paravati, the cause of the society had been taken up by the Police Paul, who was making many efforts on its behalf. Early in 1874 some of the leaders of the Telugu Mali community in Bombay had invited Phule to address them, and had formed a branch of the society. Ramayya Vyankayya Ayyavaru, Narasinharao Sayabu Vadnala, Jaya Ellappa Lingu, and Vyanku Baloji Kalevar were leading the efforts in Bombay, and earring out many reforms in the community. In the village of Bhilar in Satara district, Govindrao Bapuji Bhilar, the *patil* of the village, had heard of the aims of the society, and lost no time in establishing a branch in Bhilar. He had given advice and won new members, and had ventured to carry out a number of marriages without the assistance of the local Brahmans. Gyanu Malharaji Jagade, a Phulmali from the village of Kavadi near Pune, had used the contacts that his position as a superintendant of labourers had brought to give advice to about fifty people, some of whom had become members. Bhikoba Balaji, of the weaver caste, had brought many people back to the path of religious truth. Dhondiram Namadev Kumbhar, a potter, and Pandarinath Abaji Chavan had toured, reading poetry and lectures that told of how cunning people exploited the ignorant *Shudras.*

The manuscript account book of the society for the period 1873 to 1876 gives us a very clear idea of the tone of much of this proselytisation. One of the standard tactics of the society was simply to distribute free copies of Phule's and other polemical works in the villages around Pune. In July 1874, books were given away free to the people of the village of Bhamburade. These books were Phule's works, *Slavery, Priestcraft Exposed,* and *A Ballad of the Chatrapati Raja Shivaji*

Bhosale. Also included were Tukaram Tatya Padaval's *A Critique of Caste Divisions*, and Dadoba Pandurang's work *A discussion on religion* that had served as a text for the Paramahansa Mandali in the 1860s. Another entry in the account book, for 24 September 1874, recorded that Phule's and Dadoba's works were also to be distributed in the town of Ahmadnagar, some sixty miles to the north-east of Pune. Phule's earlier efforts to couch his work in language that could be easily understood by a popular audience meant that his books were particularly suited to distribution in this way.

This emphasis on active proselytisation may well have been an indirect borrowing from protestant missionary strategies. The role of the Satyashodhak 'adviser' was not to win acceptance for his spiritual authority in the way, for example, that Krishnarao Bhalekar had accepted the spiritual authority of Jangali Maharaj when he made him his *guru*. Rather, his purpose was to provide information and a commentary on the issues of caste and religious worship, so that every individual would be given a basis of religious 'truth', on which he might make his own decisions. The conviction that the society was a purveyor of religious truth and light, surrounded on all sides by darkness and error, was also strongly reminiscent of the missionaries' sense of their role.

Projects of education also figured very largely in the early activities of the society. This emphasis on education was to provide one of the most important themes of the broader non-Brahman movement as it developed towards the end of the century. Education came to be seen as the panacea for almost every social and religious evil. Non-Brahman leaders regarded it as having three purposes. First, it provided the occupational skills, from basic literacy to fluent English, that the lower castes needed if they were to win a share of employment in administration and the professions, proportionate to their numbers in the population of the Bombay Presidency. Second, a western secular education seemed to offer intellectual emancipation from many of the doctrines of Brahmanic Hinduism, from the belief in divine or magical powers active in the natural world, to the idea that any particular individual or religious group possessed the means to control such powers. Finally, education would help to bring about a reformation of popular manners. The idea of such a reformation was to take a central place in the programme of every non-Brahman activist and polemicist. Many were convinced that a combination of harmful social customs, such as child marriage, heavy expenditure on weddings, and the reluctance to educate women, undermined the ability of the lower castes to reach any sort of secular prosperity and well-being, let alone to compete for a share of the occupational and educational benefits dispensed by the British government. Added to these harmful customs were what non-Brahman leaders saw as the besetting vices of the lower castes, particularly the rural communities, which had been given the sanction of long usage. These included drinking, habitual debt, the reluctance to continue working hard when stores of grain were full after a good harvest, the holding of village *tamashas,* with the drunkenness and lewd singing and dancing that often accompanied them, gambling, prostitution, quarrelsomeness and litigation, and even the predilection of the cultivators for spending too much time gossiping and smoking with their neighbours. Two of these problems, drinking and debt, would have been a cause for concern in any circumstances. The question of debt was, of course, to the forefront of every discussion concerning the well-being of the rural communities. There was also a growing body of opinion in the Presidency that the excise policy of the government of Bombay served to increase drunkenness and alchoholism by licensing growing numbers of liquor shops, from which it drew a large revenue. However, non-Brahman leaders regarded the more perennial 'vices' of the lower castes as equally damaging. The traditional religious preceptors of the cultivators had signally failed even to recognise the existence of a problem. A proper secular education would attack the root of these vices, which lay in the ignorance of the people.

In the report of the society's activities in the year beginning September 1875, therefore, eighteen out of the twenty-nine resolutions that it contained were concerned with education. Vishram Ramji Gholay, of the *gavali* caste of cow-herds, now employed as a surgeon in government service, and Ramasheth Bapusheth Uravane, a wealthy Pune merchant, agreed to provide a prize for the best essay written by a *Shudra* on the differences between Indian agriculture and agriculture abroad, and the best means of bringing Indian agriculture up to the same standard. Krishnarao Bhalekar was planning to start a night school in his village of Bhamburade for those who did not have the leisure to study during the day. The society decided that it would pay a servant Rs 5 a month to collect up the children of the *Shudras* from the streets of Pune and shepherd them to school. This would stop them from picking up bad habits, and encourage a taste for learning. Some members of the society, including Phule, were delegated to conduct examinations amongst the children of the *Shudras* at two of the government Marathi schools in Pune, and to distribute prizes and sweets. A sub-committee was appointed to look into the possibility of opening a boarding-house in Pune, so that young *Shudra* students could come to Pune to study under proper supervision. The society had opened a school in the nearby village of Hadapsar. The intention had been that the society should contribute Rs 4 towards its running costs, while the villagers were to make up the remaining Rs 6 themselves. Either the villagers were too poor, however, or the society had yet to get its message understood, for the villagers had failed to raise their amount, and the school had to be closed. The report also recorded two very early examples of what was to become one of the most important and controversial of non-Brahman strategies in the struggle to improve the lower caste communities' share of educational benefits: the demand that a limited positive discrimination should be exercised in their favour. The society had petitioned Mr Cook, the principal of the Engineering College in Pune, to take a few poor students free, and he had agreed to do this. Mr Chatfield, the Director of Public Instruction in the Presidency, had likewise been approached, and he had agreed that of 1,000 free places given annually in the government schools, five should go to poor children of the *Shudra* castes.

Linked with this emphasis on education was a concern with public articulacy. The leaders of the society felt that their own members, and the *Shudra* communities at large, lacked the experience necessary to make coherent and convincing public speeches, or to express themselves confidently in writing, whether in letters to newspapers, or in framing petitions such as those asking for preferential treatment. Their lady of the influence and personal contacts bestowed by government employment had already meant that these groups had a low social and political visibility in public life. Their inarticulacy only compounded this inconspicuousness. In its early years, therefore, the Samaj arranged essay and debating competitions to sharpen up their members' skills in public speaking and writing. The *Dnyanodaya* newspaper of 1 June 1876 reported on the first competition, which had been held on the 22 May. The subjects appointed were the advantages and disadvantages brought upon the country first by the worship of idols, and secondly by the institution of caste. Candidates, of whom there were five, wrote an essay on either subject, and read it out before the assembled members. Dr Gholay, then president of the society, explained the purpose of the competition in his address. He made it clear that the society had a definite rival in mind in its sense that its members had to compete for public attention: the Pune Sarvajanik Sabha. Some years before, the Sabha had set up its own debating society. The children of the *Shudras* did not have the confidence to go there and speak, and so it was necessary that they should first be able to practise amongst themselves. Having once acquired these skills, they would launch themselves upon the more public forum of the Sabha's society. Another competition was held in 1877, in which the subjects were the condition of the untouchables, and the reasons why the *Shudras* were always the first to die whenever famines occurred in India. The subject for the 1878 competition, which was sponsored by Krishnarao Bhalekar, Tukaram Hanamant Pinjan, and Ramasheth Bapusheth Uravane, was to explain why it was that:

> Some people of the Shudra caste, into which were born the hero Chatrapati Maharaja Shivaji, and the great rulers of states, Shinde, Holkar, Gayakavad and others, do not feel it a humiliation when they perform tasks such as looking after the shoes of Brahmans. When, however, some of the Brahman caste go from house to house begging alms, they would scorn even to touch the shawls of Shudra Rajas and princes, let alone their shoes.

Religious Innovation in the Satyashodhak Samaj

This capacity for a common commitment to secular welfare was, however, only to be the outward symbol of a deeper sense of unity and independence amongst the lower caste communities that the leaders of the society sought to create. Crucial to the realisation of this unity were matters of religious worship and ritual. Phule and others hoped that the society would take the lead in establishing the idea of the *Shudras* as a new moral community, independent of Brahmanic Hinduism. The Society would express this spirit through the worship of a Supreme God that transcended all conventional religious confessions, including Hinduism, and by taking into their own hands the conduct of all ceremonies and other social occasions which required a religious sanctification through the performance of ritual.

The decision to dispense with Brahman priests struck, as the leaders of the society intended, at the very heart of existing Hindu ideas about the proper means of access to divine power. By insisting that God was available to all his human creatures, that no intermediary was necessary for the invocation of divine power, the society attempted to remove any justification for the special sanctity of Brahmans. However, the very radicalism of the society here opened possibilities for difficulty and conflict that were proportionately great. Struggling to establish a fragile basis of co-operation between a range of different caste groups and already established leaders, the society was not in the best position to withstand religious controversy.

Not the least of its difficulties was to agree upon the nature and characteristics of the Supreme God. There was the problem of ritual and worship itself. Members of the society were encouraged to carry out their own, and yet it was not clear who would provide the specialised knowledge of ritual techniques that was required or, indeed, whether members should attempt to copy Brahmanic rituals at all, or should try to devise new ones of their own. The claim to *Kshatriya* status, that characterised both Phule's account of the real identity of the *Shudra* castes, and which we have seen as a persistent concern in the Maratha-*kunbi* complex itself, compounded the problems of devising suitable religious ceremonies for the members of the society. Phule had hoped that these great rural communities of the Maratha-*kunbis* would form the natural constituency of the Satyashodhak Samaj. He had taken up the issue of *Kshatriya* status both because he saw it as one of their perennial concerns, and because it symbolised a longer tradition of conflict with Brahman religious opinion. The idea of a *Kshatriya* identity depended for its radicalism upon Phule's larger interpretation of ancient Indian history. Unless it was placed against the background idea of the Aryan invasions and the expropriation of the original *Kshatriyas* of ancient India, such claims by Satyashodhak members became little more than an ordinary attempt at Sanskritisation. The appeal and ideological effectiveness of Phule's scheme derived directly from this tension or ambiguity. In the Satyashodhak Samaj, there were always to be differences of emphasis on this point, with some groups concerned to claim an elite status and ritual that they felt was only the proper due of the Marathas, and others interested much more in a direct attack on all forms of Brahman power. The differences between these were to emerge in the matter of ritual, as the former group sought to have Vedic ritual performed for themselves that seemed to the latter too similar for comfort to the Brahmanic forms of worship rejected by the society.

Conformity amongst members was another very delicate matter. There was nothing in the rules of the society that directly forbade the employment of Brahman priests. Almost certainly, Phule and other leaders felt that this was too tricky an issue for direct legislation. The closest that the rules came to mentioning it was in the second article of the vow that members took on joining, where they undertook not to do anything which would undermine the idea of a basic religious equality, bestowed on all men by their Creator. As we shall see, however, not all members of the society seemed able to give such an uncompromising demonstration of their radicalism. This led to difficulties and tensions with others less cautious. Members often joined the society not as individuals but as families, and this made the problem of conformity more difficult. Often, the older members of the family resisted such dramatic religious innovation, and put pressure on their younger members not to go to the extreme of dispensing with Brahman priests altogether.

There was also conflict within the larger Mali and Marathi-*kunbi* communities in Pune, as the more conservative sections watched with trepidation the emergence of an organised body that threatened both established religious practices, and existing structures of authority within the castes. As we shall see, the emergence of a number of quite new institutions and organisations within the broader non-Brahman movement represented both a challenge to older caste authority, and the creation of quite different foci of power, for the control of which new leaders were to compete. The construction of new sources of power, with the ability to transcend older communities based on caste, provoked a fierce rivalry amongst non-Brahman leaders. This instability was quite disproportionate to the real ideological differences between

Another perennial problem that confronted the Satyashodhak Samaj lay in defining the exact status of its members in relation to the broader Hindu community. The question of whether or not they were still Hindus was a very awkward one, frequently seized on with glee by their opponents, and avoided as a clear decision by members themselves. Non-Hindus were free to join the society, which seemed to confirm the impression of separation from ordinary Hindus. While, however, the members of the society were reluctant to portray themselves as ordinary Hindus, they were even more anxious to avoid declaring that they had actually left the Hindu community.

We will turn now to look in more detail at the rituals and modes of worship employed by members of the society. These were of two kinds. The first were concerned with giving expression to the bonds of the new community, and conferring sanctity on these bonds by the invocation of divine power. The second were concerned with all of the normal ceremonial occasions in the lives of members, for which some new provision had to be made if Brahman priests were not employed. The first of these drew directly upon Phule's rewriting of important aspects of popular religious culture. How he imposed a new meaning on the figure of Khandoba, the guardian deity of western Maharashtra. 'Khandoba' had been the tide given to the lieutenants of King Bali in pre-Aryan India. The rite of picking up the *tali* in Khandoba worship derived from King Bali's practice of throwing down a *vida*, or roll of betel leaves, to be picked up by whoever among his troops dared to take on a particularly difficult enterprise. At the time of taking their vows, new members of the Satyashodhak Samaj were called on to perform this rite of picking up the *tali.* Tukaram Hanamant Pinjan, who was a member of the society from its earliest days, recalled the rite:

The materials for the tali were put into a brass dish: turmeric, red powder, pieces of sugar, fragments of coconut, coriander, betel leaves and betel nut. Whilst picking up the tali, he would take the names of Jotiba, Khandoba, Bahiroba and other gods, shouting 'Chang Bhala to Bahiri', 'Yelakot' and so on.

Phule himself described Gyanoba Sasane's decision to become a member: 'After I had convinced him, Sasane picked up the vida and entered the Samaj.' There are also references in the society's account book to the purchase of materials for the rite. On 22 October 1873 there were bought 'materials for the vida'. An entry for 23 February 1874 towed the purchase of coconut and turmeric, and small boxes to hold them. In the moment of the ritual, therefore, the new member became one with the most daring of King Bali's supporters, volunteering to take up the struggle against Brahman power.

The Report of the Society for 1873-5 described other changes in ritual:

> Some members of this Samaj and their families have given up a number of foolish religious customs. These are the fast at Haratalika; the celebrations for Ganesh Chaturthi on the fourth day of the light half of Bhadarapad; the Krishipanchami; giving food to Brahmans, worshipping their feet and drinking the water touched by them, for the worship of ancestors in the dark half of Bhadarapad; and making a great noise at the celebration of the Holi fire on the fifteenth of the light half of Phalgun.

The feast of Haratalika is on the third day of the light half of the month of Bhadrapad, and is the day of worship of the goddess Paravati, consort of Shiva, by married women. The following day, the fourth day of the light half of Bhadarapad, celebrates the birthday of the god Ganesh. The fifth day, *Rshipanchami*, is devoted to the worship of the seven *rshis* or sages of ancient India. Some members, then, had clearly attempted to comply with the first article in the society's vows: to worship only one Supreme God. It is not clear whether any other forms of worship were substituted for these three days, which might have been linked with Phule's reinterpretations. For the fourth item, the worship of ancestors during the dark half of Bhadarapad, Phule had certainly provided a substitute meaning: it recalled the ceremonies carried out by the *Kshatriyas* of ancient India in honour of the dead killed in battle between Vaman and Bali. We do not have any evidence that this was used to replace the conventional ceremonies. Both the two reports of the society and the subsequent recollections of its members were understandably reticent about these details of its religious practices. In the society's account book, however, there is a brief but definite reference to the celebration of King Bali. The entry for 10 November 1874 registered 'Expenses for the feast of Bali Pratipada, the first day of the light half of Kartik'. This was the normal day, during the Hindu festival of Divali, for the worship of King Bali, but the account book did not usually record expenses for particular festival days. This was also one of the days that Phule had made the centrepiece of the struggle between Bali and Vaman. It seems very likely, therefore, that the figure of Bali enjoyed a special place in the observances of the society in its early days.

We turn now to the conduct of more conventional ceremonies by the society. By far the most important of these was marriage. The report for 1873-5 took greatest pride in reporting the conduct of marriages without the aid of Brahman priests. Two such marriages had taken place in Pune, and eleven in the nearby village of Bhilar, conducted by the *patil* of the village, who had just become a member. In introducing the subject of the marriages, the 1875 report criticised the extortionate demands of the Brahman priests at the marriages of *Shudras*, and the refusal of the former to carry out the ceremony in the proper fashion unless they were paid in full. The society had therefore determined to conduct its own ceremonies, without the assistance of Brahmans, to ensure that marriages were carried out in a proper fashion and without undue expense.

Phule wrote a long account of one of the two Pune weddings, which was published in the *Satyadipika* newspaper. Phule's young friend, Gyanoba Sasane, then aged twenty-two, had arranged, with Phule's help, to marry Kashibai, the 14-year-old daughter of Narayanrao Vithoba Shinde, of Paravati village, near Pune. Phule persuaded Sasane to join the Satyashodhak Samaj, and to conduct the marriage according to the society's beliefs. Sasane's parents appealed to him to arrange a conventional wedding, but without success. Then, however, some of the conservatives in the Mali caste came out to Sasane's village of Hadapsar, and roused some of the villagers against this proposed assault upon their ancestral religion. They gathered at night outside Sasane's house, shouting threats and abuse. Sasane was greatly shaken by this, and went to Phule to tell him that he had changed his mind, Phule urged him to take courage and assured him that they were living under the protection of British justice, and Sasane returned to his former resolve. The opposition within the Mali caste continued, led, Phule said, by prominent members of a more conservative temperament, who feared that the society would undermine their authority. These opponents employed agents to visit Mali families to warn them that if they joined the society, they would have no choice but to become Christians. When Phule realised the extent of the opposition, he wrote to his fellow Satyashodhak, Rajanna Lingu, a Telugu Mali and well-known Pune lawyer. Lingu persuaded Gangaram Bhau Mhaske, a prominent public figure in Pune, and a well-wisher of the society, to arrange for police protection. The marriage went ahead according to plan, although the conservative Mali party arranged for the simultaneous marriages of two 2-year-old girls as a gesture of protest against the violation of Hindu beliefs. Neither this account nor the 1875 report of the society, however, went into any detail about the content of these new ceremonies, or Who actually conducted them.

This controversial religious initiative proved, at first, very difficult to sustain. Members were free to conduct their marriages and other important family ceremonies in the conventional manner, and it is clear that those who elected to have theirs done without Brahmans were a small minority. The second report of the society, for the year 1875-6, made no mention of marriages at all, but concentrated upon the programmes of education and social welfare carried out by the society. Indeed, references in this report suggest that there was a widespread reluctance among members to conform fully with the society's principles, particularly where the observance of caste differences and the conduct of ritual were concerned. The report opened by recording that 'Dr Vishram Ramji Gholay suggested that all members should try to begin to behave, as far as they were able, according to the rules that all members agreed to at the anniversary of the Society last year.'Towards the end the report grew more explicit: 'It is not feasible for many of our people to conduct themselves according to the second clause of the ninth of the rules that were decided upon by the General Meeting of the Society last year. Accordingly, this rule has been lifted for the present year.' The fourth clause of the ninth rule was also to be removed since 'it was included in the third clause of the twenty-third rule'. This ninth rule was the society's vow, and these alterations attenuated it severely, only a year after the members had agreed upon it. Most important was the suspension of the crucial second clause of the vow, in which members committed themselves not to observe social and religious inequalities. Very shortly after its foundation, therefore, the leaders of the society found that they would have to make compromises to allow for their less venturesome followers.

Conflict and the Problem of Leadership

Within three years of its foundation, the society encountered equally severe problems amongst its leadership. As a new focus of power and organisation, it was natural that the society should meet with some hostility from existing leaders within the Mali and Maratha-kunbi communities. However, struggles for leadership within the society proved just as damaging. The most violent of these struggles took place between Phule and Krishnarao Bhalekar, the young radical from the village of Bhamburade. It began in 1875, and continued sporadically right up until Phule's death in 1890. The immediate object of the dispute was the control of a printing press mat had been given to the Pune society by two wealthy members of the Bombay branch, Vyanku Baloji Kalevar and Ramayya Vyankayya Ayyavani. The deeper issue was Phule's personal authority within the society.

In these first three years of its existence, Phule does not seem to have played a very prominent formal role in the society's affairs. It is not clear who was first made President. In the report of 1875, Phule appeared as the society's Treasurer, while in 1876 he acted only as one of the twelve members on the managing committee, with the offices of president and vice-president going to Vishram Ramji Gholay and Laksmanrao Hari Shinde respectively. It is very difficult to find direct references to the extent of his informal authority within the society. What is clear, however, is that he was able both to withold control of the printing press from Bhalekar, and to suppress all reference to the dispute in the society's reports. It is only from Bhalekar's later comments that we learn of the bitterness that the dispute aroused. Unfortunately, we have only Bhalekar's account of the quarrel, and no explanation on Phule's side for his refusal to allow Bhalekar to carry out his plan to use the press to start what would have been the first non-Brahman newspaper. The society's account book recorded the arrival of the printing press from Bombay on 24 November 1874. It had cost Rs 1,200, and its purpose was 'that we should publish before our compassionate English Government what the aims of the society are, and what difficulties and troubles the Shudra people suffer from the Brahman servants of the Government'. Thereafter, from November 1874 until January 1876, the account book recorded a good deal of money being spent on the accommodation and maintenance of the press, but it was never brought into operation. An entry for 5 January 1876 listed the expenses of packing the press up. Only a week later, on 12 January, the society had got in an outside contractor for the printing of 1,000 copies of its rules. The report for 1875-6 remarked only that 'for about a year there has been correspondence between members here and in Bombay over the rights to the press, and so they have taken it back'.

Bhalekar gave a more impassioned account of the affair. After the pess had arrived, it had merely lain idle, while members had worried about the problem of libel that might arise from conducting a non-Brahman newspaper. Seeing their reluctance, Bhalekar declared that he would take on the responsibility of running a newspaper, and asked for the press to be rented to him. Most of the members were in favour of the idea, having been impressed with Bhalekar's already considerable record of activity on behalf of the lower castes. 'But the gentleman who was responsible for allowing the press to lie idle for two years disagreed. He did not like the idea that this young lad might become more important, and make him appear timid and incompetent. So he raised all sorts of objections before the society, and in the end returned the press to Bombay.' Undeterred, Bhalekar set about acquiring his own press with the help of a Bombay supporter, Muktaji Appaji Kambale. He brought it to Pune, and in January 1877 brought out the first issue of the weekly *Din Bandhu* newspaper, with a circulation of 300 copies.

There is no evidence that Phule refused to allow Bhalekar to conduct a newspaper for reasons of ideological disagreement. Throughout his career, Bhalekar's position on the crucial issues of religion and caste remained very close to Phule's. The dispute was rather an illustration of the difficulties of leadership that were caused by the intensely opposi-tional nature of the Satyashodhak Samaj, and its novelty as a focus of power. Phule had striven, often in the face of bitter opposition, to maintain a consistent platform of resistance to Brahman power. He had made considerable personal sacrifices in the course of the struggle, beginning with his banishment from his father's house, with a young wife and few resources of his own. The stresses and privations of such a position, kept up for more than twenty-five years, almost certainly made Phule possessive of his leadership. Bhalekar, then aged twenty-six years to Phule's fifty, had already demonstrated considerable intellectual independence and capacity for organisation. He himself remarked on his own irreverence and liking for argument. At Phule's first visit to his village of Bhamburade in 1867, Bhalekar had shown no hesitation in getting up and criticising his speech: 'In order to show up the mistakes in what he said (I was young at the time, and had a great liking for argument) I got up and made a speech of my own.' Phule may have felt that the purposes of the society would be served better by preserving a strong and united leadership than by allowing a major new initiative on the part of such a determinedly independent and enthusiastic member. The amounts of money that were spent on the press, ultimately to no purpose, aggravated feelings on either side.

Phule's decision did not resolve the problem of authority in the society. Bhalekar himself remained loyal to its larger aims, but never lost his resentment of Phule, and his sense of grievance at the lack of appreciation shown towards his considerable efforts. Bhalekar's alienation led to the loss of some of the society's impetus. In 1878, and again in 1879, he organised debating competitions on his own initiative. An announcement in the *Dnyanodaya* newspaper of 28 February 1878 gave notice of the first of these: 'The undersigned humbly beg to inform all members of the Satyashodhak Samaj that some wise members wish to hold a competition for the reading and writing of essays, on 10 March 1878, according to the rules of our Society, that our people should learn to read and write fluently.' There is no indication that the society itself organised a competition after 1877.

There were other signs, muted and indirect, of restiveness amongst some of the members. Certainly, several were not unwilling to support Bhalekar in his efforts. Ramasheth Bapusheth Uravane and Tukaram Hanamant Pinjan were co-signatories of the letter to the *Dnyanodaya*. Another member, Dadji Sakharam Chavan, put his name to the announcement of the 1879 competition, given in the *Dnyanodaya* of 13 March 1879. In 1877 the president of the society, Dr Vishram Ramji Gholay, resigned, according to Bhalekar because he found it hard to work with Phule. The report of the society for 1875-6 also gave indications that all was not well. The secretary, Narayan Tukaram Nagarakar, praised the work that members had done. But there was still a great need for support from intelligent, wealthy, and hardworking people. 'While the numbers of such people in the society do not increase, and while the members that there are do not attend the society regularly, it will not flourish as it should. Every member should be quite clear about this. The society has taken in hand a work of very great importance, but the work is not going ahead as fast as we would have wished.' Another indication of flagging enthusiasm was that only 67 people are recorded in this report as paying any kind of subscription, against a claimed membership of 316. The society had Rs 766 in its funds at the time, but most of this was contributed by a few of the wealthier members, and by Phule himself.

The problem of authority in the society was not alone in causing this loss of unity and energy towards the end of the decade. Equally important was the resistance that it encountered amongst the very Mali and Maratha-*kunbi* castes whose cause it claimed to champion. This emerged clearly in a letter written to Bhalekar's *Din Bandhu* newspaper by Narayan Meghaji Lokhande, a rising young member of the society in Bombay. The Satyashodhak Samaj and its progenitor, Jotirao Phule, had taken up the important work of giving education to the *Shudras,* and striving to improve their condition. However, Lokhande said, wealthy and influential *Shudras* had not given Phule the support that he deserved. This was because they took a very poor view of Phule's hostility to Brahmans. But, Lokhande continued:

> My brothers, you are making a great mistake. The fashion for calling themselves Brahmans that these people have taken up is absolutely against the Shastras, and so they commit a great sin in the eyes of God. To you, a Brahman is your guru in religion, and we revere him more than God himself. Therefore, he should look on you as a parent would his child. But this is not at all the case. These Brahmans do not make haste, in the way that you would, to help your child out of difficulty. On the contrary, they strive to increase your troubles. In some villages, Brahmans have seized the property of the Shudras and made them homeless and destitute. So, my friends, are you not making a mistake?

Despite all these difficulties, the leaders of the Satyashodhak Samaj had succeeded, against formidable odds, in laying down a precedent for non-Brahman organisation. Both the tradition of organised radicalism instituted by the society, and the experience of planning a common venture, were to be extremely valuable in the future.

Membership of the Early Satyashodhak Samaj

In this early stage of its existence, the society drew its support from Pune and its immediately adjacent villages, and from Bombay. Very often, however, members had only moved to Pune and Bombay within one or two generations. The leaders of the society were Mali or Telugu Mali by caste. Malis also made up a large proportion of its support, although a very wide range of castes was represented within the membership. A high proportion of the most prominent members were engaged in commerce as merchants and contractors, and often formed business connections in addition to their common ideological commitments. A considerable number were also employed in local government administration, or had a profession.

We will look first at a few of the more prominent members, about whom we have most information. Narayan Meghaji Lokhande (1848-1907) ranked alongside Phule and Bhalekar as a Satyashodhak campaigner and polemicist. He was the son of a poor Mali from Thana district. After a secondary school education, he went to work in Bombay as a clerk in a railway office, then in a post office, and finally as a store-keeper in a cotton mill. He joined the Satyashodhak Samaj in 1874. He undertook extensive organisational activity from the late 1870s, concerning himself especially with the condition of workers in the cotton mills in Bombay. Early in 1880, he founded the Mill Hands Association, which agitated for shorter working hours and better conditions for labourers. He wrote prolifically in the *Din Bandhu* newspaper, which he took over as editor from Bhalekar in May 1880. Lokhande's work contained an important difference of ideological emphasis from that of Phule and Bhalekar. The latter had always remained wary of making direct claims to a Maratha status for the lower castes. Lokhande showed no such hesitation in laying claim to the Maratha name. As editor of the *Din Bandhu,* he made it a central ideological project to identify the Maratha name with all of Maharashtra's agricultural and labouring castes. He spent much editorial energy in denigrating rival interpretations - either that the name should be applied only to the Maratha-*kunbis,* or that all Marathi-speaking Hindus might claim the tide.

Ramayya Vyankayya Ayyavaru was an important activist and polemicist during the 1870s. He was one of the Telugu Mali community in Bombay who made up a large proportion of the society's Bombay support. Ayyavaru was a wealthy contractor, with a strong interest in social and religious reform. He took the lead in forming the Bombay branch of the society and, with Vyanku Baloji Kalevar, another Telugu Mali contractor, purchased the ill-fated printing press. He founded an institute for women in Bombay, and was active in the Nitiprasarak Mandali, founded in 1882, which contained many members of the society, and which strove to spread ideas of moral reform without bias towards any existing religion. Ayyavaru and Phule came into conflict when the former published a pamphlet, entitled *A Request to Our Christian Brothers,* which reproached Christians for their aggressive claims to a monopoly of religious truth. However, Ayyavaru remained insistently loyal to the broader aims of the Satyashodhak Samaj, and carried its traditions of activism into the next century.

Vishram Ramji Gholay (1838-1900), the president of the society in 1875-6, was of the *gavali* caste, and came of a family with a strong tradition of service in the Maratha armies. His grandfathers had been the commanders of the fort of Anjanavel, and his father had entered the army as a *Subedhar,* or Indian officer, under British rule. He went to Grant Medical College in Bombay, and came to Pune as an assistant surgeon in 1874, and joined the society. He was a very generous contributor to the society's funds for educational projects. He made great efforts on the society's behalf throughout the 188os, assisting at the reception given to Sayajirao, the Maharaja of Baroda, giving advice when members from Otur, in Junnar district, were taken to court by the village Brahmans for having conducted their own marriage ceremonies, and attending on Phule when he became ill in 1888.

We turn now to the composition of the larger membership of the society. A number of members were employed in the administration and the professions. A list of sixty-seven members given at the back of the report for 1875-6 included four doctors, two 'head writers', two 'writers', a head clerk, a police inspector, a Deputy Collector, an overseer, and a government pensioner. Other lists of members give some indication of their occupations. Hanumanrao Bapuji Sahane, Narayan Tukaram Nagarakar, Nana Karkhanavis, Narayanrao Kada-lak, Vinayak Babaji Dengale, and Namadev Mahadev Dasturakar all returned themselves as 'writers', or clerks in private employment. Muraraji Vithoba Musil was a clerk in a local government department. Bapuji Hari Shinde was a head accountant in the government service at Buldhana. Rajanna Lingu, a Telugu Mali, was a prominent lawyer in Pune. Yashavantrao Raghoba Kambale was a railway inspector. Gyanu Jayakar was a *Jamadar*, or commander of troops in the Bombay army. Viththal Tulsiram Hirave was a soldier stationed in Pune. There was also a sprinkling of students. Vinayakrao Babaji was a matriculation candidate. Dayaram Kirad was a matriculation student receiving aid from the society because of the poverty of his family. Tukaram Chavan went to engineering college, paid for by the society.

An even larger proportion of members were merchants, traders, and contractors. Most of the Telugu Mali members in Bombay came into this category. Jaya Karadi Lingu, Vyanku Baloji Kalevar, Narasinha Sayabu Vadnala, Nagu Sayaji, and Devaji Ellapa were all Bombay merchants and contractors who contributed substantially to the society's funds, and took its programmes of education and religious reform to their own communities. Mali members in Pune included a number of prominent merchants and contractors. Ramasheth Bapusheth Uravane was a wealthy merchant, trading in sugar, and a close friend of Phule's. Ramachandra Hari Shinde, on the managing committee of the society in 1875, was a contractor, in business for a time with Bhalekar in the company set up by Phule, called the Pune Commercial and Contracting Company. Babaji Manaji Dengale was a Pune trader. Gyanu

Malharaji Jagade of Pune, and Gopal Manaske of Bhamburade were *mestres,* superintendents of labourers in construction projects. Although Malis were the largest part of the membership, other castes were represented. Bhikoba Baloba Sali and Tukaram Bahiroba Sali were of the Sali or weaver caste. Ravaji bin Balaji Jadhav and Sakhu Bapu Mahar were of the untouchable Mahar caste. Damodar Bapuji Shimpi and Sadguru Bhivaji Shimpi were of the Shimpi caste of tailors. Dhondiram Namadev Kumbhar, who was to become a formidable polemicist of the society, was a potter or bricklayer. Raju Baba was of the Vanjari caste of grain-carriers. There were two Muslims, Ajjam Elija Shaleman, and Babanabhai Musulman. Govindrao Bapuji Patil, of Bhilar village in the Satara district, was a Maratha-*kunbi.* The society was dominated, then, by well-to-do merchants, tradesmen, and professional men, but also attracted poorer and more obscure Mali families, as well as a small number of members from other castes. They found the society, and its accompanying ideology, attractive for several different reasons.

First, and most obviously, they experienced the sense of incongruity almost always felt by a newly urbanised and upwardly mobile group. In secular terms, they occupied a position of affluence and local respectability, but their low ritual status, as *Shudras,* remained unchanged. This sense of disparity was heightened by the publicity that was given to the actual contents of Hindu religious texts, especially those that specified the very low ritual status of *Shudras,* such as Manu's Laws.

Such discrepancies were by no means unusual in Hindu society, as individual castes flourished and declined. An adjustment of ritual position was usually possible in some form of Sanskritisation. Yet the intellectual climate in Pune and Bombay was characterised by a public hostility to older Brahman models of behaviour, and by intense debate about individual and social values.

The attractiveness of Satyashodhak ideas for these groups derived from their close personal experience of the advantages enjoyed by Brahmans in the local institutions of British administration. As contractors and professional men dealing very frequently with local government institutions, they came into close contact with Brahman officials and administrators. This would have magnified both their conviction of the economic and social advantages enjoyed by Brahmans, and their feeling of an undue dependence on them. Besides them, the Malis and other lower castes seemed woefully lacking in the ability to secure such rewards. The most likely way to acquire this ability lay in organisation, not just of the Malis, but of all lower castes. This reflected the conviction of a connection between the religious and the administrative and occupational power of Brahmans that came to stand at the very heart of Satyashodhak ideology. Members of the society were convinced that only a very broadly-based movement would be able to persuade the British government that it did itself, and society as a whole, a great disservice in directing so many educational and occupational advantages towards Brahmans.

Such a body would be able to claim with conviction that these benefits should be directed towards the great bulk of Maharashtra's cultivating and labouring castes, the real substance of her society, and the representatives of her history and culture. Both of these concerns came together in giving great appeal to Phule's *Kshatriya* ideology, set out in the works that were adopted as Satyashodhak texts. For these early supporters of the Samaj, the idea that their 'real' identity was that of the dispossessed *Kshatriyas* of ancient India served the social and religious purpose that might otherwise have been met by the claim to a higher conventional ritual status, and by a change in social practices towards a Brahmanic model of behaviour. There was also a strong political dimension to the assertion of *Kshatriya* status. Pratapsinh Bhosale's insistence on his status as a *Kshatriya* was nothing less than a claim to the position of secular authority that belonged to a kingly ruler. It represented an assertion of his own leadership of Hindu society against what he saw as a Chitpavan Brahman effort simultaneously to usurp his secular authority, and to undermine its religious legitimation by consigning the Bhosales to the ranks of the *Shudras.* In asserting an original *Kshatriya* status for all lower castes, now withheld by conventional Brahmanic religion, Phule and his urban following in the 1870s made the deliberate Link with this political dimension of traditional Maratha claims to a *Kshatriya* ritual status. Lacking the obvious genealogical basis for their arguments that Pratapsinh possessed, they made their claim in the context of the larger argument that the virtues of the warrior and the cultivator had been the central force in the shaping of Maharashtra's traditions and culture. To their representatives in nineteenth-century society belonged the position of social and political leadership that Brahmans had assumed, and upon which the latter had consolidated their hold under British rule. These representatives were the peasant and urban lower castes, the true *Kshatriyas* of nineteenth-century Maharashtra. This immediately prompts the question as to what connection the lives of merchants and contractors, urbanised and relatively affluent, could have possessed with these elements in Maharashtra's traditional society and culture to give the identification with the warrior and the cultivator any real meaning.

Yet there were two vital links. First, as Malis, they did belong to the large body of Maharashtra's cultivator castes with which these traditional occupations were associated, and the period of their urbanisation was relatively short. Two, the very nature of their occupations as merchants and contractors meant that they maintained their contact both with the urban environment in which their awareness of injustice was sharpened.

This duality of the early support of the Satyashodhak Samaj is beautifully illustrated in an anecdote about Phule told by his friend and business colleague, Gyanoba Sasane. Sasane had accompanied Phule to inspect his orchards outside Pune. When all the workers had stopped for their mid-day meal, Phule got up and started to drive the well-bucket himself, singing as he did so. The labourers laughed to see him, whereupon Phule turned to explain. He was just a cultivator in his bones, he said. What was more, all plain cultivators sang at their work. It was only those who did not toil with their hands that had the leisure to sit with musical instruments.

REFERENCES

M.R. Lederle, *Philosophical Trends in Modern Maharashtra,* Popular Prakashan, Bombay 1976, p. 80. J. Masselos, *Towards Nationalism: Group Affiliations and the Politics of Public Associations in Nineteenth Century Western India,* Popular Prakashan, Bombay 1974, pp. 81-5.

R.C. Zaehner, *Hinduism,* Oxford University Press 1980, pp. 125-46. G.A. Deleury, *The Cult of Vithoba,* Deccan College Postgraduate and Research Institute, Pune 1960. J. Lele *(ed.), Tradition and Modernity in Bhakti Movements,* E. J. Brill, Leiden 1981.

J.T.F. Jordens, *Dayananda Sarasvati: His Life and Ideas,* Oxford University Press, Delhi 1978, pp. 127-59.

Christine Dobbin, *Urban Leadership in Western India: Politics and Communities in Bombay City, 1840-1885,* Oxford University Press, 1972, pp. 65-70.

P.S. Patil, *The Life of Mahatma Jotirao Phule,* Chikhali 1927 (Marathi), pp. 84-6.

R.C. Dhere, *Santasahitya ani Lokasahitya: Kahi Anubandh,* Pune, 1978 (Marathi), pp. 92-121.

Tukaram Tatya Padaval, *A Critique of Caste Divisions,* Bombay, 1865.

R.C. Dhere, *Santasahitya ani Lokasahitya,* pp. 118-19.

Gyanoba Sasane, MS autobiography (Marathi), unpaginated. This MS is in Dr R. M. Paul's collection. It was written down, to Sasane's dictation, by a poor boy in Hadapsar, after Sasane had arranged for him to receive a small monthly allowance from the Scottish mission in the village, so that he could attend the village school.

Tukaram Hanamant Pinjan to Mukundrao Patil, 11 July 1923. This letter is reprinted in *Purogami Satyashodhak,* Pune, vol 3, no. I, January-March 1977.

The Report of the Pune Satyashodhak Samaj, from 24 September 1873 to 24 September 1875, Dnyanprakash Press, Pune 1877 (Marathi), p. 1.

The Report of the Pune Satyashodhak Samaj, from 24 September 1873 to 24 September 1875, P. 8.

The Report of the Pune Satyashodhak Samaj, from 24 September 1873 to 24 September 1875, pp. 1-6.

Dhananjay Keer, *Mahatma Jotirao Phooley, Father of Indian Social Revolution*, Popular Prakashan, Bombay 1974, pp. 161-4.

The Report of the Pune Satyashodhak Samaj, from 24 September 1875 to 24 September 1876, pp. 2-4.

Reported in the *Dnyanodaya* (English-Marathi), 12 April 1877.

Dnyanodaya, 28 February 1878. This is a reference to the powerful Shinde family, who were supposed to have started their service of the peshwas as the bearers of their slippers.

Satyadipika (Marathi), June 1874.

The Report of the Punt Satyashodhak Samaj, from 24 September 1873 to 24 September 1875, p. 4.

The Report of the Pune Satyashodhak Samaj, from 24 September 1875 to 24 September 1876, p. 1.

Krishnarao Bhalekar, *A Short History of Krishnarao Bhalekar*, Bhalekar MSS, Dr R. M. Paul Collection, Pune.

Ramayya Vyankayya Ayyavaru, *A Request to Our Christian Brothers*, Bombay, 1887.

8

Dynamics of Dalit Society

RAMABAI

Due to the efforts of Pandita Ramabai there was a beginning of education for girls and many great learned Arya Brahmans began to educate their helpless ignorant women to redress the errors of their rishi ancestors, but there may be many negative results of our critical writing about the tyrannical statements of the merciless Aryan bookwriters on women. Mainly this: fearing that when the cruel wickedness of the Aryan books come to the attention of the daughters and bhat-Brahmans they will make mincemeat of all the legends of the temples and gods and mockingly reject them, and that besides, in most Brahman families a continual quarrel between mothers-in-law and daughters-in-law will arise and cause numerous tensions, many bhat-bhikshuks will stop sending their daughters and daughters-in-law to school and naturally will not give them even so much a glimpse of our *Satsar* book.

Phule wrote this in a pamphlet in 1885 in response to attacks on two women, Tarabai Shinde and Pandita Ramabai. In 1882 Ramabai had come to Pune, founded the Arya Mahila Samaj and then, shortly after, departed for England where she converted to Christianity. For this, she was condemned by even the moderate brahmins who had originally sponsored her efforts. Tarabai, a daughter of one of Phule's Maratha colleagues in the Satyashodak Samaj, had written a bitter and hard-hitting attack on Hindu patriarchy, *Stri-Purush Tulna*

("Comparison of Women and Men") in 1882. Both women evoked waves of reaction, Ramabai in the wider world of the English-educated Brahman intellectuals, Tarabai in Phule's own Satyashodhak circles; and Phule defended both.

Pandita Ramabai was by far the better known of the two women and, in spite of her conversion to Christianity, accepted much of the framework of the Brahman intellectuals of the time. She called her organisation (undoubtedly the first autonomous women's organisation in India) the Arya Mahila Samaj and focused her main English book on "the high-caste Hindu woman". She also continued to retain many Brahmanic habits, in particular vegetarianism, as a symbol of her Indian identity—perhaps a necessary symbol for her in the face of often racist church pressure--and accepted the identification of "India" with "Hindu" and the Aryan model justification for caste hierarchy, arguing that the complete dependence and ignorance of women had been the cause of "the present degradation of the Hindu nation."

> Without doubt, 'caste' originated in the economic division of labour. The talented and most intelligent portion of the Aryan Hindus became, as was natural, the governing body of the entire race.

In spite of this and for all the frequent mildness of her language, it was Pandita Ramabai who was the first to proclaim, with great clarity, backed by her personal refusal to remain a Hindu, that the Sanskritic core of Hinduism was irrevocably and essentially anti-woman:

> Those who diligently and impartially read Sanskrit literature in the original, cannot fail to recognise the law-giver Manu as one of those hundreds who have done their best to make women hateful beings in the world's eye.... I can say honestly and truthfully, that I have never read any sacred book in Sanskrit literature without meeting this kind of hateful sentiment about women.

Thus, her conversion testimony stressed that there were

> ...only two things on which all those books, the Dharma Shastras, the sacred epics, the Puranas and the modern poets, the popular preachers of the present day and orthodox high-caste men, were agreed: that women of high and low caste as a class, were bad, very bad, worse than demons, as unholy as untruth, and that they could not get Moksha as men [could].

In spite of her initial acceptance of most of the assumptions of Hindu nationalism, when it came to her own experience, this daughter of a wandering and reformist Brahman, the only woman of her time to have been educated in the sacred language, who had fought her way forward to be recognised by the intellectuals of her time, had come to condemn the core of Hinduism as fundamentally patriarchal.

TARABAI SHINDE

We know little of Tarabai Shinde's life and virtually nothing of what happened to her after she wrote her book. It is clear that she did not go on to achieve the autonomy she so clearly strove for, and whether she ever managed to carve out even a small space for herself in the confined world of the nineteenth century Maratha landholding elite is something we shall perhaps never know. *Stri-Purush Tulna* is her sole known testament, and the sound of a voice not-so-far-heard is its beginning:

> Since this is my first effort at writing, being helpless, bound and without a voice in the prisonhouse of the endless Maratha customs, this essay has extremely harsh language. But seeing that the new terrible examples of men's arrogance and one-sided morality that appear every day are ignored and all blame is put on women, my mind has been filled with the pride of women's position and gone into utmost turmoil.

Tarabai was referring to the debate on widows who were blamed for trying to dispose their babies, the implications of sexual assaults on them being ignored. She was concerned about more than just atrocities; she attacked the whole pattern of life laid out for women.

> What is *stri dharma?* Endless devotion to a single husband, behaving according to his whims. Even if he beats her, curses her, keeps a prostitute, drinks, robs the treasury, takes bribes, when he returns home she should worship him as a god, as if Krishna Maharaj himself had come from stealing the milk of the Gavalis... There are a million reasons for breaking *pativrata.*

And she went on from this to a scornful, satirical attack on the gods and Rishis of the Puranas themselves:

> Now, even with five husbands didn't Draupadi have to worry about Kama Maharaj's intentions?... [What about Satyavati and Kunti?] One agreed to the whims of a rishi in order to remove the bad odour from her body, the other obeyed a mantra! What wonderful gods! What wonderful rishis!

Stri-Purush Tulna takes the form of a diffuse and bitter polemic. It is not a reasoned, direct critique of the Hindu scriptures based on conceptual analysis, but a satirical attack on them in a language of familiarity. This was in fact the way in which many working class and peasant women talked about the stories they were so familiar with. The *Ramayana* and the *Mahabharata* were a part of the lives of the majority but this did not necessarily make them part of a religion, as was made out by religious spokesmen. When Hindu theorists began to turn such texts into "scriptures", women like Tarabai and Ramabai had to attack and reject them. Ramabai tried to create a different institutional framework with different human relations, and spent a lifetime in the service of high (and low) caste widows, whose position represented the most dire fate of women at the time. Tarabai, who was not in a position to do as much, expressed her rebellion in a bitter rhetorical attack on the structures of patriarchy:

> It was a woman, Savitri, who went to the court of Yama in order to save the life of her husband. But leave aside Yama's court, have you heard of any men who have gone even a step on the path towards it? Just as a woman loses her auspiciousness and so has to bury her face like a convict

> and live all her life in darkness, do you have to shave your beard and live like a hermit the rest of your life if your wife dies? If any smart alec god gave you a certificate to take another woman on the tenth day after your wife has died, then show it to me!

In their different ways, women like Tarabai and Ramabai were already, in the nineteenth century, raising their voices against what Partha Chatterjee has described as the "nationalist resolution of the women's question." This rested on separating the material and cultural spheres and making women the guardians of the home, its moral and spiritual essence: "What was necessary was to cultivate the material techniques of modern western civilisation while retaining and strengthening the distinctive spiritual essence of the national culture." In looking to this solution of "eastern morals and western science", there seems to have been no qualitative distinction between reformist Hindus and Hindu nationalists. This was insufficient for women who wanted to be considered complete human beings, since it was the "eastern morals" which oppressed them.

Unlike the Arya Samajists, Ramabai could not see the present state of women simply as "degeneration". Unlike the Brahmo Samajists and men like Gandhi, she could not turn to idealised versions of the Vedas and Upanishads to convince herself that the "essence" of Hindu spiritualism could be saved from its casteist and patriarchal excrescences. Ramabai, like Phule and the later militant Dalits, had to reject Hinduism. Similarly, Tarabai could not see rishis and gods as symbols of divinity without accepting her own position as an inferior. Yet how is it that so many of the later and more highly placed women activists came to compromise on these issues? The answer is partly, of course, that they were forced to: compromise was a way to achieve small gains.

With the emergence of Hindu nationalism in the late nineteenth century had forced even the moderate social reformism of the upper castes to retreat, the women's movement slowly took on an organised form. It emerged with some autonomy in the 1920s with the founding of the All-India Women's Congress and similar organisations. These upper caste and elite women's organisations worked within the Hindu framework and spoke of Sita and Savitri as ideals for women, not as symbols of male oppression. They praised the freedom of the Vedic period, and depicted purdah and other evils as resulting from the social conditions of the Muslim invasion, if not from the Muslims themselves. They fought for and eventually got implemented in some formula a new Hindu code giving substantial, though hardly equal rights to women in such sensitive areas as property and divorce. But they were embarassed by the fact that a Dalit, Ambedkar was the chairman of its drafting committee; and they had no organisation to combat the street demonstrations organised by the fundamentalists. Besides this, by leaving Muslim women out of the bill, they left a dangerous legacy for the firmentation of communal feelings in years to come.

Agrarian women seem to have had their own forms of action that reinterpreted tradition more actively but very often also remained within the framework of the Hindu discourse while building an organisational space for women. Kapil Kumar describes the role of women led by laggi (a Kurmi) in the Oudh Kisan Sabha, supported by Baba Ramchandra (a Maharashtrian Brahman). This led to the founding of a women's front, the Kishanin Sabha which focused both on giving women land rights, and attacking male polygamy and reforming family relations. Like the Kisanin Sabha argued for monogomy. Its rules stated that all relationships should be treated as legitimate and that women should be respected even if they did not produce children. In addition, while using local religious traditions like celebrating a success with a *yagya* to a village goddess) there was also a reinterpretation of tradition. Thus Kaikeyi was praised for sending Rama to the jungle, and Sita was woman who acted on her own: "Did not Rama tell Sita not to accompany him to the forest but Sita on her own decided to go?"

There is very little historical evidence, and even less effort to uncover what may exist, of the actual discourse and actions of working class and peasant women throughout this period while their elite sisters were yielding to the male formulations of Hindu nationalist themes, whether those of Hindu raj or Ram raj. Sumanta Banerjee offers a clue to what could be done in his depiction of lower class women's culture in nineteenth-century Calcutta, while talking of the *kheur*, a popular form of songs on the Radha-Krishna theme, which evolved into a kind of drama of repartee. He cites one example in which Ambalika protests when her mother Satyavati urges her to have union with Vyasa to beget a child:

People say
as a girl you used to row a boat in the river.
Seeing your beauty, tempted by your lotus-bud,
the great Parashar stung you, and
there was a hue and cry:
You've done it once,
You don't have anything to fear.
Now you can do as much as you want to,
no one will say anything.
If it has to be done,
Why don't you do it, mother?

Similar forms of expression were used by many lower class women. Similar biting dialogues were apparently also used in the Satyashodhak *tamashas* of the 1920s in Maharashtra and seem to have been common to *tamasha* culture in most parts of India. The logical style of the Ambalika song (if you think it's so great, do it yourself) provoked an uproar a century later in the intellectual circles of Bombay (at the time of the founding of the Dalit Panthers in 1972) when a prominent Marathi writer said that "prostitutes do work necessary to society and so should be given respect", and Raja Dhale won himself temporary fame, saying, "If Durgabai thinks the work deserves so much respect, why doesn't she do it herself?"

The powerful critiques of the early feminists, women like Ramabai and Tarabai and their male supporters, focused on crucial issues of patriarchy and sexuality, attacking the double standard of *pativrata*. Many women upheld the value of monogamy and others used legends and mythology to mock all impositions of sexual standards, though no explicit claims to sexual freedom were raised among reformers and radicals. Later leaders of the women's movement during the colonial period, identified with the dominant Hindu reformist cultural trend underlying the Congress organisations and in so doing, accepted the basic framework of brahmanical patriarchy. But it was early feminists like Ramabai and Tarabai who were closer to the general attitude of lower class and peasant women in taking the *puranas* as stories and not scriptures, and seeing them as representing the many facets of male oppression rather than as divinely-ordained ideals of human relationships.

Hinduism as Aryan Conquest: The Dalit Radicals of the 1920s

The mobilization of the oppressed and exploited sections of society—the peasants, Dalits, women and low castes that Phule had spoken of as *shudras* and *ati-shudras*—occurred on a large scale in the 1920s and 1930s, under varying leaderships and with varying ideologies. They took part in nationalist campaigns, some of them hailing Gandhi as a kind of messianic figure; they organised unions and Kisan Sabhas; they staged strikes, anti-rent campaigns and revenue/tax boycotts; they fought for forest and village commons. It was an era, following the World War-I and the Russian Revolution, when the masses were coming on to the stage of history.

Inevitably, the specificities of caste exploitation could not be ignored in India. Many low-caste activists of the 1920s, organising as non-Brahmans and Dalits, were drawn to an anti-caste, anti-Brahman, even anti-Hindu ideology of the kind that Phule had formulated. Since few outside Maharashtra had heard of Phule, most likely it was the Tamil non-Brahman movement which had the most influence as the strongest initiator of "non-Aryan" themes. Yet so pervasive were these that it is clear the themes struck a deep mass resonance everywhere. The very use of "Aryan" discourse by the elite was evoking a common response which, in its turn, was to force the elite to revise this discourse significantly. The non-Brahman movements in Maharashtra and Tamil Nadu, as well as the Dalit movements arising in places as distant as the Punjab and Karnataka, all began to argue in terms of the Aryan conquest and Brahman exploitation through religion.

The names of most Dalit movements—Ad-Dharm in Punjab, Adi-Hindu in U.P. and Hyderabad, Adi-Dravida, Adi-Andhra and Adi-Karnataka in south India—indicated a common claim to being original inhabitants. This was exemplified early in Maharashtra, where a pre-Ambedkar Dalit leader, Kisan Faguji Bansode (1870-1946), warned his caste Hindu friends in 1909 that:

> The Aryans—your ancestors—conquered us and gave us unbearable harassment. At that time we were your conquest, you treated us even worse than slaves and subjected us to any torture you wanted. But now we are no longer your subjects, we have no service relationship with you, we are not your slaves or serfs.... We have had enough of the harassment and torture of the Hindus.

Bansode, an educator and journalist, represented a generation of educated Mahar leaders that arose in Nagpur, where Mahars often had some land and formed forty per cent of the workers in an emerging textile industry. He, like many other of the regional Mahar leadership, later turned away from such themes, identifying with Hinduism through devotion to the Mahar saint Chokamela, and Ambedkar in fact had to fight this group to establish his own leadership in Vidarbha. However, by the 1920s, the new Dalit or "adi" movements, with an ideological claim to being heirs of a "non-Aryan" or "original Indian" equalitarian tradition, began to take off in many regions of India.

In Andhra, where the process was affected by the militant Dravidianism of the Madras presidency, the commercialised coastal areas produced both a mobile Dalit agricultural labourer class and a small educated section. A proposed conference of Dalits in Vijayawada in 1917, sponsored by reformist Hindus, was to be called the First Provincial Panchama Mahajana Sabha but changed its name, in a mood of revolt, to the Adi-Andhra Mahajana Sabha on the grounds that "the so-called Panchamas were the original sons of the soil and they were the rulers of the country." The Dalits were in a militant mood; the major temple in the city closed down for the three days of their conference. For over a decade and a half after that, until they became absorbed as "harijans" into the Congress and Communist movements, coastal Andhra Dalits held conferences as Adi-Andhras. By the 1931 census, nearly a third of the Malas and Madigas of the Madras presidency had given their identity as Adi-Andhra.

The Vijayawada Conference was presided over by Bhagyareddy Varma (1888-1939), a Hyderabad Dalit originally named Madari Bhagaiah, who had been organising Adi-Hindu conferences since 1912. Hyderabad had a vigorous, though factionalised, petty bourgeois Dalit group, which began to pick up the Adi-Hindu identity in the 1920s. By 1930 the state census indicated a rather vigorous cultural debate:

> The Adi-Dravida Educational League argued that, judged by the history, philosophy and civilization of the Adi-Dravidas, the real aborigines of the Deccan, the depressed classes are, as a community, entirely separate and distinct from the followers of Vedic religion, called Hindus. The League's contention was that Hinduism is not the ancestral religion of the aborigines of Hindustan; that the non-Vedic communities of India object to being called Hindu because

> of their inherited abhorance of the doctrines of the Manusmruti and like scriptures, who have distinguished themselves from caste Hindus for centuries past, that the Vedic religion which the Aryans brought in the wake of their invasion was actively practiced upon the non-Vedic aborigines, and that the aborigines, coming under the influence of the Hindus, gradually and half-consciously adopted Hindu ideas and prejudices.

In Hyderabad, thus, Tamil Dalits identified themselves as Adi-Dravidas. Telugu-speaking Dalits called themselves Adi-Hindus but a large section of them gave this a militant, anti-Brahman interpretation. Bhagyareddy Varma was a major figure in this group, later identifying with Buddhism and giving tacit support to a younger generation of radicals who became followers of Ambedkar. In faraway U.P. too, where Varma travelled for conferences, a new radical identity arose. Its leading ideologue was an untouchable ascetic from Mainpuri district who had briefly been a member of the Arya Samaj. He left it out of disgust and began to organise the Dalits on the basis of an Adi-Hindu identity. Oiling himself, rather defiantly, Acchutananda, he argued:

> The untouchables, the so-called harijans, are in fact adi-Hindu, i.e. the original or autochthonous Nagas or Dasas of the north and the Dravidas of the south of the subcontinent, and they are the undisputed, heavenly owners of Bharat. All others are immigrants to the land, including the Aryans, who conquered the original populations not by valour but by deceit and manipulation ... by usurping others' rights, subjugating the peace-loving and rendering the self-sufficient people indigents and slaves. Those who ardently believed in equality were ranked, and ranked lowest. The Hindus and untouchables have since always remained poles apart.

In Punjab, a Dalit named Mangoo Ram, also originally a part of the Arya Samaj, began an Ad-Dharm movement in which the Dalits by 1926, had proclaimed themselves a separate *quaum* (community) in a conference in a village of Hoshiarpur district. As the report of the Ad-Dharm Mandal described the Aryan conquest:

> During this time of great achievements, the Aryans heard about the original land's civilization and came there. They learned the art of fighting from the local inhabitants, and then turned against them. There were many wars—six hundred years of fighting—and then the Aryans finally defeated our ancestors, the local inhabitants. Our forefathers ... were pushed back into the jungles and the mountains ... from that time to this time the Hindu Aryans have suppressed the original people.

Again there was a concern for official record of identity. By the 1931 census, nearly 500,000 Ad-Dharmis were reported.

Mangoo Ram, Acchutanand, Bhagyareddy Varma and Kisan Bansode were all of a generation slightly older than Ambedkar. They represented a new movement, they organised on the basis of some mobility of village untouchables— some going into new factories and industries, some overseas to plantations or as soldiers in the Indian army, others claiming small holdings of land deriving from traditional village service-claims or even acquired from factory or other earnings. Spearheading the Dalit organizations was a growing, though still small, educated or semi-educated leadership. Various activities were taken up in this period. On the one hand, social reform included efforts to abolish devadasi traditions and sub-caste differences, and giving up drinking or meat-eating. On the other hand, organising occurred on economic issues concerning factory and mill workers and efforts to acquire land.

While much of this involved linkages with reformist Hindus and acceptance of a basic Hinduist discourse, it was the "adi" ideologies, based on non-Aryan racial theories, that provided the framework for the most militant expressions. It was not that all Dalits, let alone all militant non-Brahmans, accepted this; there were in every region those who chose instead to identify themselves as Hindus, fighting for temple entry, for instance. A significant set of Dalit leaders even went over to the Hindu Mahasabha. But the adi ideologies were pervasive ideas that won a popular base, as census reports show, and expressed the powerful emotional resistance to brahmanism and caste hierarchy that was embodied in Dalit organisations everywhere in the colonial period. (They also had links with the themes of the non-Brahman movements of the Madras and Bombay presidencies, and most of the militant Dalits also had some kind of alliance policy with the non-Brahmans.)

However, while these expressions bore similarities to the ideology of Phule, there were crucial differences from Phule's period that were reflected in the 1920s' non-Brahman-Dalit versions of the non-Aryan themes. First, a whole period of the construction of Hinduism had intervened, with the formulation of an increasingly sophisticated ideology of Hindu nationalism and its spread. The founding of major organisations such as the Hindu Mahasabha and the Rashtriya Swayamsevak Sangh (RSS) occurred in this period. While the RSS remained an aloof, indrawn cadre organisation, organisations like the Mahasabha and the Arya Samaj undertook campaigns to win over low castes. The *shuddhi* campaign (designed to "purify" Dalits or convert them back from Islam) was carried out primarily in the Punjab but the ideological appeals that went along with this had a much wider spread. These identified Dalits as part of the "Hindu fold", and began to emphasise the low-caste origin of figures such as Valmiki and Vyasa to show that Dalits too had a part in the "creation of its great literature". Hindu nationalist upper castes were revising and reinterpreting the racial aspect of their identity to stress a Hindu unity encompassing the caste hierarchy. By the 1930s, it was clear that this reinterpretation had an appeal: not only were large sections of non-Brahmans identifying themselves as Hindus and claiming kshatriya status through the medium of caste conferences, but many important Dalit leaders were also won over, with some like M.S. Rajah of Tamil Nadu and G.A. Gavai of Nagpur even ready to join the Hindu Mahasabha.

On the other hand, the Dalit activists, peasants and workers of the time confronted the formulation of a radical class ideology by a new left intelligentsia. Young Indian socialists and communists led militant struggles that attracted large sections of the exploited and gave them a vision of an equalitarian society, but they avoided the recognition of caste and stressed a mechanical class framework that sought to override traditional identities rather than reinterpret them. It is striking that in the painful confrontation between Gandhi and Ambedkar after the Second Round Table Conference, when both Gandhians and Hindu Mahasabhaites tried to mobilize forces against the followers of Ambedkar and promote their solution to the issue, there was no prominent leftist even concerned about caste. Nehru in his autobiography remarks again and again that he saw Gandhi's harijan campaign as diversionary. It led to the diversion of the people's attention from the objective of full independence to the mundane cause of the upliftment of harijans.

There were many aspects of this resistance to dealing with caste. There was an inability to even recognise identities such as the Adi-Andhra; the communists universally adopted the Gandhian term "harijan" without much concern for whether it would appeal to the people concerned. They also saw themselves, without much trouble, as Hindu (perhaps as "Hindu atheists"). At the same time, communist class ideology defined the industrially-employed working class as advanced, while peasants (so crucial to Phule) were seen as backward, either feudal or "petty bourgeois". State exploitation (such as the exploitation of the peasantry by means of taxes and land revenue) was ignored, while only private property owners (moneylenders, zamindars, etc.) were the appropriate objects of class, as opposed to "national" struggle.

As G.P. Deshpande has argued, Phule was making an effort to formulate a kind of universalistic ideology. He did not identify the oppressed and exploited shudras and ati-shudras as a set of castes so much as a peasant community, nor was the community strictly identified in racial terms. Non-Aryan was, after all, a negative category. In the 1920s, in contrast, the communists were putting forward another universalistic ideology. This one did not recognise community/caste as a node of exploitation; it threw all non-class categories into the realm of the superstructure, relegated to secondary consequence since they were only cultural/ideological constructs. *The formation of a class ideology of this type created a caste ideology of a specific type in reaction*, one which set up caste in opposition to class as a cultural/social factor, a non-economic factor.

In this context, with the strong ideological winds of Hindu nationalism (even in the modified form of Gandhism) and class struggle blowing all around them, the alternative "adi" identity theories put forward by Dalit radicals became racial ones. This can be seen in the above quotations. The Aryans as a people with one religion (Hinduism) were seen as basically confronting (conquering and enslaving) the non-Aryans as a people with a different religion. Sometimes the conquering Aryan caste/community was seen in larger terms (as "all-caste Hinduism"), sometimes in smaller terms " (only as the "upper castes"), but, more often, it was increasingly seen as a racially and religiously solidified group, "the Hindus" Phule had refused to legitimise Hinduism even as the religion of the supposed upper castes, seeing it only as a tool of exploitation. The later radicals also condemned Hinduism but began to see it more and more as a reality.

The communists saw the national movement as basically the only valid non-class struggle of the period, progressive because imperialism had to be fought in order to achieve a democratic revolution that would advance the development of the productive forces (i.e. industrialisation). This resulted in the Dalit and non-Brahman movements being stigmatised as pro-British, the communists refusing to recognise the legitimacy of taking the fight against the Indian elite (or

"Indian feudalism") as central.

Thus two opposing ideologies prevailed among the toiling masses, one arguing from the standpoint of being original inhabitants or non-Aryans, and the other basing itself on the theory of class struggle. With the failure, in particular, of the more all-encompassing Marxist theory to incorporate the problems of caste in India, the broad movement of the oppressed was split into a class movement and a caste movement. There was no synthesis, no development of an integrated ideology and, as a result, those lower castes/ classes who did get drawn into the national struggle or the left-led working class movement, gave up the sharpness of their anti-caste fight. Beneath the folds of the Congress and its hegemonic claim over almost all other political movements, a large number of forces and identities simmered but remained unconnected and ineffective.

The most significant attempt to transcend this fragmentation in the 1930s and 1940s was made by Dr. B.R. Ambedkar, one of the great democratic leaders of the twentieth century.

Hinduism as Counter-Revolution—B.R. Ambedkar

> It must be recognised that there never has been a common Indian culture, that historically there have been three Indias, Brahmanic India, Buddhist India and Hindu India, each with its own culture.... It must be recognised that the history of India before the Muslim invasions is the history of a mortal conflict between Brahmanism and Buddhism.

Dr. Bhimrao Ramji Ambedkar (1891-1956; known as "Babasaheb" in the movement) came into politics claiming the heritage of the non-Brahman movement. Between 1917-20 he returned to India after getting his degree in law in the U.S. He gave up service in Baroda state after insults were heaped upon him as an untouchable. Settling in Bombay as a professor at Sydenham College, he associated with Shahu Maharaj of Kolhapur (notorious to nationalists as anti-Brahman and pro-British) in his initial political organising. The autonomy of the Dalit movement was his concern, but it was to be an autonomy in alliance with non-Brahmans. At the first Depressed Classes conference in Nagpur in 1920, which he attended in the company of Shahu Maharaj, he attacked not only nationalist spokesmen, but also Vitthal Ramji Shinde, the most prominent non-Dalit social reformer claiming to lead the "uplift of untouchables."

Ambedkar's emergence into politics was cautious. Very gradually he gathered a team around him, of educated and semi-educated Mahar boys, as well as a few upper-caste sympathisers, forming the Bahishkrut Hitakarni Sabha, which began to hold conferences around the province. In 1926, an explosive movement resulted when a conference at Mahad in the Konkan ended with a struggle to drink water from the town tank. The Mahad satyagraha, the first "untouchable liberation movement," did not succeed in getting water but did end with the public burning of the *Manusmriti.* The campaign was partly spontaneous and partly planned; Mahad had been chosen as a place where Ambedkar had significant caste Hindu support, where a tenant movement uniting Mahar and Kunbi peasants was beginning (which developed into the biggest anti-landlord movement in Maharashtra in the 1930s), and where the municipality had already passed a resolution to open public places to untouchables.

By the time of the Simon Commission Ambedkar had clearly emerged as the most articulate Dalit leader in the country with a significant mass base, and it was natural that he should be invited to the Round Table Conference. This led to the clash with Gandhi over the issue of an award of separate electorates to untouchables. For Gandhi, the integrity of Hindu society with the untouchables as its indissoluble part was a central and emotional question. The confrontation over Gandhi's fast and the Poona Pact (1932) disillusioned Ambedkar once and for all about Hindu reformism; it inaugurated his radical period which led to an announcement in 1935 that he was "born a Hindu but would not die a Hindu" and the founding in 1936, of the Independent Labour Party (ILP), a worker-peasant party with a red flag. The "conversion announcement" set off ferment throughout the country, while the ILP went on to become the biggest opposition party in the Bombay legislative council.

The 1930s was a decade of ferment, with growing nationalist agitations and workers' and peasants' struggles. The ILP grew and became the only party in India which led struggles against capitalists and landlords along with agitations against caste oppression, calling for a radical opposition to the "Brahman-bourgeois Congress" and seeking to pull in non-Brahmans as well as Dalits. While Ambedkar himself did not support a non-Aryan theory of Dalit-Shudra identity, poems and songs published in his weekly *Janata* show how pervasive these ideas were, and how they linked anti-caste radicalism with calls for class struggle:

> Bhils, Gonds, Dravids, their Bharat was beautiful,
> They were the people, the culture was theirs, the rule was theirs;
> The Aryas infiltrated all this, they brought their power to Bharat
> and Dravidans were suppressed...
> Brahmans, Kshatriyas, Vaishyas, all became owners
> Drinking the blood of slaves, making the Shudras into machines.
> The Brahmans, Kshatriyas and Banias got all the ownership rights.
> All these three call themselves brothers, they come together in times of crisis
> And work to split the Shudras who have become workers.
> "Congress," "Hindu Mahasabha," "Muslim League" are all agents of the rich,
> The "Independent Labour Party" is our true house...
> Take up the weapon of Janata

> Throw off the bloody magic of the owners' atrocities,
> Rise workers! Rise peasants! Hindustan is ours,
> Humanity will be built on labour,
> This is our birth right!

The ILP led some major combined struggles in this period. The most notable of these was the anti-landlord agitation in the Konkan region of Maharashtra which brought together Kunbi and Mahar tenants against mainly Brahman landlords, climaxing in a march of some 25,000 peasants to Bombay in 1938. This was followed by a massive one-day united textile workers' strike against the "black bill" of the Congress government which outlawed strikes. Communists were involved in both of these, and at the massive peasant rally Ambedkar proclaimed, though very ambiguously, an admiration for Marxism:

> I have definitely read studiously more books on the Communist philosophy than all the Communist leaders here. However beautiful the Communist philosophy is in these books ... the test of it has to be given in practice. And if work is done from that perspective, I feel that the labour and length of time needed to win success in Russia will not be so much needed in India ... in regard to the toilers class struggle, I feel the Communist philosophy to be closer to us.

The 1930s was thus the period in which Ambedkar expressed most strongly his major themes of unity and militancy: unity of workers and peasants, of Dalits and non-Brahmans (Shudras), and unity with opposition parties against the Congress. It is striking that all through this period (as later) it was the dominant caste peasants who were the main perpetrators of atrocities against Dalits in villages, and the latter under Ambedkar fought this vigorously. Nevertheless at a broader level he called for and tried to build a unity of Dalits with the Kunbi-Marathas, associated with the non-Brahman party and praised Shahu Maharaj as well as Phule. Ambedkar's position here was that at the caste level, brahmanism was the main enemy, just as capitalism and landlordism were the main enemies in class terms. He consistently argued for the left and non-Brahman/Dalit forces to come together to form a political alternative that would fight both the Indian ruling classes and imperialism. Thus, for example, following the 1938 peasant and worker struggles, he met with Periyar and Swami Sahajanand, the peasant leader of Bihar, in an attempt to form a broad front. Similarly, he tried to dissuade the non-Brahman leaders of Maharashtra from merging their movement with the Congress, arguing that it would only make them the "hamals" or coolies of a brahman leadership.

Yet the 1930s failed to consolidate a radical alternative to the Congress. Apart from the ability of the Congress under Gandhi to win mass support, the main barrier was the argument of the left that the main contradiction was with imperialism and that the Congress represented an "anti-imperialist united front." The movements dissolved, the Communists supported the British Government during the 'anti-fascist' war, and Ambedkar retreated from his radicalism to turn the ILP, which had been limited only to Maharashtra, into a much narrower but more all India Scheduled Caste Federation (founded 1942). His goal now was to get whatever concessions he could from the British out of an independence he now saw as inevitable. He rapidly accepted a position as Labour Minister in the British government, then as Law Minister in the independent regime of Nehru. Ambedkar still saw the Congress as a 'brahman-bourgeois' party, but since there was little he could do about it he turned to reformist interest-group politcs.

Ambedkar had always seen the necessity of both economic and social measures for the liberation of the Dalits. But the acceptance of a mechanical Marxist framework led him to see these as separate entities and not interwoven in the way that Phule had. On the economic front, he mostly began to follow a Nehruvian-left line. While he had written two major books in the early 1920s on fiscal and monetary policy which by and large reflected a neoclassical perspective though with a severe critique of British rule; in the 1930s and 1940s he switched to a socialistic framework that took for granted the necessity of state-guided industrial development but did not confront the problem of high-caste domination over the state machinery. This was expressed in his book *States and Minorities,* written as a submission to the constitutional convention on behalf of the Scheduled Caste Federation. Economics, though, was not by this time his major concern. He was putting most of his intellectual energy into the question of the historical roots of the caste system and India's cultural identity.

Ambedkar began with a rejection not only of Marxist "class theory" but also of the kind of "caste thoery" represented by the non-Aryan identity claims of other Dalit radicals of his time. This was seen in two books published during his lifetime, *Who were the Shudras?* and *The Untouchables,* and but it was his unpublished manuscripts, *Revolution and Counter-Revolution in Ancient India* and *The Untouchables: Children of India's Ghetto* which show the breadth of his attempt to articulate a historical theory. *Revolution and Counter-Revolution* represents his major theoretical analysis, and begins with a firm rejection of the Aryan theory of caste: 'The Aryans were not a race. The Aryans were a collection of people. The cement that held these together was their interest in the maintenance of a type of culture called Aryan culture." As he had earlier made clear:

> As a matter of fact the caste system came into being long after the different races of India had commingled in blood and culture. To hold that distinctions of caste are really distinctions of race and to treat different castes as though they were so many different races is a gross perversion of the facts. What affinity is there between the Brahman of the Punjab and the Brahman of Madras? What affinity is there between the Untouchable of Bengal and the Untouchable of Madras?... The Brahman of the Punjab is racially the same

> stock as the Chamar of the Punjab and the Brahman of Madras is the same race as the Pariah of Madras. Caste system does not demarcate racial division.

It was not that Ambedkar denied "racial" elements completely; for example, he referred to the early Magadha-Mauryan empires as being the work of "Nagas". He simply argued they should not be given causal priority in explaining caste. In his view, all the Varnas included some kind of racial mixture; for instance the original "shudras" were a tribe of kshatriya Aryans who had been degraded due to conflicts with Brahmans, only later being assimilated with the conquered darker-skinned non-Aryans. Similarly he rejected an analysis in terms of economic factors. In his famous phrase, somewhat similar to the way he discussed race, "caste is not a division of labour; it is a division of labourers."

Caste was thus neither racial nor economic. What then were the main explanatory factors, the motive of historical change that produced the caste system, this "social division of the people"? With class and race rejected, and violence ignored, the emphasis is on ideological and religious factors. In Ambedkar's analysis these are interwoven as civilisational forces that produced the conflicts and changes in Indian society. Without a knowledge of the Indus valley civilisation, he differentiated three major phases, as noted above, with the central element in them being the conflict between Hinduism as representing inequalitarian and oppressive elements, and Buddhism as the advanced, egalitarian and rational mode: (a) brahmanism (the Vedic period, basically tribal in nature and characterised by *varna* among the Vedic Aryans, though this was not based on birth); (b) the "revolutionary" period of Buddhism, marked by the rise of the Magadha and Mauryan states and bringing about a great advance in the status of women and shudras whose position had become degraded in the last stages of the Vedic period; and (c) the "counter-revolutionary" period of Hinduism marked by the *Manusmriti*, the transformation of *varna* into caste, and the complete downgrading of shudras and women.

> The triumphant Brahmanism began an onslaught on both the Shudras and the women in pursuit of the old idea, namely servility, and Brahmanism did succeed in making the Shudras and the women the servile classes: Shudras the serfs to the three higher classes and the women the serfs to their husbands. Of the black deeds committed by Brahmanism after its triumph over Buddhism this one is the blackest. There is no parallel in history for so foul deeds of degradation committed by a class of usurpers in the name of class domination.

It has to be noted here that in using the term 'shudra' Ambedkar was clearly not referring to the untouchables, whom he saw as "broken men" settled outside the villages; he was referring to the non-Brahman masses whom he saw, along with untouchables and tribals, as victims of the caste, system. By the 1940s, however, his hope that there would be a unified struggle was at a low ebb, and he was in his political writings treating "Hindus" as a "majority" that included non-Brahmans and was posed against such minorities as Muslims and Dalits.

Nevertheless, Ambedkar's longer-term strategy was to break up that majority, to dissolve "Hinduism" itself, and to do so by building a unity of Dalits and middle castes (non-Brahmans) which would be both a caste and a class unity of peasants and workers, against the brahman-bourgeois Congress. The last years of his life saw a return to this kind of united front, expressed in the change of his Scheduled Caste Federation into the (hopefully non-caste) Republican Party. It participated in the Samyukta Maharashtra Samiti, organised to fight for a Marathi-speaking state and which was actually the first full left-democratic front of opposition parties. Ambedkar, in fact, had argued that the united front should continue even after the winning of a Marathi-speaking state, and fight for the interests of the rural poor; and a massive land satyagraha led by his lieutenant Dadasaheb Gaikwad and communist peasant leaders followed in both 1956 and 1965.

Yet, the end of Ambedkar's life is remembered by the masses of his Dalit followers neither for the class unity of peasants and workers nor for the renewed effort at forming the Republican Party as a broad-based organisation but for his conversion to Buddhism along with nearly a million Dalits in Nagpur. For Ambedkar, and for the militant Dalits who followed him, Hinduism remained in the final analysis a religion of caste that had to be renounced and destroyed if the masses of India were to win liberation. He had written in 1936, in confrontation with Gandhi and Punjab anti-caste radicals, that it was necessary to deal with religion. Indian socialists, he noted:

> will be compelled to take account of caste after the revolution if (they) do not take account of it before revolution. This is only another way of saying that, turn in any direction you like, caste is the monster that crosses your path. You cannot have political reform, you cannot have economic reform, unless you kill this monster.

But this, he went on to argue, required that "you must destroy the Religion of the Shrutis and the Shastras. Nothing else will succeed." "You will succeed in saving Hinduism if you kill Brahmanism," he argued, softening his blow with suggested reforms for Hinduism. It is perhaps this kind of language that has provided a thin wedge for the Bhartiya Janata Party (B.J.P.) to try to co-opt even Ambedkar as a "Hindu reformer." But such Hindu reformism would have required the rejection of all the sacred books of the Hindus, of Rama and Krishna as ideals, and in the end Ambedkar was unwilling to believe this was possible. His unpublished writings are harsh in their overall critique:

> Is there then no principle in Hinduism [to] which all Hindus, no matter what their other differences are, feel bound to

render willing obedience? It seems to me there is, and that principle is the principle of caste.

The way to liberation, then, involved economic and ideological struggle, and Ambedkar never gave up the former. But his stress was on ideological/cultural struggle, and though he could not succeed in fully integrating it with an economic alternative, he gave it a sharpness that would remain: the challenge before socialists—to deal with the "monster that would always cross their path," the issue of caste and its religious justifications.

Hinduism as Delhi Rule: Periyar and the National Question

As the colonial period drew to an end the surface waves of Indian politics were dominated by the issue of Muslim separatism and Hindu identity, Hinduism came to be a taken-for-granted identity, whether it was the moderate and liberal version most Congressmen subscribed to, or the increasingly virulent form of Hindu nationalism. The latter, growing throughout the 1920s and 1930s, began increasingly to emphasise not only blood and territory (race, religion and nation) but also language, projecting Sanskrit/Hindi as the quintessentially "Indian" languages. This had a significant north Indian bias. *Hindi-Hindu-Hindustan,* the emotive slogan of north Indian fundamentalism, had a powerful negative side: the equation of language, religion and nation encouraged not only those with a different religious identity but also those with a separate linguistic identity to see themselves as a different "nation". Thus the other side of the powerful centralising tendency of Hindu fundamentalism was that many anti-caste movements turned to a regional and anti-northern, as well as anti-Brahman identification.

Caste is not ethnicity, and Ambedkar above all had insisted on this distinction and taken a resolutely all-Indian, Dravidian forces. The DK gave birth to the Dravida Munnetra Kazhagham (DMK) which gave up the separatist demand, and then to the All-India Dravida Munnetra Kazhagham (AIADMK) which capitalised on the charisma of its superstar leader and asserted an all-India identity, allied with Congress and eventually propped up its dead hero's film star companion as a temperamental dictatorial leader. The major problem of the Dravidian movement remained the difficulty of winning Dalit support, something Phule had put at the centre of his strategy. In Tamil Nadu, it was not the radical Ambedkar but the Hindu Mahasabhaite M.C. Rajah who was the most well-known Dalit leader, and his alienation from the Dravidian movement was the other side of the distancing of the movement itself from Dalits. The south thus witnessed a powerful non-Brahman movement and a strong opposition to "Hinduism" but more than in any other region was plagued by splits between communists and Dravidians, and Dalits and non-Brahmans.

The currents of regional or subnational (linguistic national) identity were thus significant during the colonial period. They overlapped in complicated ways with claims to a non-Hindu religious identity, but they nearly always shared a framework of opposition to a brahman-bania, Delhi-based centralised rule. The logical outcome of these movements was not necessarily towards the establishment of an independent nation-state; demands for independence were often raised, but the thrust was just as much on a decentralised, federal structure with much more autonomous regions than in the Indian union which came into existence. The triumph of the Congress finally represented both a triumph of a "Hindu" identity and of a centralised, Delhi-based state in the Indian subcontinent.

Brahman Socialism and the Hindu Rate of Growth

During the colonial period the overwhelmingly Brahman Indian elite fashioned an upgraded "Hinduism" which reinterpreted Indian identity and Indian history in a way that could draw low castes, women, adivasis and others into a "national community" whose core was conceived to be the Vedic, Aryan, brahmanic tradition. Whether it was Tilak and the Ganapati festival, Vivekananda and Ramakrishna, or Dayananda and the Arya Samaj, largely high-caste symbols were used to define the heart of this tradition. Even after Hindutva theorists began to argue that the Aryans actually originated in the subcontinent, the notion of Aryans as a core group was kept. And, while the militant "Hindu nationalists" of the RSS and Hindu Mahasabha gave this a more virulent anti-Muslim character by making Hinduism the centre of the Indian state, there were disturbing similarities between their imaging of Indian history and that of proclaimed secularists such as Nehru or even Dange.

While continuing to use such emotive Hindu terminology as Ram Raj and identifying himself fully with this tradition, Gandhi nevertheless sought to give it a major reinterpretation by proclaiming non-violence and truth as its core. He also offered the basis for a different path of development with his notion of *gram swaraj* and a decentralised, village-centred economy. But this was so inextricably linked with Ram Raj and Hindu-Vedantist anti-technological and anti-sexual ideas of limiting wants, as to discredit it among those— like Ambedkar—concerned with rationality and a need to lift Indians out of their current, colonially-induced poverty.

In the end Gandhi fell a victim to the Hindu nationalists themselves who were furious at what they saw as his responsibility for Partition. Yet, ironically, contemporary "revisionist" historical scholarship is stressing the role of the Congress leadership in choosing Partition, since a united India would inevitably have been a decentralised and federated one giving too many concessions to the Muslim-majority areas and only a truncated India could offer the centralised state structure they demanded.

Forces countering the Hindu majority interpretation of Indian society and history existed throughout the colonial period, pre-dating the overriding preoccupation with the "Muslim problem". This is clearly shown in the work of Jotiba Phule. But these forces were fragmented and remained subordinated. The Communists themselves who claimed to be the main "class" opposition to the "bourgeois" Congress could not offer a serious challenge at the level of mass mobilization, in spite of their considerable working class base and such sporadic tempests as the Telengana revolt. Worse, they never even tried to counter its Hinduist interpretation of history, with the most well known Communist excursion into historical interpretation, Dange's *India: From Primitive Communism to Slavery*, also beginning with the Aryans. The non-brahman/Satyashodhak movement in Maharashtra was absorbed in the 1930s; that in Tamil Nadu evolved into a more long-lasting Dravidian movement but one which was even more split from left and Dalit-trends. The radical voices of early feminists were buried under the weight of a more compromising and upper class pre-independence women's movement. The peripheries, such as the north-east, remained remote, without influence on "all India" developments. In this context, the Dalit movement from the 1920s sought to carry on a cultural and economic challenge to the dominant elite, but the efforts of leaders like Ambedkar and numerous others throughout the country had no hopes of achieving hegemony on their own, without the basic shudra-ati-shudra unity which Phule had projected and which Ambedkar also wished to build.

It was the Congress which triumphed. The usual categorisation of the Congress by the left, as representing some form of "bourgeois" (national, monopoly, comprador) or "bourgeois-landlord" force, simply misses much reality. Ambedkar's "bourgeois-brahman" or more aptly bourgeois (bania)-bureaucratic (brahman) would be more accurate. With the assassination of Gandhi marking the end of an era of struggle, the suave and sophisticated Nehru was the natural leader of the party. With the Second Five-Year Plan a "socialist pattern of development"—a focus on heavy industrialisation and the state sector—was chosen. This was influenced by the powerful successes claimed by the Soviet Union, by the overwhelming swing of all newly independent countries towards state-controlled development, and by a consensus even among "development economists" on such issues. But the "Nehru model" had its specific Hindu character from the beginning. As Nehru himself described the choice of socialism over capitalism:

> The old culture managed to live through many a fierce storm and tempest, but, though it kept its outer form, it lost its real content. Today it is fighting silently and desperately against a new and all-powerful opponent—the *bania* civilisation of the capitalist West. It will succumb to this newcomer, for the West brings science and science brings food for the hungry millions. But the West also brings an antidote to the evils of this cut-throat civilisation—the principles of socialism for cooperation, and service to the community for the common good. This is not so unlike the old Brahman ideal of service, but it means the brahmanisation (not in the religious sense, of course) of all classes and groups and the abolition of class distinctions. It may be that when India puts on her new garment, as she must, for the old is torn and tattered, she will have it cut in this fashion, so as to make it conform both to present conditions and her old thought.

The left critique of Congress socialism has been that it was capitalist reformism because it did not admit of working class leadership. This is insufficient. It was worse than that. It was brahmanism, of course idealised by Nehru in terms of "service" and "cooperation", but with a clear implication that these meant management; socialism was identified with planning and the public sector, with Statism. That it could mean something very different, the rule of the shudras (the working classes), never seems to have occurred to Nehru. The only thing he had against the Gandhian notion of "trusteeship", apparently, was that it could be that of private capitalists, the hated banias. Brahmanic trusteeship in the hands of a public sector was another matter.

Gandhi had opposed a heavy industrially-powered development, arguing that "by using Manchester cloth we only waste our money; but by reproducing Manchester in India we save our money at the price of our blood because our very moral being will be sapped." "Reproducing Manchester", only under state ownership, was precisely what India's new ruling elite set out to do. Neither Gandhi nor any of the well-known Gandhian economists could offer a rational basis for a decentralised development; Gandhism remained at the moral level, and efforts to promote khadi and village industries remained a matter of government patronage which had little to do with real self reliance. Industrialisation was a goal no third world country rejected; and the overwhelming consensus of development theory at the time of Indian independence made the Nehru-Mahalanobis type of planning and the focus on the public sector practically inevitable. But the costs of the path not taken were borne by a major section of the toiling people whose poverty remained as oppressive as ever.

The brahmanic socialism of the Nehruvian model of development created a powerful superstructure—a heavy industrial base, a scientific and technological establishment, an extensive university system, a glittering cultural scene. The growth rate it involved, aptly nicknamed the "Hindu rate of growth" by economist Raj Krishna was, at 3.5 per cent, quite respectable by previous history of economic growth but was barely 1.5 per cent per capita annually in the first three decades after Independence: it rose slightly in the 1980s so that the per capita growth rate was 1.9 per cent from 1965-1990. But this was significantly lower than the 2.9 per cent for all other low income countries and 5.8 per cent for China in the same period. As the South Commission put it,

> Growth was not high enough to trickle down ... in India, growth in the first three post-war decades was much slower

> than the average for the developing countries. The rise in India's per capita income, of the order of about 1.5 per cent per year, was too small to secure a significant improvement in the living standards of the masses of the people.

Because of the stress on import-substitution using capital-intensive measures, insufficient industrial employment was generated, and most of the burden was borne by agriculture. The primary sector, mainly agriculture, which had employed an estimated 75 per cent of the population producing 54 per cent of national income at the end of British rule, was still, by 1991, employing 67 per cent of the workforce, but its share of GDP had come down to 31 per cent meaning in effect that nearly as many in agriculture were getting a much smaller proportion of the total income. This immiserated primary sector threw off its surplus labour, the large majority of them not getting well-protected jobs in factories but becoming the growing "unorganised sector" living in slums in cities and small towns.

In terms of human welfare this meant that the islands of growth in industry and agriculture did not result in significant welfare gains for the majority. The average lifespan rose to 58 for women and 60 for men by 1990, a significant gain from 44 and 46 respectively in 1965 and from the drastic situation of the colonial period when life expectancy did not reach 30 until 1941. But it was a stunted and undernourished population surviving on an average of only 2229 calories per day, and India remains the only major country in the world where women continue to live shorter lives than men. Between 1980 and 1990, as an international survey on hunger showed, 41 per cent of children below four years of age were classified as underweight and 30 per cent of babies were born with low birth weights. 20 per cent of the population even in the 1980s were without access to health facilities; 24 per cent of the urban and 50 per cent of the rural population were without access to safe water; and 28 per cent of urban and 40 per cent of the rural population were classified as below an absolute poverty level. By the World Bank's figures, in absolute numbers there were 420 million poor and 250 million "extremely poor"; of the poor, 77 per cent were estimated to be rural. This was, according to the Bank, a decline since 1972, but sheer numbers still made India the largest poor country in the world, housing over one-third of the world's poor.

This was a far cry from the dreams both of India's freedom fighters, who had fought not only for independence but also for prosperity and equality, and of the Dalit and non-Brahman critics who had insisted above all on equality. Today, whether or not the new economic policies will actually succeed in their professed goals, whether inequalitarian capitalism or a more sustainable development will follow, the pressure for liberalisation comes more from the failures of this earlier statist regime, the Nehruvian model, than from influences exerted by imperialist institutions.

How much was this stagnant, bureaucratically top-heavy, impoverished form of development related to a caste system in which (according to the later Mandal Commission report) the public sector continued to be brahman-dominated, i.e. with 15 per cent "forward castes" holding nearly 70 per cent of all positions and 90 per cent of Class I positions? There has been, strikingly, little effort to join an analysis of the specific nature of India's developmental path to a critique of the caste system as a crucial part of its social structure.

A recent attempt has been made by a liberal economist, Deepak Lal, who argues in *The Hindu Equilibrium* that the caste system represented a form of labour organisation that led to a stagnant but relatively high level of living standards by pre-capitalist norms, with a "predatory state" or "revenue state" living mainly off the surplus from agriculture. The most oppressive feature of British rule, according to Lal, lay not in any positive blocking of development but in failing to break through this equilibrium. With independence and a mainly brahmanic elite inheriting the hoary bureaucracy, the "casteist revenue economy" got "a new lease of life in the modern ideological garb of fabian socialism." Lal thus connects brahmanism, the caste system, the hostility to a market economy and preference for a bureaucratically-controlled command economy with slow growth in both agriculture and industry. In a sense, (to use more Marxist language) in seeing the main contradiction of the colonial period as with caste-feudalism rather than imperialism, many aspects of this argument resonate with the political positions argued by Phule, Periyar and Ambedkar.

Equally striking has been a recent article in the *Economic and Political Weekly* by B.P.R Vithal on "the roots of Hindu fundamentalism," arguing that in fact Hindu traditions could be sustained only with a growth rate of between 0 and 3 per cent and "if we get on to a trajectory of a consistently faster rate of growth (and) it merely succeeds in breaking present moulds there will be a rootlessness which can be dangerous in a large country like ours." M. Shivaiah has argued from a Dalit perspective, that this position amounts to a justification for an alliance with the B.J.P. and that Vithal, a high-level IAS official, represents a widespread trend in the bureaucracy.

Along with linkages of brahmanism and bureaucraticisation, we can argue that the general orientation to an idealistic, abstract intellectualism (a socialism which conceives that slogans of *garibi hatao* are the equivalent of eradicating poverty, that passing laws and schemes is sufficient, that solving a problem theoretically is the equivalent of solving it empirically) can be called a characteristic of brahmanism. These are all highly contentious issues, but they do suggest that breaking through the high-caste monopoly of political and administrative positions, along with breaking the hold of the bureaucracy and political structure on the economy itself (not to be confused with establishing a positive welfare, infrastructural and guiding role for the state), is a necessary condition for achieving a healthy economic growth.

In any event, whatever position we may take in the debate about causes, the problems of economic stagnation, mass marginalisation, immiseration of the majority of those connected with agriculture and traditional artisan manufactures, are very real ones. They are not simply the problems of the 1980s.

Hinduism as Feudal Backwardness: The Dalit Panthers

> The present Congress rule is essentially a continuation of the old Hindu feudalism which kept the Dalits deprived of power, wealth and status for thousands of years ... the entire state machinery is dominated by the feudal interests, who for thousands of years, under religious sanctions, controlled all the wealth and power, who today own most of the agricultural land industry, economic resources and all other instruments of power....
>
> *Who is a dalit?* Members of scheduled castes and tribes, neo-Buddhists, the working people, the landless and poor peasants, women and all those who are being exploited politically, economically and in the name of religion.
>
> Who *are our friends?* Revolutionary parties set to break down the caste system and class rule. Left parties that are left in a true sense. All other sections of society that are suffering due to economic and political oppression.
>
> *Who are our enemies?* Power, wealth, price. Landlords, capitalists, moneylenders and their lackeys.
>
> Those parties who indulge in religious or casteist politics and the government which depends on them... We do not want a little place in Brahman Alley. We want the rule of the whole land.
>
> We are not looking at persons but a system. Change of heart, liberal education, etc. will not end our state of exploitation. When we gather a revolutionary mass, rouse the people, out of the struggle of this giant mass will come the tidal wave of revolution.

This quote is from the manifesto of the Dalit Panthers, a militant organisation of Dalit youth. Born in Bombay in 1972, with its leadership drawn from a new generation of young poets and writers, and founded against the backdrop of increasing rural and urban tensions—it was a period in which atrocities against Dalits in the villages, often of brutal and horrifying forms, seemed on the increase—the Dalit Panthers proved to be the spark that set off a wave of organising efforts throughout the country. In Karnataka, a dispute over a cultural issue (a Dalit minister was forced to resign after describing conventional Kannada literature as *cattle feed*) led to widespread clashes throughout the state between Dalits and caste Hindus. The Dalits raised the slogan, "Throw the Brahmans into the gutter along with the Gita" and eventually formed the Dalit Sangarsh Samiti with branches all over the state. In Bihar, a revived Naxalite movement sprang up among the Dalits, with issues of honour or *izsat* (mainly the protection of Dalit women against landlord molestation) and agricultural wages being central. In Tamil Nadu, Ambedkarite organisations began to be founded in many villages. Other areas were slower to pick up the cue: a Dalit Panther unit was formed in Gujarat in 1980 after widespread upper-caste rioting in protest against reservations; an Andhra Dalit Mahasabha was formed in 1984 after a brutal massacre of Dalits in the village of Karamchedu. Whatever its form in each region, a new movement was enveloping most of the country, and the question "will the caste war turn into a class war?" almost began to replace the more conventional, "will the Green Revolution turn into a red one?"

Individual efforts were also underway to give a new theoretical articulation to the class-caste struggle. This question was taken up by V.T. Rajshekar of Bangalore, the founder-editor of *Dalit Voice* and though he swung fairly quickly to an emphasis almost solely on caste struggle, his articulate, aggressive and often vitriolic journalism won him readers throughout the country and among Dalits abroad. A more Marxist attempt at integration was made by Sharad Patil, a district organiser of the CPI(M) in the tribal belt of Maharashtra.

He took time off from his party work to study Sanskrit as a basis for a theoretical interpretation of Indian history, produced a new approach, "Marxism-Phule-Ambedkarism" and then a new party, the Satyashodhak Communist Party. In Andhra, Kancha Ilaiah of the Naxalite tradition began to theorise the role of both patriarchy and caste. Theory almost inevitably led to political action. Though the Panthers themselves were born in the context of a great disillusionment with the traditional Ambedkarite Republican Party, and even leaped to fame with an electoral boycott in 1974 that significantly benefited the communist candidate in the heart of Bombay's working class area, the thrust of the movement took them into electoral as well as revolutionary politics. One of the most important of the new parties was founded by a Punjabi Dalit, Kanshi Ram, who had been turned into an Ambedkarite after his experiences in Maharashtra. Kanshi Ram avoided the Panthers and the more flashy Dalit agitations of the time, and began with an organisation of Dalit, backward caste and minority government employees. He developed this by 1980 into the Bahujan Samaj Party, with its base mainly in north and north-west India and an ability to cut drastically into the taken-forgranted "vote banks" of the Congress. Another was the Bharatiya Republican Party, founded at almost the same time by Prakash Ambedkar, the grandson of Dr. Ambedkar. With the Buddhist revival, and a wave of conversions to Islam that was overplayed by the Hindutva forces to stress a "danger to Hinduism", the new ferment was clearly covering all aspects of social life.

The Panthers had been the starring point of this ferment and their thrust was to universalise the Dalit identity as proletarian experience. This differentiated it from the Dalit movement of Ambedkar's time, which had accepted the separation of economic and cultural spheres, of class and caste, sometimes ignoring the economic sphere substantially. It also contrasted with the first new left upsurge in India, the Naxalite revolt, with its rural orientation and Maoist fervour for agrarian revolution. Now, after the Naxalites had been crushed in Bombay, the bastion of Indian capitalism itself, economic exploitation and cultural oppression intertwined to define a new Dalit revolt—linked in imagery if not in terms of a concrete socio-economic analysis.

Many factors brought about the Dalit Panther phenomenon: the economic crisis which had been unfolding since the middle 1960s, the disillusionment with the history of corruption and co-opting of the party founded by Ambedkar; the spread of education; and the nature of the capitalist city as a communications centre. It is true, of course to say that the poets and activists of the Dalit movement were *petty bourgeois* or *middle class*; but what was striking was the changing nature of this middle class and its increased spread. In Ambedkar's time this consisted of only a very small section of educated dalits who could provide the core of activists for a movement; by the 1970s education and the gains from reservations had produced a widespread section. It ranged upwards to a few high-level government employees and political leaders and downwards to the villages, where in most areas some minimal education of the boys of the most conscious Dalit castes, Mahars, Chambhars, etc. was practically universal and was slowly beginning to include the girls as well. The nature of the. Indian education system made them vulnerable to the modernistic upgradings of Hindu ideologies found in school books; but simultaneously the ability to read and write proved a powerful weapon for the movement.

Both education, whatever its limitations, and the communications network of the time made a range of contemporary and historical world events a reality for an increasing number of the poor themselves. The Vietnam revolution, the Chinese revolution, the Black movement and Black poetry, Marxism, the women's movement, the new left, were all part of the cultural mix that represented a world-wide phenomenon. In describing Bombay from its red light districts to its mixed culture and language, the images of Namdev Dhasal, greatest of the early Dalit poets and a Panther founder, show a stretch in time, from the crystalised images of India's past to the age of revolutions. They show the consciousness born out of a classic industrialised world juxtaposed with the miseries of village immigrants whose ignorance was symbolised in the mother:

In the eighteenth century the whole human race was
turned upside down,
but even today you haven't heard of it...
Mother, your son is not a child.
He is the son of this age's rebellion,
he can see clearly the injustice, himself as victim,
governmental machinery, means of living, power of toil,
mines of coal and steel, warehouses, factories,
there: protection, guarantee of food and money,
my face, lying in the dust, separated from all of this.

The early Dalit uprising had a strong Naxalite tinge; Dalits identified themselves as modern and proletarian and saw their enemy—Hinduism—as feudal backwardness. Militancy was a crucial aspect of this. To cite a Dalit activist of the Bombay slums, "We knew nothing of what was written in the Manifesto. All we knew was that if someone put his hand on your sister—cut it off!" This near nihilist mood and fierce anger distinguished it from early twentieth century movements and made the Dalit Panthers specifically and the whole new Dalit movement generally, an aspect of a worldwide "new left" upsurge. Indeed, it was at this time that the term "Dalit" or downtrodden, the 1930s' and 1940s' Marathi/Hindi translation of this British category of "Depressed Classes," became widespread: a militant alternative to the Gandhian term "Harijan" and the colourless governmental "Scheduled Castes".

The combining of economic and cultural radicalism was also common to many new left movements of the period. Whereas the traditional Indian left, including the Naxalites, during almost this entire period scarcely spoke of cultural issues or critiqued Hinduism as such, for the young Dalit poets, economic and cultural exploitation were interwoven from the beginning. The Manifesto (written under a pronounced Naxalite ideological influence), after condemning Hinduism as feudalism, had really nothing to say about caste issues; the poetry however spoke of caste, of Buddha, of Brahmans, of Shambuk and Ekalavya just as it spoke of poverty and the meaninglessness of parliamentary democracy. It ranged over all of Indian history and mythology, claiming a new past as well as laying claim to the future. For the poets it was as important to curse both god and the modern university as it was to expose capitalism—

> One day I cursed that mother-fucker god
> He just laughed shamelessly.
> My neighbour, a born-to-the-pen Brahman, was shocked.
> He looked at me with his castor-oil face...
> I cursed another good hot curse
> The university buildings shuddered and sank waste-deep.
> All at once scholars began doing research
> into what makes people angry...

Their modernism was turned against the caste system, as much as it was turned against economic exploitation:

> I stand today at the very end
> of the twentieth century.
> All around me is in flame...
> Taking in one hand the sun, in the other the moon,
> I am conscious of my resolve,
> the worth of the blood of Ekalavya's broken finger.

Marxism, as known in India, had separated class and caste oppressions; now the two were sought to be joined. This new project laid the ground for the upsurges of the 1970s and 1980s. The Panthers, in fact, rose and fell like a flash. Their first split came within only two years, rhetorically structured on the lines of "Buddhism versus Marxism Raja Dhale, leader of the Buddhist faction, claimed that his opponent

Namdev Dhasal was a tool in the hands of the Marxists. Much of the intense Dalit debate at this time took place at a seemingly crude level ("Who is your father: Ambedkar or Marx?") but behind it lay a great fear of being controlled by articulate, sophisticated Brahman radicals. And the leftists to a large degree laid themselves open to attack by their ignorance of the rules of the anti-caste discourse. (For example, the apparently trivial but symbolically important mistakes of spelling Phule's name as "Jyotiba" in the brahmanical fashion rather than "Jotiba" after the village deity continued to be made again and again by upper-caste communists).

Nevertheless, the fragmentation of the Panthers was only an episode in a long upsurge. Not only did Dalits continue to organise and fight back but they also provided major themes of revolt to other new assertions of the rime. If the proletarianisation of Dalit identity was a new universalism, a new claim to being a kind of vanguard it was also an effort to define the entire Indian revolution in terms of the upsurge of the low castes, the theme of "we are the proletariat" being expressed in numerous poems and constantly in speeches. It was typical, for instance, that the then Panther leader Arun Kamble, speaking of the Mandal Commission and the need for unity between Dalits and non-Brahmans at a Visham Nirmulan conference in the early 1980s, could argue for a "kunbization" of Marathas (i.e. accepting their identity as toiling peasants rather than as "village rulers"), and end with the assertion: "We want dalitistan but not dalitistan as a separate country; we are 98.5%, we are the majority, *India shall become dalitistan!*." Dalits were, on such platforms, beginning to define identities and ideologies for other sections of the exploited.

The 1970s saw not only the rise of a new low-caste upsurge, but also the spread of a kind of *Dalit consciousness* to many other movements. This came to signify the uniting of social and economic issues. It was taken up for instance by A.K. Roy, an independent Marxist leader of mine workers and the Jharkhand movement. In a pamphlet called *The New Dalit Revolution* published in 1980, Roy attacked the entire upper-caste leadership of left movements, attempted to theorise the geographical/social basis of Indian hierarchy in terms of the interaction between a hilly tribal area, a river bank-centered feudal civilisation, and a port city-centered colonial civilisation. Roy called for a fresh "discovery of India" through the participation of intellectuals in movements.

> Whether the Indian bourgeoisie is black or white, big or small has very little bearing on the politics of the country. What really matters are two basic features: caste system with uneven development of history and its interaction with the belated capitalism percolating from the top...
>
> The communists have prepared various blueprints of revolution like National Democratic Revolution, Peoples' Democratic Revolution, New Democratic Revolution, and many other forms using mysterious terms hardly understood or even remembered by their own followers, not to speak of the toiling millions at large, while India needs a simple New Dalit Revolution, a policy of red and green flag combining the struggles for social emancipation with that against economic exploitation to storm the citadel of colonialism in the country.

Roy went on to assert the need for a cultural revolution within the Indian left, insisting that the symbols of the people should not be Rama or Krishna but those of the low-caste masses—often local, tribal and peasant leaders such as Birsa Munda (leader of an adivasi revolt in the nineteenth century), or Veer Narayan Singh (the adivasi chieftain who fought Aurangzeb):

> The culture of the people, struggle of the oppressed like that of Birsa Munda of Chotanagpur and Veer Narayan Singh of Chhattisgarh would be highlighted which is now obscured and would be restored to its rightful place above the wars and conspiracies of the feudal kings and colonial rulers which now crowd the pages of history. From Buddha to Lenin it would be a unique journey, a new search for a spirit of emancipating millions, *a new religion not only a new*

> *parly,* out to make a new history for mankind without exploitation, subjugation and with justice.

The Dalit Politics

The "unique journey" that A.K. Roy had called for seemed to be beginning in the 1970s. Several youth went to the villages, new activists rose from the masses, social turmoil increased as economic and political pressures mounted, and new voices rose as other low-caste and oppressed sections joined the Dalits in organising.

Dalit themes were expressed also by tribals, for instance by Waharu Sonavane, an adivasi poet-activist coming out of a Marxist-led movement of mainly Bhil agricultural labourers and poor peasants of Maharashtra. He was an activist sensitive from the beginning to cultural issues but by the late 1980s these were becoming dominant themes, as he challenged the dominance of non-tribals in adivasi-based movements. He began to argue that the adivasis who had been fragmented by religious identity and political parties, should come together. But while he was ready to include B.J.P. adivasi politicians in this coming together, Waharu clearly identified with the heritage of *rakshasas,* dismissing Rama as an exploiter and giving a unique adivasi perspective on the entire non-Aryan theme.

> A strong alliance between a minority of Brahmans and a handful of rajas took one after the other adivasi tribe under their control on the basis of violence and aggression. They made them into slaves and disarmed toiling peasants paying taxes to rajas, and settled them in villages to enlarge their kingdoms through settled agriculture. Between the sixth century B.C., that is the period of Buddha, and the fifth centuries A.D. a defined caste hierarchy and jajmani system was established. Most free adivasi tribes became toiling castes giving surplus to rajas and brahman-dominated feudal society! This society had the capacity to slowly transform adivasi tribes and absorb them in the hierarchy, but at lower levels. *We were those who faced this but remained free!...* When the adivasis of that time began to resist the atrocities

> against them, the Aryans became enraged. Then the Aryans went to the ruler of that time, their raja Shri Ramachandra, with the demand 'protect us from the rakshasas, our herds need open fields.' Rama gave a promise. Under the leadership of Ramchandraji adivasis of that time were slaughtered as rakshasas and crushed.[1]

The 1980s were marked not only by the assertion of Dalits and other low castes, but also by the rise of other new social movements, of peasants fighting against their exploitation by the market and state, of women, of tribal and caste Hindu peasants fighting against environmental destruction and displacement. These movements began to identify at least in part with a critique of Hinduism and to put forward new cultural themes that began to converge with those of the Dalit and anti-caste movement, and sometimes drew on this tradition.

In the new post-1975 women's movement, for example, there was initially a strong rejection by feminists of religion as such, with the underlying theme that "all religions are patriarchal and oppress women" replacing the pre-independence tendency to take Sita and Savitri as ideals of womenhood. For some time, this religious-cultural critique remained akt an abstract level; then in the late 1980s, partly under the impact of the rise of fundamentalism, many women activists began to look for aspects of their own tradition that they could identify with. But this identification, much more than the earlier acceptance of a Hindu (or Muslim) framework, was a criticla one. Madhu Kishwar of the well-known women's magazine *Manushi* called for a "defence of our dharma" and wrote of women bhakti saints, but simultaneously made a strong attack on the militaristic and aggressive depiction of Rama by the fundamentalists. Feminists now tended to look to what some called "even more fundamental religious traditions: at the role played by *devis* or goddesses in Indian tradition, the co-opting of that role and ways it might be recovered. In the words of a song by Kamla Bhasin,

Every woman in this country is dishonoured, degraded,
With your hand on your heart, say, how can such a country be free
In this country, they say, there are goddesses without number,
Tell me, have they loosened even a link of our chains?
Have we gained anything of honour from the veil?
Beneath the veil we have remained smothered, beneath the veil we burned...
Make the veil into a flag, unfurl it evverywhere,
We will bring humanity's rule to this land.
You will not be able to challenge the power of women now
We are resolved to take on even the form of Kali Mata.

By the late 1980s Dalit and other low-caste women, and feminists from south India were also making themselves herd. They tried to recover non-Aryan and anti-Brahman traditions, took Sita as a symbol of oppression rather than an ideal, and argued that the Ramayana represented the triumph of patriarchy over matriarchy. Ruth Manorama, a Dalit Christian from Bangalore involved in organising slum dwellers, begin to speak of the "triply oppressed", focusing on brahmanism as a major factor in women's oppression but not sparing Dalit men from her vitriolic criticisms. By the 1991 National Women's Studies Conference in Calcutta two minority community feminists, Flavia Agnes and Razia Patel, were openly attacking "Hindu hegemony" in the dominant women's movement.

Within the environmental movement also, a similar development saw the emergence of culturally radical themes contesting a dominant trend that identified, though more ambiguously than in the colonial period, with a reformist Hinduism. Middle-class environmentalism had been Gandhian in inspiration, mounting a strong ideological attack on western civilisation and western science and technology that included a tendency to idealise Indian traditional culture. This even involved some indifference to or idealisation of caste, with the most important academic study of the "ecological history of India" giving what was in effect a functionalist justification of caste as a system of ecological adaption. But even here there was a new note, with "ecofeminists" like Vandana Shiva emphasising the mother-goddess theme in women's writing as the protector of nature and identifying it with the tradition of "Prakriti" Environmental mass movements based on peasants and other low castes very often used more anti-Brahman traditions. Thus a movement for water rights on the river Ganga used the symbol of Ekalavya, partly because the fishing communities they organised identified themselves with Ekalavya, while a strong local peasant struggle in southern Maharashtra for a peasant-built small dam identified itself with the tradition of Phule and named it the Bali Raja Memorial Dam. Gradually activists connected with tribal and peasant anti-caste traditions began to challenge the tendency of middle-class environmentalists to overlook the exploitative aspects of caste-linked traditions.

Bali Raja became an important symbol for other mass movements in Maharashtra as well. A group working on anti-caste issues among the other backward castes in the Vidarbha region took this as a major theme of yearly celebration, and it also became a central symbolism used by the most powerful mass movement in the state, the Shetkari Sanghatna. Its leader, Sharad Joshi, though himself a Brahman, used the symbols of the people to explicate his "Bharat versus India" Contradiction in society between the (mainly urban) exploitating sections and the (mainly rural) exploited. Gandhian models were evoked to stress that village and agriculture-centered development had to be followed rather than one based on state-controlled heavy industry. This was no longer Ram Raj but Bali's kingdom, and the 1989 Nanded conference of the Shetkari Sanghatana took the popular peasant saying but turned it into an affirmation: "troubles and sorrows *will go;* the kingdom of Bali *will come.*" What is Bali's kingdom? Sharad Joshi queried later, and identified it with what was then being talked of everywhere as sustainable development: "not a goal but a direction, a direction that means producing more for peoples' needs but without destroying the foundations of production...."

Thus, at least in the west and south, the new peasant movement for higher crop prices was identifying itself with popular and anti-Brahman traditions. The Shetkari Sanghatana not only used Bali Raja along with Shivaji and Phule but was also by the early 1990s, in the context of a campaign for women's land rights, describing Rama as an oppressor of Sita. The Rayat Singh used anti-caste themes form a Lohiaite tradition and tried to make alliances with the Dalit movement in Karnataka. On the other hand, however, leaders of the farmers' movement in the Hindi belt such as Mahendra Singh Tikait, the U.P. jat, spoke an anti-brahmanic language but also identified with more orthodox versions of Hinduism.

There was thus an extreme unevenness in the culture of popular movements in the 1980s: a spread of the challenge to orthodox Hindu traditions, but marked at points with what, from the Dalit point of view, was a compromise with brahmanism on the part of some sections, and at others with a readiness to identify with other religious and cultural fundamentalisms as a counter to brahmanic Hinduism. These counter-fundamentalisms were perhaps strongest in the complex movements arising in the peripheral nationalities. In Punjab, opposition to brahman-bania Delhi rule involved an identification with Sikh religious traditions that at points turned into a strong fundamentalism, including efforts to regulate women's dress and suppression of intellectual enquiry. In Kashmir, Islamic and socialist tendencies were mixed in a guerrilla armed struggle against the centre and often involved the exertion of controls over women. In Assam, much of the movement from 1980 onwards seemed to be dominated by high-caste Hindu students, and the Hindu fundamentalists tried to take advantage of this by arguing for accepting "Hindu refugees" but resisting "Muslim encroachers". The more militant armed struggle group, the United Liberation Front of Assam, the ULFA, on the other hand, picked up the theme of north-eastern uniqueness: their Assam, never conquered by Hindus or Muslims, was very largely "Mongoloid, Tibeto-Mongoloid, and Austric" in contrast to the Aryan-Dravidian mainland, as their petition before the General Assembly of the U.N. put it.

There were interesting Dalit responses to all of these: *Dalit Voice* for example, rejected the Assam movement as brahman-dominated, but identified itself with Sikhs and Muslims. It stressed that one of the assassins of Indira Gandhi was a Dalit (a Mazhabi Sikh), and argued that Islam was liberatory for women. Kanshi Ram's Bahujan Samaj Party also built-up one of its strongest political bases in Punjab in a similar manner. Thus in many ways the 1980s saw, below the surface of the growth of Hindutva and Congress corruption, complex processes of cultural dialogue. Compared to the colonial period, there was intense interaction between the various forms of opposition to the Indian state, with the left forces also involved in various ways. Yet the period was still marked by ongoing contradictions and a failure to evolve a total liberatory theory.

The logic of Dalit politics, it may be argued, involved three major emerging themes:

(a) a challenge to the very definition of Hinduism as the majority religion and the core of Indian tradition; an insistence that it was rather a brahmanic Hinduism that represented the hegemony of an elite over that tradition, and that this hegemony had to be overthrown;

(b) a spreading of this theme beyond Dalits themselves to involve all the sections of those oppressed, exploited and marginalised by the processes of caste exploitation, including adivasis and other backward castes (the former shudras), peasants, women, and oppressed nationalties;

(c) a synthesis of a new economic and political direction with the cultural challenge.

For Dalit politics to succeed, it may be argued, all of these were necessary. And the story of the 1980s was in large part a failure to achieve this.

In many ways a united challenge did indeed seem to be emerging in the last half of the decade. There was an upsurge of movements and even after the mid-decade trauma of Operation Bluestar, the assassination of Indira Gandhi and the Delhi massacre of Sikhs put a hiatus to this, a new rise was seen almost immediately after. V.P. Singh symbolised this rise but what was crucial about his movement was not simply the political processes that gave birth to the Janata Dal and the National Front and which also, brought these into an alliance with the Left but the fact that it drew with it a growing upsurge of the new social movements. V.P. Singh associated with Sharad Joshi and Datta Samant, while issues such as social justice (the Mandal Commission), remunerative prices, debt write-off and decentralisation became central to the rhetoric of the new front, with even environmental themes beginning to gain a new voice. Thus, to many throughout the country, V.P. Singh clearly represented a new kind of class and caste challenge:

> There is to be sure a lot of fear behind the sneer.There is fear that the so-called backward classes and Harijans will make a determined bid for power at the national level and thus put an end to the elitist rule that has prevailed since 1985... Girilal Jain has gone to the length of suggesting that only Brahmans can hold India together, while one of his columnists finds the cohorts of Devi Lal tribes and groups condemned by the British as criminals and therefore capable of 'criminalising' the political apparatus... Devi Lal is nothing short of an apparition. He would bring the jats, the gujars, ahirs — the narods — to power in Delhi; with them will come the mobilized peasants of the entire Hindi belt and the politically mobilized Dalits of Rajasthan and Maharashtra.

> They will rampage the imperial superstructure built in forty years of Independence, with the glitter of five-star hotels and the feasty social and political culture of the English-speaking elite....

However, the opposition challenge could not achieve the kind of integrated cultural and economic alternative required by the logic of Dalit politics. There were crucial, even yawning gaps in the whole process. It was at one level hijacked by politicians, seen symbolically in the fact that it was the corrupt Haryana patriarch, Devi Lal, who was taken as representative of the "farmers' movement," while V.P. Singh himself and his political lieutenant, Ram Vilas Paswan, fairly smothered the presence of independent Dalit leaders and movements in coming to "represent" the issues of the anti-caste movement. But this also implied a failure of the leadership of these movements; the farmers' movement suffered a major split in 1989; women and environemntalists remained fragmented and unable to cope with the processes of the political arena, and the Dalit movement itself, in spite of significant political clout, was far from uniting. By 1988-89 Kanshi Ram's Bahujan Samaj Party in north India, and the Bharatiya Republican Party of Prakash Ambedkar in Maharashtra had achieved renewed strength, yet they remained at odds with each other and could not mobilize a coordinated political force. Dalits and their low caste and minority allies remained on the margins of politics, unable to cope effectively with the co-opting processes of the Congress and of the opposition political parties.

There was no common economic programme. The left (and the political parties) paid lip service to issues like remunerative prices but did not systematically analyse the State exploitation of the peasantry that lay behind it; socialists talked of decentralisation and even made it a rhetorical centre of the proposed Eighth Plan, but continued to assume that surpluses would flow from the villages to the centre and then be transferred back to the villages and districts as a form of decentralisation. The Left gave reluctant assent to caste reservation in the Mandal Commission but continued to insist on an "economic criterion" which finally got actualised in 1992 when a Supreme Court judgement demanded the exclusion of "the creamy layer". There was a tendency to seek refuge in old slogans which could perhaps inspire activists but not the masses of people. Behind this uncertainty about the economic programme was a rising crisis of the socialist model itself—with its failures so clearly revealed in Russia and Eastern Europe, mass confidence in what had been traditionally seen as the alternative to an exploitative society was vanishing, and no new alternative to both capitalism and Statism was being articulated at the political level.

The upsurge failed. The new Dalit movement was, by the 1990s, still strong but floundering: V.P. Singh's government was short-lived, racked by factionalism and scandal, unable to implement its major programmes, unable to give a new direction. It fell in October 1990 under the impact of the second Ayodhya campaign and the rath yatra led by L.K. Advani; it was replaced by the caretaker regime of Chandrasekhar and then by renewed Congress rule. The opposition seemingly rallied again for the elections of 1991 when for the first time perhaps in Indian history, there was a democratic-left alliance (the National Front/Left Front alliance) opposing *both* Congress and the Hindu rightist forces headed by the B.J.P..

Yet this alliance, with no common programme, and with large sections of the popular movements that had been with V.P Singh in 1989 now alienated, was ineffective in the 1991 elections. Their percentage share of the votes was not so bad; a shaky Congress government that came to power with its lowest share of popular votes so far (and it was estimated that the assassination of Rajiv Gandhi, coming traumatically in the middle of a hot, gruelling campaign, gave them a 10 per cent sympathy vote) and the NF-LF total was slightly higher than that of the B.J.P. Nevertheless, the solid and ominous upsurge of the forces of Hindu raj dominated the scene. Even when the new Narasimha Rao-led Congress government made a seemingly sudden turn to a market economy, apparently jumping straight into the lap of the IMF and the World Bank, the left opposition forces could do little other than attempt an increasingly negative defence of the Nehruvian model and the promises of secularism and socialism that it had represented. There was little awareness of the need of confront the fact that the traditional forms of both secularism and socialism were outmoded and discredited.

Worse was to come. There was no political force capable of rallying the people in opposition to the Congress and for a different kind of development, an "alternative structural transformation." The Congress itself was discredited; yet it seemed impossible to loosen its stranglehold on power. The B.J.P. began to step up campaigns of militant Hinduism, large numbers of embittered, directionless youth, including now fanaticized women, flocked to the banner of Rama. December 6, 1992 saw the storming and demolition of the old mosque at Ayodhya while police stood by. The days after saw hundreds of people die in police firing and rioting, as enraged and alienated Muslims rose in fury and the provoked Hindus and the police turned on them. Then a final round of mainly anti-Muslim pogroms in early January 1993 turned Bombay, the pride of Indain capitalism and cosmopolitanism, over to the vultures of destruction as gangs held the streets for days, rampaging, attacking stabbing and burning property. Contractors, gangsters, politicians all had their hands in the communal cauldron, but it appeared to be burning with its own logic. Fanatics such as Shiv Sena's Bal Thackeray could now openly say to *Time* magazine that "Have (Indian Muslims) behaved like the Jews in Nazi Germany? If so, there is nothing wrong if they are treated as Jews were in Nazi Germany... In politics (we follow) Shivaji. In religion it's Shiva. The third eye is now opening." No one dared arrest him.

A sense of despair began to overtake many activists and movement participants, as they felt both cultural and economic developments were getting out of control. Clearly the political and economic parameters of the Indian state since independence had gone awry, and simple economistic explanations of communalism no longer seemed adequate. The growing challenge of religious fundamentalism everywhere made it necessary for democratic and revolutionary forces to deal with issues of identity: A consensus was developing that secularism could not remain an abstract ideal, but had to be identified with the popular traditions of communities.

Yet, large sections of the Indian left and progressive movements, saw these popular traditions in "Hindu" and brahmanic terms. There was a visible turn to liberal Hindu and Muslim traditions/celebration of "bhakti-sufi" movements, and a plethora of references to Vivekananda as a symbol of progressiveness, to the point where a columnist of *The Week* could mock the communists' turn to a "Red Hindutva".

Were the Communists forgetting the Phule-Ambedkar traditions that many of them had praised in the centenary years of 1989 and 1990? Were they making another compromise with the political forces now perceived as dominant, with a more traditional Hinduism? The Dalits were not particularly surprised; it was a confirmation of the position many took that the political parties and social and cultural institutions were hopelessly upper-caste dominated. The Dalits were clearly alienated. Baburao Bagul, an award-win-rang writer and a one-time communist party member, had condemned the hegemony of Hinduistic themes in the national movement; in Europe, he said, nationalism and the bourgeois revolution had a progressive content and people had fought religious authority, but in India, nationalism "was turned into a form of... ancestor worship." Bagul went on to argue that, since

"Hindus are the majority," there was little to hope for from the Indian tradition:

> Democratic socialism which is based on liberty, equality and fraternity is the philosophy of the modern age. And this philosophy has no roots in the Indian psychic and mystical value-structure. The literature of the saints has not provided any valuable alternative in the form of ideals. On the other hand, fascism, varna domination, here-worship, pride, scorn, malice and hatred—all these have solid literary and inellectual support.

Obviously the logic of Dalit politics led beyond just the cultural issues of Dalits as such and represented a need for a broad economic and political thrust. It also called for a unity and alliance between movements, between different sections of the oppressed and exploited. This could not effectively take place, and by the beginning of the 1990s, reactionary forces seemed to be on the rise. More prominently in Uttar Pradesh politics we have observing this upward mobility.

9

Dalits and Social Justice

Social Justice, vague and vagarious in its semantics has been constitutional claptrap since January 26th, 1950 and whenever the downtrodden have sought justice on the basis of equality in the context of total deprivations in the past, this chameleon chant 'social justice' has played hide and seek with the victim sector of Indian humanity known popularly as the Scheduled Castes and Scheduled Tribes. They are large groups which suffer adversities, social and educational, economic and cultural, struggling to join the mainstream. They too have so far not succeeded in securing for themselves what the great Preamble to the Constitution has pledged to the people of India. While it is assumed that the pariahs, the melchchas and the antyajas of Bharat have constitutional title to the blessings of socio-economic justice, equality of status and opportunity as well as fraternity assuring basic dignity, the actualisation of these fruits of freedom has been but paper-togged illusions emanating from State Secretariats and Planning Commissions. Far too long have the political echelons of various hues hidden the truth of their lies regarding social justice, and now, during the Ambedkar Centenary Year, militancy in the demand for right and Justice has catalysed these deprived and desperate sections of society. The rhetoric of social justice has been the opium of the sup pressed people all these decades. A new hope will rise from the ashes of the past, a power from the social proletariat to claim back their just rights. It is very apt here to quote a young tribal intellectual Zamora:

"One day, the fields will stay green
and the earth black, sweet and wet.
Our children will grow tall on that earth
and our children's children.
And they will be free as the mountain trees and birds.
They will wake each day, happy to be alive
knowing the land was conquered once more, for them.
Oneday...
Now we plough dry fields
each furrow wet with blood".

As the bonded labour of the status quo, no longer are they in a mood to continue. As the eternal tenants of an extortionate order they will not submit any more. Statesmanship, legislative, administrative and judicial, must sharpen our perspective of history, and with dynamic sensitivity conscientise the democratic process into becoming a radical locomotive of social transformation. These weakest sections of society, sometimes described as harijans and girijans, are many millions strong and their unheard cries and unseen tears have given place to clenched fists and angry eyes. True, even to-day their voice is muffled, their wails ignored and their lives are but long nights.

Once the wielders of power show the will to liberate these categories of Indian society there will be a great upsurge of equality, a new awareness of dignity and an outpouring of untapped energies as a new human resource at the service of the Nation. Only then can there be true *fraternity*, homogenising the suppressed sector with the upper classes. Mere legislative prescriptions cannot abolish deeply entrenched social abuses and economic bondages. A radical rupture with the status quo ante involves not merely legislative mandates and administrative directives but activist cadres with a passion for the cause and able to mobilise the victims of injustices into liberating themselves. This Operation Freedom of the *Panchama* Proletariat is itself a struggle and constitutes the current phase of the battle for swaraj of the suppressed human sector. The Statute Book of India contains many legislations designed to lift the Dalits, to abolish their disabilities and to give them special opportunities for advancement in education and employment. Bonded labour is by law abolished. Untouchability, by Constitution, is forbidden. The Civil Rights Act goes a long way to eliminate injustice inflicted on the Dalits. Specially stern punishments are prescribed for commission of offences against Scheduled Castes and Tribes, but these magic remedies sleep as paper tigers. The social evils continue. The economic wrongs go on. The law is dead, vis a vis these unfortunates. There are plans and sub-plans, schemes and projects worked out by the Administration at the Central and State levels. There are special reservations for employment and education and these facilities look like reverse discrimination. But what are the raw realities? Tolstoy's biting words set the tone for a social audit of the performance:

> "The abolition of slavery has gone on for a long time. Rome abolished slavery. America abolished it, and we did, but only the words were abolished, not the thing".

Discrimination against the Scheduled Castes and the practice of untouchability persist though only in certain parts of the country. Even today, serfdom and bonded labour implicating Dalit families continues. All the laws and constitutional prescriptions notwithstanding, enforcement is a flop, a fraud. Investigation into offences against the Scheduled Castes and Tribes is often done by hostile policemen. Gang rapes of these backward women rarely reach the court and if they do they hardly survive to end in conviction. The truth is that neither the Police nor the Court has any emotional involvement or sufficient social commitment where, on the one side, is the feudal order and, on the other side, is the Dalit brother or sister. What is of moment and accounts for the law's betrayal is the implicit hostility of the dominant classes to legislative measures which are merely the skin-deep homage paid to social justice.

The situation is no different even regarding the special provisions made for lifting the lot of the S.C./S.T. sections at the educational and employment levels. Whatever the quantum of reservation in official orders, the fact remains that in *actual figures* only flimsy percentages get the benefit How many I.A.S. or I.P.S. Officers are there among the S.C./S.T.? How many Chief Ministers and Chief Justices are there from among these backward-most groups? Indeed, how many Attorneys General, Solicitors General, Advocates General or other high Law Officers or Judicial echelons in the High Court and Supreme Court have ever been appointed from the S.C./S.T.? How many S.C./S.T. cadres occupy the highest posts in the various professions in the country? How many great artists, singers and dancers and professors and scientists, have been drawn from the S.C./S.T.? It is clear that the alleged special advantages extended to the Scheduled Castes and Tribes are a hoax or gross exaggeration. I will cite two examples to illustrate how one can practise deception through reservations on paper, the Dalits getting absolutely little or nothing in actual fact. Suppose you reserve 75% of the judgeships in the Supreme for the S.C./S.T. categories. It is well known that ordinarily recruitment to the Supreme Court Judgeships is made from among High Court Judges. If there are no S.C./S.T. judges in the High Courts the mere fact of reservation of a high percentage does not secure a single seat on the bench in the Supreme Court for the S.C./S.T.. Similarly, you rarely come across a judge from these 'untouchables' on the High Court benches because there are few Advocates belonging to these categories. Similarly, by attaching certain qualifications which cannot be fulfilled by the S.C./S.T. one may successfully defeat reservation percentages. It happened in Kerala that there was reservation for the tribals in the matter of appointment as mahouts employed by Government in trapping and training of elephants in centres maintained by the Government; but since the minimum qualification of matriculation was prescribed no tribal could get even a mahout's post altho' they were traditionally living in forests where the elephants roamed wild. One can multiply instances to demonstrate that in the higher categories of posts where State Power can be exercised the S.C./S.T. are successfully kept out even while making it appear that 22.5% is reserved for them right through.

The grievance against the SC/S.T. whose population bears a proportion of 22.5% is that they are getting reservation of 22.5% even in high posts. The truth is that in 1979 the S.C. got 4.75% and the ST. 0.94% in Class I services. In 1981 in Class I. the S.C. got 4.62% and the S.T. 0.97%. Out of the total of 370 High Court judges as on March 16, 1982 only 4 were from amongst S.C. and none from the S.T. It is thus clear that in the bureaucracy and the Judiciary not to speak even the Ministry from time to time, the S.C. and S.T. have been suffering great discrimination in actual facts. Untouchability is still writ large.

In the field of higher education also, the actuals fall far less than the formal percentages of reservation. Mahatma Phule whom Dr. B.R. Ambedkar admired stressed that *adisudras* suffered because of lack of education. Dr. Ambedkar himself argued:

> "I firmly believe in the efficacy of education as a panacea for our social evils. The problem of lower order in this country is not only economic but also cultural. It is not enough to house them, feed them and then to leave them to serve the higher classes as was the ancient ideal of this country. It is even more necessary to remove from them that feeling of inferiority which has shunted their growth and made them slaves of others and to create in them a consciousness of significance of life for themselves and for their country of which they have been cruelly robbed by the current social order of this country. I am convinced that nothing can achieve this except the spread of higher education."

Therefore reservation in access to higher education is a *sine qua non* of Dalit uplift. The illiteracy rate of the S.C./S.T.

is abysmal and therefore attracting them into attractive high standard, even English medium schools is a compulsive need if abolition of backwardness is the desideratum. Unfortunately the State has done little to *actualise* admissions without dropouts of the S.C./S.T. children into Convent School, English Medium Schools, or any schools for that matter. Special concessions and financial attractions to bring in Dalit children on a massive basis is the desideratum if the *mlecha* masses are to awake and arise. In the matter of higher education, mere reservations liberalising age restrictions and minimum marks could not do. More must be done. Special training and coaching, tuition geared to overcoming handicaps should be a first priority if reservation in education is to bear fruit. In scientific and technological fields preferential treatment should be extended to the S.C/S.T. Until these minimum steps are taken educational untouchability and invisible *Chathurvarna* will survive the Constitution. What we need is a social revolution, an educational revolution and a public services revolution through crash programmes and mass line methodology. Navodaya schools, from this angle are a new hoaxes. *Antyodaya* in the "widest commonalty spread" is the "consummation devoutly to be wished".

There is the question of merit urged against them altho' the truth is that given better environment, better opportunities, better training and special coaching, they can more than successfully compete with the so called upper classes. Give them education in the L.K.G., U.K.G. and the Doon Schools, the St. Stephens College or Miranda House or other high class Colleges with sophistications woven into the courses and the careers; they will beat the best. The wisest Indian of ancient India, Thiruvalluvar, was a Dalit by birth. The most devout composers in ancient Tamil countries like Alwars were of Dalit origin. The retort by Dr. B.R. Ambedkar on this point is worth quoting:

> "The Hindus wanted the Vedas, and they sent for Veda Vyasa who was not a caste Hindu. The Hindus wanted an

> epic, and they sent for Valmiki who was an untouchable. The Hindus wanted a Constitution and they sent for me".

It is society, the disabling environment, the penurious privations and the long disease from intellectual, industrial, educational and cultural opportunities and social suppressions for sinful centuries which have kept these millions of Indian humans in dark and depressed serfdom. What an irony that the culpable classes charge the victims with the guilt of 'reservations' which are a paltry part of history's reparations!

All the Mandal fury, with blood in the streets, against evolving an egalitarian synthesis out of competing inequalities is based upon a misunderstanding of the actual facts. It is a terrible pity that people do not look beneath the reservation' percentages. They will then realise, once they lift the veil, and see 'the petty done and the undone vast' that we have miles to go and promises to keep if equal justice to the handicapped social groups is the goal. What is more, when a few members of the S.C./S.T. get a little education, they forsake the lower layers in their own communities and engage themselves in selfish pursuits of promoting their own families. Dr. B.R. Amedkar way back in 1956 bitingly observed:

> 'The educated — highly educated class (from Dalit-Shoshit Samaj) have betrayed me. I had expected that after acquiring education — higher education, they will serve the society. But I see here a crowd of clerks who — are engaged in feeding their own stomach!" Dr. B.R. Ambedkhar, March 18, 1956 of Ramlila Groud, Agra.

What we find as a fact is that even when some benefit accrues to some members of the S.C./S.T. they are cornered by a few families, the pariahs being always the panths and the desperate Dalits at the dismal bottom layers of the S.C./ S.T. segment continuing for ever as the dreg.

The general development of the masses of these *mlecha* sections — a categorical imperative if fraternity is the condition of social stability — can be achieved only by massive economic programmes which can make dynamic impact. While jobs and education are extremely important, as Dr. B.R. Ambedkar emphasised, equality and homogeneity are a far cry if the landless Dalit is not given land, the penniless pariah is not given opportunities to start small factories, the bonded woman is not liberated from servitude so as to enable her to pursue a vocation and the Dalit youth, now illiterate and disorganised and drawn into delinquent and destitute situations, are given effective opportunities to enter the professions and public services in large numbers through short courses and on-going education. Do not the rich and the powerful *to-day* bypass merit through capitation fees, graft, nepotism and buying marks? More than all, the humblest levels of the harijans and girijans must be reached and raised by special projects, and other backward classes should not permitted to rob these Least Developed Castes of their hope of standing up and entering offices of State to exercise power.

It is fallacious to imagine that because there are reserved seats in legislatures for the S.C. and S.T. they wield political power. No. They are divided among the political parties and, with "the three line whip", act according to the directives of the dominant classes in the Parties. This causes disunity and debility in political action. The remedy for this malady is Dr. B.R. Ambedkar's exhortations: "Political power is the master key by which you can open each and every lock". His message to the Panchama proletariat still holds good: "Educate! Unite! and Agitate!"

10

Gandhi on Status of Untouchables

The stigma of untouchability is fairly old in our society. It generated social hatred and discriminatory feeling of high and low, and as a result the later category suffered for centuries in the hands of the former. Time and again, ceaseless efforts were made by social reformers to alleviate the status of down-trodden and bring them to a level by which they could breathe and subsist with some confidence in the society. This was, however, a most complex problem, the complete or satisfactory solution of which could not be evolved in spite of efforts by prominent personalities including social reformers, educationists and political leaders of our society. For example, Buddha, Mahavira, Kabir, Nanak, Dayanand and others played their social and religious role at one time or the other. Besides numerous socio-religious reform movements had deep linkage with the cause of the untouchables who were labelled as a serious stigma on the fair name of Hinduism. The idea of social discrimination dawned on Gandhi in South Africa where he engaged himself against the discriminatory attitude of the South African Government against Indians. The problem was akin to that of untouchability as the migrants were treated as inferior to the local population which enjoyed numerous basic rights legally denied to Indians. As a youngman Gandhi began to realise how much hellish was their life which had weakened their social and moral fabric essential for the growth of physical and economic faculties of human beings. In India, too, he was confronted with this problem when he came back to his motherland in 1915, during the second year of the World War-I.

For him the reconstruction of the life of the nation was of utmost significance. This could be achieved by alleviating the social status of the untouchables. He always called untouchability as a cruel and inhuman institution. It violated human dignity. He did not believe that the imperial ambitions of Britain were alone responsible for our slavery, but it was the neglect of our national duty which was primarily responsible for it. A reformed India, he stated, would be a free India.

Untouchability in its extreme form always caused him so much pain, because he considered himself to be a Hindu of Hindus saturated with the spirit of Hinduism. As he always regarded it *at* an excrescence in Hinduism, he had even no hesitation in renouncing Hinduism itself. To remove untouchability was a penance that caste Hindus owed to Hinduism and to themselves. Thus the purification required was not of untouchables, but of the so-called superior castes.

The apathy of the high-caste Hindus worried him much. He, however, dealt with them as best as he could. During his discussion with Harijans, at Ahmedabad, he opined, 'This is a movement for the purification of Hinduism. Think what contribution you can make to it. If you bestir yourselves, if you shed your unclean habits, if you reform your way of living, irrespective of what the high-caste Hindus do, I assure you their superiority of birth will automatically disappear, Superiority consists in clean and pure living and I assure you that in spite of your unclean occupations you can live cleaner and purer lives than the rest of us. Yours is a service without which the community cannot do. I want you to be conscious of the dignity of your profession, to learn to practise it in a dean manner and I am sure you will be able to dictate your terms. Depend on yourself, stand on your own legs and work your own salvation'.

Gandhi believed that the so-called caste Hindus had a personal obligation to fulfil towards the Harijans which they must do unconditionally and it was to be their atonement. Whether in this world or the next, it is for each one to free oneself from bondage by one's own effort. Harijans should not look upon themselves as lowly, weak or crippled'.

Gandhi asked the Harijans to magnify their own faults so that they appeared to be as big as mountains and then make constant efforts to overcome them. In it lay the key to obtaining the rights which they wanted. 'Never believe that since others have the same faults we need not mind our own. No matter what others do, it is your dharma to overcome the feelings which you find in yourselves .... You will not be able, at the behest of others, to overcome what you yourselves do not look upon as failings. Hence, it should suffice to say that you should shake off whatever faults you can find in yourselves.'

In the process of regeneration of the nation, Gandhi waged an incessant and systematic war. 'If we are children of the same God how can there be any rank among us.' For him, there was only one *varna* in India—the *Sudras*. Indeed the *Sudras* are those who serve. He wished that all the Hindus voluntarily call themselves *Sudras*.

He was critical of any person who would claim superiority over fellow-men. In his opinion there was no such thing as inherited or acquired superiority. He was happy and felt satisfied to call himself a scavenger, a spinner, a weaver and favourer. He wrote in the *Harijan*, 'I have intentionally described myself as a *Bhangi*.' In man made social ladder I want to be at the bottom.

He indeed was much pained to see the appalling plight of untouchables in various regions of the country. Its eradication greatly agitated his mind and he devised ways and means, from time to time, through his speeches and writings. He wrote in *Navajivan*, 'By passing resolutions and talking about their problem we have raised hopes in them. It was absolutely necessary to do this. It was necessary also that hopes should be raised in them and to tell those antyaja friend that what has happened should be sufficient answer to them. Another answer can be that they lay the entire burden on me. I can understand the sting in their words. They accuse me of being satisfied with the more or less that I do myself and of being gullible enough to be taken in by others who only befool me. However, if I do something, there are others who may be doing less but still they do it'.

Gandhi called Harijans as men of God and believed that all the religions of the world describe God pre-eminently as the Friend of the friendless. Help of the helpless and Protector of the weak. He stated that the rest of the world apart, in India who could be more friendless, helpless or weaker than the forty millions or more Hindus of India who were classified as 'untouchables'. If, therefore, any body of people could be fitly described as men of God, they were surely these helpless, friendless and despised people. He opined, 'when Caste Hindus have of their own inner conviction and, therefore, voluntarily, got rid of the present day untouchability, we shall all be called Harijans; for according to my humble opinion, Caste Hindus will then have found favour with God and may, therefore, be fitly described as His men'.

Through his speeches in public and writings in *Young India* and *Harijan,* he emphasised the problem of untouchability and its removal from its roots. He hated untouchability with his entire soul.

The Mahatma had the feeling that in Hinduism there was no sanction for treating a single human being as untouchable. The Bhagavadgita has never taught that a *Chandala* was in any inferior to a Brahmana. 'A Brahmana ceases to be a Brahmana, immediately he becomes insolvent and considers himself a superior being.' Gandhi regarded himself a Sanatani Hindu, because he obeyed the eternal precepts of the faith as embodied in the Shastras as he understood them. He had no doubt that there are many interpolations in the Smritis and the other scriptural books. He rejected as interpolations everything in the Smritis or other writings that was inconsistent with Truth and Non-violence or other fundamental and universal principles of ethics. He opined, 'The idea of superiority and inferiority is repugnant to the most elementary principles of morality. A Brahmana who considers himself superior to any single creature of God ceases to be a Brahmana. If we are children of the same God, how can there be any rank among us ?.... What will happen to the body, if these members begin to quarrel about rank ? . . . . The verses in the Smritis about Sudras deserve to be summarily rejected as being contrary to the spirit of humanity.'

Gandhi was quite sure in his mind that untouchability would not be removed by the force even of law. It could only be removed, he opined, when the majority of Hindus realized that it was a crime against God and man and were ashamed of it. In other words, it was a process of conversion, i.e.. purification, of the Hindu heart. The aid of law had to be invoked when it hindered or interfered with the progress of the reform as when, in spite of the willingness of the trustees and the temple-going public, the law prohibited the opening of a particular temple.

He assessed the social position of untouchables as follows: "Socially they are lepers. Economically they are worse than slaves. Religiously they are denied entrance to places we miscall 'houses of God'. They are denied the use, on the same terms as the Caste Hindus, of public roads, public schools, public hospitals, public wells, public taps, public parks and the like .... The wonder is that they are at all able to eke out an existence or that they still remain within the Hindu fold. They are too downtrodden to rise in revolt against their suppressors. ... It is only ceaseless effort that can raise these downtrodden fellow beings from degradation, purify

Hinduism and raise the whole Hindu society and with it the whole of India".

Regarding inter-dining and inter-marriage, the Mahatma opined that marrying and dining were matters of individual concern and no one had a right to ask to choose a girl for wife or to dine with anybody against his will. He, however, elaborated his point thus: "But my answer is at the same time 'yes' because if a person refused to take food touched by another person on the ground of untouchability or inferiority, he is observing untouchability. In other words, untouchability cannot constitute any ground for restraint on interdining or marriage."

An important organisation, known as the Harijan Sevak Sangh which was not a part of the Congress, was the outcome of the fast, the Mahatma undertook in 1932 when he was in jail. G.D. Birla was its President and Thakkar Bapa its Secretary. ...'it is the duty of Harijan workers and Caste Hindus to do sweepers' work themselves. . . . These reforms do not cost much. They require intelligence, hard work and love of an ideal. We may not relegate sweepers' work to one particular class. Therefore all should learn it in the same way as cooking. Each person should be his own sweeper. If this ideal were to be put into practice in society, the miserable condition of sweepers would at once be rectified'.

The system of forced labour exacted by petty landowners from Harijans and other classes called backward is almost universal in India. The petty landlords are mostly Hindus. 'It is the privilege of Harijan Sevaks, no matter to what organisation they belong to befriend Harijans, to study their condition in detail, to approach Savarna Hindus and show them as gently as possible what their duty is towards those whom they have treated as outcastes of society and deprived even of legal rights.'

Gandhiji always preached to the Harijans cleanliness,

abstention from carrion-eating and intoxicating drinks and drugs, necessity of taking education themselves and giving it co their children, also abstention from eating the leavings from Caste Hindus' plates. He stated, 'On the contrary, I suggest to Caste Hindus that the shortcomings are not inherent to Harijans but that they are due to our criminal neglect of— even deliberate suppression of— these brethren of ours .... We must approach Harijans as penitents or debtors, not as their patrons or creditors extending generosity to the undeserving'.

Gandhi also recommended that common schools and wells should be opened where the existing ones were not available for Harijans either owing to the violent and successful opposition of the neighbours or some other unavoidable cause: Harijans, he opined, could not be left uncared for in matters of necessary services till public opinion had ripened. 'National schools, to be worth the name in terms of Swaraj for the attainment of which they have been brought into existence, must be conducted with a view to advancing the national programme in so far as it is applicable to educational institutions. Thus, for instance, national schools must be the most potent means of educating the 'untouchables' and abolishing the curse of untouchability from the schools. Whilst in theory the (present national) schools are open to the 'untouchables' very few, as a matter of fact, have untouchable children in them .... I have no hesitation in advising that teachers should run the risk of closing down their schools if the condition of running them requires the exclusion of untouchables. Thus the Mahatma emphasised the fact that preliminary training should consist in teaching Harijan children manners, good speech and good conduct. 'A Harijan child sits anyhow; dresses anyhow; his eyes, ears, teeth, hair, nails, nose are often full of dirt; many never know what it is to have a wash.... Their lesson should begin for the first three months with teaching them cleanliness. They should be taught also how to eat properly .... If this preliminary training is to be given in all Harijan schools, pamphlets giving detailed instructions for teachers in their languages should be prepared and distributed, and inspectors of schools be required during their inspection to examine teachers and pupils on this head and to send full reports of the progress made in this direction'.

Actually, Gandhi never reconciled himself to untouchability. He always regarded it as an excrescence in Hinduism. He stated emphatically that a religion that established the worship of the cow could not possibly countenance or warrant a cruel and inhuman boycott of human beings. '. . . I should be content to be torn to pieces rather than disown the suppressed classes. Hindus will certainly never deserve freedom, nor get it if they allow their noble religion to be disgraced by the retention of the taint of untouchability.'

He warned the Hindu brethren against the tendency which he saw of exploiting the suppressed classes for a political end. He stated that to remove untouchability was a penance that Caste Hindus owed to Hinduism and to themselves. The purification required was not of "untouchability" but of the so-called superior castes. There was no vice that was special to the "untouchables", not even dirt and insanitation. 'It is our arrogance which blinds us, superior Hindus, to our own blemishes and which magnifies those of our downtrodden brethren whom we have suppressed and whom we keep under suppression .... That religion and that nation will be blotted out of the face of the earth which pins its faith to injustice, untruth or violence. God is Light, not darkness. God is Love, not hate, God is truth, not untruth. God alone is great. We His creatures are but dust. Let us be humble and recognise the place of the lowliest of His creatures. Krishna honoured Sudama in his rags as he honoured no one else. Love is the root of religion.'

For the opening of the roads was not the final but the first step in the ladder of reform. Temples in general, public wells, public schools must be open to the untouchables equally with the Caste Hindus.

'I want my Harijan brother, if he wishes, to share this temple worship with the millions of his co-religionists the so-called Caste men. It is the latter's duty to throw open their temples to their Harijan brethren. Temple worship supplies the felt spiritual want of the human race. It admits of reform. But it will live as long as man lives.'

Mahatma regarded untouchability as the greatest blot on Hinduism. I regret untouchability as the greatest blot on Hinduism. This idea was not brought home to me by my bitter experience during the South African struggle. is not due to the fact that I was once an agnostic. It is equally wrong to think—as some people do-that I have taken my views from my study of Christian religious literature. These views date as far back as the time when I was neither enamoured of, nor was acquainted with the Bible or the followers of the *Bible.*

While at school I would often happen to touch the 'untouchables', and as I never would conceal the fact from my parents, my mother would tell me that the shortest cut to purification after the unholy touch was to cancel the touch by touching any Mussalman passing by. And simply out of reverence and regard for my mother I often did so, but never did so believing it to be a religious obligation. After some time we shifted to Porbandar, where I made my first acquaintance with Sanskrit. I was not yet put into an English school, and my brother and I were placed in charge of a Brahmin, who taught us *Ramaraksha* and *Vishnu Puja.* The text *"Jale Vishnuh Sthale Vishnuh"* (there is the Lord present in water, there is the Lord present in earth) has never gone out of my memory. A motherly old dame used to live close by. Now it happened that I was very timid then, and would conjure up ghosts and goblins whenever the lights went out and it was dark. The old order, to disabuse me of fears, suggested that I should mutter the *Ramaraksha* texts whenever I was afraid, and all evil spirits would fly away. This I did and, as I thought, with good effect. I could never believe then that there was any text in the *Ramaraksha* pointing to the contact of the untouchables as a sin. I did not understand its meaning then, or understood it very imperfectly. But I was confident that *Ramaraksha,* which could destroy all fear of ghosts, could not be countenancing any such thing as fear of contact with the untouchables.

The *Ramayana* used to be regularly read in our family. As Brahmin called Ladha Maharaj used to read it. He was stricken with leprosy, and was confident that a regular reading of the *Ramayana* would cure him of leprosy, and in-deed, he was cured of it. 'How can the *Ramayana*', I thought to myself, 'in which one who is regarded now-a-days as an untouchable took Rama across the Ganges in his boat, countenance the idea of any human beings being untouchable on the ground that they were polluted souls ?" The fact that we address God as the 'purifier of the polluted' and by similar appellations, shows that it is a sin to regard anyone born in Hinduism as polluted or untouchable—that it is Satanic to do so. I have hence been never tired of repeating that is a great sin. I do not pretend that this thing had crystallised as a conviction in me at the age of twelve, but I do say that I did then regard untouchability as a sin. I narrate this story for the information of the Vaishnavas and orthodox Hindus.

I have always claimed to be a Sanatani Hindu. It is not that I am quite innocent of the scriptures. I am not a profound scholar of Sanskrit. I have read the *Vedas* and the *Upanishads* only in translation. Naturally therefore, mine is not a scholarly study of them. My knowledge of them is in no way profound, but I have studied them as I should do as a Hindu and I claim to have grasped their true spirit. By the time I had reached the age of 21, I had studied other religions also.

There was a time when I was wavering between Hinduism and Christianity. When I recovered my balance of mind, I felt that to me salvation was possible only through the Hindu religion and my faith in Hinduism grew deeper and more enlightened.

But even then I believed that untouchability was no part of Hinduism; and that if it was, such Hinduism was not for me.

True Hinduism does not regard untouchability as a sin. I do not want to enter into any controversy regarding the interpretation of the *Shastras*. It might be difficult for me to establish my point by quoting authorities from the *Bhagavat* or *Manusmriti*. But I claim to have understood the spirit of Hinduism. Hinduism has sinned in giving sanction to untouchability. It has degraded us, made us the pariahs of the Empire. Even the Mussalmans caught the sinful contagion from us, and in South Africa, in East Africa and in Canada, the Mussalmans no less than Hindus came to be regarded as pariahs. All this evil has resulted from the sin of untouchability.

I may here recall my proposition, which is this: So long as the Hindus wilfully regard untouchability as part of their religion, as long as the mass of Hindus consider it a sin to touch a section of their brethren, Swaraj is impossible of attainment. Yudhishtira would not enter heaven without his dog. How can, then, the descendants of that Yudhishtira expect to obtain Swaraj without the untouchables ? What crimes for which we condemn the Government as Satanaic have not we been guilty of towards our untouchable brethren?

We are guilty of having suppressed our brethren; we make them crawl on their bellies; we have made them rub their noses on the ground; with eyes red with rage, we push them out of railway compartments—what more than this has British rule done ? What charge that we bring against

Dyer and O'Dwyer may not others, and even our own people, lay at our door ? We ought to purge ourselves of this pollution. It is idle to talk of Swaraj so long as we do not protect the weak and the helpless, or so long as it is possible for a single Swarajist to injure the feelings of any individual. Swaraj means that not a single Hindu or Muslim shall for a moment arrogantly think that he can crush with impunity meek Hindus or Muslims. Unless this condition is fulfilled we will gain Swaraj only to lose it the next moment. We are no better than the brutes until we have purged ourselves of the sins we have committed against our weaker brethren.

But I have faith in me still. In the course of my peregrinations in India I have realised that the spirit of kindness of which the poet Tulsidas sings so eloquently, which forms the cornerstone of the Jain and Vaishnava religions, which is the quintessence of the *Bhagavat,* and which every verse of the *Gita* is saturated with— this kindness, this love, this charity, is slowly but steadily gaining ground in the hearts of the masses of this country.

Many a fracas between Hindus and Mussalmans is still heard of. There are still many of those who do not scruple to wrong one another. But as to the net result, I feel that kindness and charity have increased. The Hindus and Mahommedans have become godfearing. We have shaken ourselves free from the hypnotism of law courts and Government schools and no longer labour under any other hallucination. I have also realised that those whom we regard as illiterate and ignorant are the very people who deserve to be called educated. They are more cultured than we, their lives are more righteous than ours. A little study of the present day mentality of the people will show that according to the popular conception, Swaraj is synonymous with Ramarajya— the establishment of the Kingdom of Righteousness on earth. If it can bring any comfort to you, my untouchable brethren, I would say that your question does not cause so much stir, as it used to do formerly. That does not mean that I expect you to cease to have misgivings about the Hindus. How can they deserve to be not mistrusted having wronged you so much ? Swami Vivekanand used to say that the untouchables were not depressed, they were suppressed by the Hindus who in turn had suppressed themselves by suppressing them.

I suppose I was at Nellore on the 6th of April. I met the untouchables there and I prayed that day as I have done today. I do want to attain *moksha.* I do not want to be reborn. But if I have to be reborn, I should be born an untouchable, so that I may share their sorrows, suffering and the affronts levelled at them, in order that I may endeavour to free myself and them from that miserable condition. I, therefore, prayed that if I should be born again, I should do so not as a Brahmin, Kshatriya, Vaishya or Sudra, but as an Atisudra.

Today is much more solemn than the sixth. It is hallowed by the memory of the massacre of thousands of innocents. And I prayed, therefore, also today that if I should die with any of my desires unfructified, with my service of the untouchables unfinished, with my Hinduism unfulfilled, I may be born again amongst the untouchables to bring my Hinduism to its fulfilment.

I love scavenging. In my Ashram, an eighteen-year-old Brahmin lad is doing the scavenger's work in order to teach the Ashram scavenger cleanliness. The lad is no reformer. He was born and bred in orthodoxy. He is a regular reader of the *Gita* and faithfully performs *sandhyavandana.* His pronunciation of Sanskrit verses is more faultless than mine. When he conducts the prayer, his soft, sweet melodies melt one into love. But he felt that his accomplishments were incomplete until he had become also a perfect sweeper, and that if he wanted the Ashram sweeper to do his work well, he must do it himself and set an example.

You should realise that you are cleaning Hindu society. You have therefore to purify your lives. You should cultivate the habit of cleanliness, so that no one may point his finger at you. Use alkali ash or earth if you cannot afford to use soap to keep yourselves clean. Some of you are given to drinking and gambling which you must get rid of. You will point your finger at the Brahmins and say that even they are given to these vices. But they are not looked upon as polluted as you are. You must not ask the Hindus to emancipate you as a matter of favour. Hindus mast do so, if they want, in their own interests. You should, therefore, make them feel ashamed by your own purity and cleanliness. I believe that we shall have purified ourselves within the next five months. If my expectations are not fulfilled, I will think that although my proposition was fundamentally correct, yet I was wrong in my calculation; and I will again say that I had erred in my calculation.

You claim to be Hindus; you read the *Bhagavat*. If, therefore, the Hindus oppress you then you should understand that the fault does not lie in the Hindu religion but in those who profess it. In order to emancipate yourselves you shall have to purify yourselves. You shall have to get rid of evil habits like drinking.

If you want to ameliorate your conditions, if you want to obtain Swaraj, you should be self-reliant. I was told in Bombay that some of you are opposed to N.C.O. and believe that salvation is only possible through the British Government. Let me tell you that you will never be able to obtain redress by discarding Hindu religion and courting the favour of a third party. Your emancipation lies in your own hands.

I have come in contact with the untouchables all over the country; and I have observed that immense possibilities lie latent in them of which neither they nor the rest of the Hindus seem to be aware. Their intellect is of original purity. I ask you to learn spinning and weaving, and if you take them up as a profession, you will keep poverty from your doors. As regards your attitude towards the *Bhangis* I will repeat what I said at Godhra. I cannot understand why you should yourselves countenance the distinction between Dheds and Bhangis. There is no difference between them. Even in normal times their occupation is as honourable as that of lawyers or Government servants.

You should now cease to accept leavings from plates, however clean they may be represented to be. Receive grain only—good, sound grain, not rotten grain—and that too only if it is courteously offered. If you are able to do all I have asked you to do, you will secure your emancipation, not in four or five months, but in so many days.

The Hindus are not sinful by nature—they are sunk in ignorance. Untouchability must be extinct in this very year. Two of the strongest desires that keep me in flesh and bone are the emancipation of the untouchables and the protection of the cow. When these two desires are fulfilled, there is Swaraj, and therein lies my own *moksha*. May God give you strength to work out your salvation.

In a huge assembly of students at Nagpur on 9 November, 1933, the Mahatma stated that he was not confined to Hinduism, and if untouchability was removed from the Hindu heart, he expected far-reaching consequences and a greatg change in Indian society. The barrier of untouchability, he said, was a great hindrance towards achievement of any kind of unity. He was, however, not sure if his dream about the removal of untouchability would be achieved during his life.

I know this tussle between English and Hindi is almost an eternal tussle. Whenever I have addressed student audiences, I have been surprised by the demand for English. You know, or ought to know, that I am a lover of the English language. But I do believe that the students of India, who are expected to throw in their lot with the teeming millions and to serve them, will be better qualified if they pay more attention to Hindi than to English. I do not say that you should not learn English; learn it by all means. But, so far as I can sec, it cannot be the language of the millions of Indian homes. It will be confined to thousands or tens of thousands, but it will not reach the millions. Therefore, I am delighted when the students ask me to speak in Hindi.

You, both the speakers, have spoken of me in terms, which if I believed to be true of myself, I do not know where I would be. But I know my place. I am a humble servant of India, and is trying to serve India, I serve humanity at large. I discovered in my early days that the service of India is not inconsistent with the service of humanity. As I grew older in years, and I hope also in wisdom, I saw that the discovery was well made, and after nearly 50 years of public life, I am able to say today that my faith in the doctrine, that the service of one's nation is not inconsistent with the service of the world, has grown. It is a good doctrine. Its acceptance alone will ease the situation in the world and stop the mutual jealousies between nations inhabiting this globe of ours. You have said truly that, in taking up this war against untouchability, I have not confined myself to Hinduism. I have said more than once that if untouchability is removed in its fulness from the Hindu heart, it will have far-reaching consequences, inasmuch as it touches millions of human beings. As I said last night to the great meeting in Nagpur, if untouchability is really removed from the Hindu heart, that is, if the high caste Hindus purge themselves of this terrible taint, we shall soon discover that we are all one and not different peoples. Hindus, Muslims. Christians, Parsis, whatever we may call ourselves. We shall feel the unity, once the barrier of untouchability is removed. As I have often said, untouchability is a hydra-headed monster, appearing in many shapes. Some of them are very subtle. If I have jealousy for any human being, that also is a species of untouchability. I do not know if my dream about the removal of untouchability will be fully realised while I am living. AH those who are religiously inclined, those who believe not in formal religion but in the essence of religion, cannot but believe in the removal of a subtle type of untouchability that affects the lives of a vast mass of humanity. If Hindu hearts can be purged of this evil, our eyes of understanding will be more and more opened. It is not possible to estimate the gain to humanity when untouchability is really removed. You can now have no difficulty in understanding why I have staked my life for this one thing.

If you, the students who have assembled here, have followed me so far and understood the implications of this mission of mine, you will soon extend the help I want from you. Many students have written to me asking what part they can take in helping this movement. It is a surprise to me that students are obliged to ask this question. The field is so vast and near you that you need not ask the question as to what you may do and what you may not. It is not a political question. It may become one, but for you and me, for the time being, it is not connected with politics. My life is governed by religion. I never lost sight of the principle that governs my life when I began dabbling in politics. As this is a humanitarian campaign, students must devote a part of their spare time, if not the whole, to the service of thousands of Harijans. By giving me this magnificent purse you have certainly equalled the brightest records of students' meetings which I have addressed in my many peregrinations throughout the length and breadth of India. But I want much more from you. I have found that, if I get many helpers who can give their spare time, much work can be done. This work cannot be done by hired labour. With hired labour we cannot go to Harijan quarters and sweep their roads, enter their houses and wash their children. I have described in the columns of the *Harijan* what students can do. A Harijan teacher has shown what a Herculean task it is for him to tackle. Even wild children are better than Harijan children. Wild children are not sunk in utter degradation, as the Harijan children are, nor do they live in such filthy surroundings. This problem cannot be tackled by hired labour. No amount of money can enable me to do this. It must be your prerogative. It is an acid test of the education received by you in schools and colleges. Your world will not be measured by your ability to make faultless English speeches. Your worth will be measured by the service you render to the poor and not by Government posts worth Rs. 60 or Rs. 600 that you may have got. I wish you would do this work in the spirit I suggest. I have not met a single student who has said that he cannot spare one hour per day. If you write your diary from day to day, you will find that you waste many a precious hour in the 365 days of the year. If you want to turn your education to good account, you will turn your attention to this work while this hurricane campaign lasts. Erstwhile students are serving Harijans within a radius of 5 miles round about Wardha. They are doing good silent work; therefore, you do not know them. I invite you to see their work. It is hard but pleasurable. It will give you joy, greater than your cricket or tennis. I have repeatedly said that money will come if I have real, intelligent, honest workers. As a boy of 18 I began my education in begging. I have seen that money can be found easily if we have the right kind of workers. Money alone will never satisfy me. I would ask you to pledge yourselves to devote a definite number of spare hours to Harijan service. As you, Mr, President, have said, I am a dreamer, I am indeed a practical dreamer. My dreams are not airy nothings. I want to convert my dreams into realities as far as possible. Therefore, I must hasten to auction the gifts I have received from you.

There was much difficulty in running schools for Harijan boys. In spite of allurements of fee-concessions and scholarships to them, their attendance in the schools was not up to the mark. The Mahatma suggested ways and means for the improvement of their lot by devising novel schemes by the teachers attached to these schools." One who is responsible for the management of over twenty-five Harijan schools writes a long letter stating the difficulties experienced in the management of the schools and ask how I would conduct them if I had the direct management thereof. I need not recount his difficulties which he has described carefully. What I am about to say is an attempt to answer them.

While we are bound to give scholarships and other help to those Harijan boys and girls who attend the established schools, there is no reason whatever slavishly to reproduce the mode and methods of those schools in the ones under our own management.

We have to recognise that we get Harijan children with great difficulty to attend any school at all. We cannot expect any degree of regularity in them and, thanks to our past criminal neglect, they are so unkept that we have, in the beginning stages, to handle them in a manner wholly different from the ordinary.

On first admission their bodies have to be minutely examined and thoroughly cleaned. Their clothes might have to be cleaned and patched. The first daily lesson, therefore, will for some time consist of applied hygiene and sanitation and simple needle-work. I should use no books probably for the whole of the first year. I should talk to them about things with which they are familiar and, doing so, correct their pronunciation and grammar and teach them new words. I should note all the new words they may learn from day to day so as to enable me to use them frequently till they have them fixed in their minds regularly. The teacher will not give discourses but adopt the conversational method. Through conversations he will give his pupils progressive instruction in history, geography and arithmetic. History will begin with that of our own times, and then, too, of events and of persons nearest us, and geography will begin with that of the neighbourhood of the school. Arithmetic will begin with the sums applicable to the pupil's houses. Having tried the method myself, I know that infinitely more knowledge can be given to the pupils through it, and without strain on them, than can be given through the orthodox methods, within a given time. Knowledge of the alphabet should be treated as a separate subject altogether. The letters should be treated as pictures which the children will first be taught to recognise and name. Writing will follow as part of the drawing lesson. Instead of making daubs of their letters, pupils should be able to make perfect copies of the models placed before them. They would not, therefore, be called upon to draw the letters till they had acquired control over their fingers and the pen. It is criminal to stunt the mental growth of a child by letting him know as much only as he can get through a book he can incoherently read in a year. We do not realise that, if a Child was cut off from the home life and was merely doomed to the school, he would be a perfect dumee for several years. He picks up information and language unconsciously through his home, not in the schoolroom. Hence do we experience the immense difference between pupils belonging to cultured homes and those belonging to uncouth homes, which are no homes in reality.

In the scheme I have adumbrated, the schoolmaster is expected to treat his occupation seriously and feel one with his pupils. I know that, in putting the scheme into operation, the want of schoolmasters of the right type is the greatest difficulty. But we shall not get the right type till we have made the right beginning.

I must postpone the consideration of the stage when we have to arm the pupils with books.

11

Dalits and the New Economic Policy

India adopted the New Economic Policy (NEP) in 1991 which constitutes a major break with the economic policy pursued since Independence. The main thrust of the NEP is on liberalisation, privatisation and globalisation. Further, the NEP is composed of two parts: (i) short-term 'stabilisation' measures such as devaluation of the Indian rupee by about 20 per cent; and (ii) long-term 'Structural Adjustment Programme' (SAP, so christened by IMF/World Bank) which, as the name suggests, is intended to restructure the Indian economy. Obviously, the scope of the SAP is so wide and comprehensive that it seeks to alter, in a major way, policies with respect to monetary and fiscal management; trade and prices; location, ownership, structure, management and control of industries; foreign capital, multinational corporations (MNCs), and technology; agriculture and other activities; investment in social sectors such as health, education and other infrastructural services. India was also a party GATT and subsequently became a member of the WTO (World Trade Organisation).

The NEP is based on the following three basic premises:

(a) Opening up of the economy would enable the country to have a greater access to modern foreign technology, which, on the one hand, would strengthen the forces of competition and efficiency; and, on the other help promote exports; and,

(b) The process of competition, both internal and external,

would help achieve optimum allocation of resources and secure their efficient utilisation;

(c) The above two together would help the country achieve a higher rate of economic growth.

Thus, in essence, the NEP aims at progressive reduction in the role of the 'state' in the economic management of the country and securing a transition of the 'centrally planned' Indian economy to a 'free market' economy. What is a matter of concern is that, among other things, the transition is going to erode, perhaps considerably, the 'welfare' role of the state. Second, the NEP has blind faith in the 'trickle-down', theory of distributing the benefits of economic growth among different socio-economic groups in the country.

Here we intend to examine in a broader macro perspective the impact of the NEP on the Dalits. Here, the term 'Dalits' is used in a comprehensive manner and includes all the depressed and disadvantaged sections of Indian society. The central argument of the paper is that in all probability the NEP, through dismantling of the welfare state, is set to affect adversely the social and economic interests of all the weaker sections, but most of all of the Dalits. Again, relevant empirical information, wherever available, is provided about the Scheduled Caste/Scheduled Tribe (S.C./S.T.) communities with a view to representing the conditions of the Dalits as a whole.

Scheduled Castes: A Socio-economic Profile

Indian society is highly stratified, with many glaring inequalities among different socio-economic groups. The worst positioned among them are the Dalits and tribals. The caste system segregated the Dalits from the rest of the society to such an extent that they were denied even the basic human rights that one must enjoy in order to ensure one's bare existence. Denial of the right to drink water from any public well and to walk on the road in broad daylight were some of the notable examples of social persecution of the Dalits at the hands of the upper-caste Hindus. They were forced to cook their food in broken earthen pots. They wore dirty clothes, if at all they did so, because their wearing clean and neat clothes would irritate the upper castes. Further, the torn and dirty clothes would enable the upper castes to easily identify Dalits. They were destined to live in kachcha houses on the outskirts of villages, because their living in pucca houses would insult the upper castes, while their living in the vicinity of a village would result in intermingling with the members of the upper castes and pollute them. This description could be infinitely extended.

The caste system could not have perpetuated for centuries only through the subjective prejudices and the idea of pollution. One of the most formidable factors that provided the enduring sustenance to the caste system was its solid economic foundation. Again, what needs to be emphasised is that the economic aspects of the caste system were sanctified by the Hindu religious scriptures and, like discrimination, they were deeply internalised.

Caste have played an ascriptive role inasmuch as it allocated economic functions in the society. Such distribution of economic activities among different individuals has been a characteristic feature of every human society, either in crude or in very complex form. But the unique feature of the caste system was that it assigned an occupation not to an individual, but to a group of individuals. A particular individual was ordained to undertake a particular occupation just because he or she belonged to a particular group, i.e., caste. This led B.R. Ambedkar to argue that the caste system did not result only in 'division of labour', but it culminated in the 'division of labourers' (Ambedkar, 1979). The former is the result of preference, choice and aptitude of an individual; the latter is independent of the individual will. The former is voluntary, while the latter is not only obligatory, but also coercive. Thus, like in the social sphere, in the economic sphere too the caste system amounted to a travesty of individual freedom.

But the effects of the birth-based occupational distribution on different castes were entirely opposite in nature. It proved to be a divine privilege to the upper castes enjoying the virtual monopoly of education, industry, trade, commerce and so on; on the other hand, it spelt disaster for the lower castes. This is because the latter were assigned the tasks involving only manual labour. They were thus prevented from earning/accumulating wealth, which restricted their needs to bare existence. What proved further deplorable, menial labour was stigmatised. Thus, the absence of freedom of occupation, low earnings (mainly in kind), implicit restriction on needs, and stigma on menial labour destroyed the economy of the lower castes. They came to be wholly dependent on the upper castes for their bare economic existence. As a result, the Dalits remained socially outcaste, economically dependent, politically powerless, and culturally backward.

Caste system thus not only creates and sustains an unequal opportunity structure which is an anathema to the egalitarian principles which are the basis of a modern democratic society. What is worse, it itensifies and perpetuates the sufferings and servitude of the disadvantaged caste-class groups by reducing their access to development benefits vis-a-vis the higher caste-class groups. In the context of the NEP, the unequal opportunity structure warrants special attention for two reasons. First, as mentioned at the beginning, the NEP is based on growth first and trickle-down benefits inherent in the post-war theories of economic growth. Second, not only have the advocates of the NEP grossly neglected the role of the caste system in the distributional aspect of the prospective gains of the NEP, but even the opponents of the NEP (mainly the 'leftists') do not seem to have paid due attention to the caste system as one of the major criteria to assess the prospective adverse impact of the NEP on Indian society.

Thus, after three-and-a-half decades of planned economic development and all the rhetoric of the 'socialistic pattern of society', the rate of literacy of these communities was barely

22 per cent and that of urbanisation 16 per cent; nearly 50 per cent of them were agricultural labourers; out of every 100 bonded labourers in the country 66 belong to the S.Cs.; their share in industrial employment was an abysmally low 4 per cent. As a consequence of all this, the extent of poverty among the S.Cs. was as high as 50 per cent as against 30 per cent for the population as a whole.

TABLE 1. SOCIO-ECONOMIC PROFILE OF THE SCHEDULED CASTES (ALL INDIA)

S.No.	Indicator	Status
1.	Population (1981)	10.48 Crore
2	Urbanisation	16.00%
3.	Literacy	21.38%
4.	Agricultural Labourers	48.22%
5.	Cultivators	28.17%
6.	Average Status of Cultivators	Marginal
7.	Industrial Employment	4.00%
8.	Percentage of People Below Poverty Line	50.00%
9.	Bonded Labourers	66.00%

Source: Government of India, 1990. *Report of the Study Group Appointed During the VII Five Year Plan to look into the Progress of the S.Cs. and S.Ts.*. New Delhi: Ministry of Social Welfare.

Size Distribution of Landholdings Among the S.Cs.

The significance of landholding as a main source of livelihood in rural areas can hardly be overemphasised. Further, access to land largely determines the overall asset-base of rural households inasmuch as size of asset-base in rural areas generally tends to vary directly with the size of landholding. Thus, size of landholding/asset-base determines the extent of access to agricultural prosperity. Again, which is equally important, it has a crucial bearing on the credit-worthiness and overall social prestige of an individual in the rural society.

Thus, in 1985-86, the percentage of marginal farmers among the S.Cs. was as high as 71 as against 58 for the population as a whole. The extent of semi-medium, medium and large farmers among the S.Cs. is obviously low compared to the general scenario. However, one also notices intra-SC farmers' inequality with respect to landholding inasmuch as less than 1 per cent of the large S.C. farmers cultivated about 11 per cent of the total land cultivated by them all, compared to 71 per cent of them cultivating less than 24 per cent (Government of India, 1990b).

The condition of agricultural labourers, most of whom belong to the S.C./S.T. communities is pathetic. They have to toil in heat, rain and cold alike to earn their bare subsistence. They stand a better chance of employment during busy agricultural seasons such as sowing and harvesting, while during lean periods they remain largely either jobless or underemployed. Constant increase in prices of essential commodities such as foodgrains depresses their already meagre purchasing power. Further, they suffer from chronic inadequacy of housing, clothing and even primary medical facilities. They can seldom afford to send their children to school because of their abject poverty and wherever they do, the drop-out rate among their children is very high. Except in a state like Kerala they are not organised or unionised and consequently their bargaining power vis-a-vis their masters is low. If they dare to make any attempt in an organised way to demand higher (in fact 'due') wages, the landed interests retaliate with all sorts of actions such as intimidation and even physical coercion. Occasionally, their houses are even burnt and their womenfolk molested with a view to 'teach them a lesson'. It is distressing to note that in some parts of the country landlords have raised 'private armies' to deal with the agricultural labourers who muster some strength and question their exploitation.

To make matters worse, the various state governments are very reluctant to revise agricultural wages upward periodically as required under the Minimum Wages Legislation enacted in 1948 and are not even enthusiastic about the implementation of the prevailing wage rates. As a result of these factors, the overall condition of agricultural labourers is pathetic and, as mentioned above, a majority of them belong to the S.C./S.T. communities. Thus, the Dalits in the country are socially depressed, economically dependent, politically marginalised, and culturally deprived and starved.

The Founding Fathers of free India's Constitution duly recognised this tragic situation of the S.C./S.T. communities and incorporated in the Constitution the principle of 'preferential treatment' in the form of the 'reservation policy' (RP). Through this policy, along with the reservation in the central and state legislatures, places for the S.C./S.T. communities in proportion to their numbers came to be reserved in the central and state government/semi-government offices as also in the educational institutions run by them, i.e., 12.5, 7.5 and 4.0 per cent for the S.Cs., the S.Ts., and the Denotified and Nomadic Tribes, in proportion to their respective population.

Thus, the purpose of the reservation policy was to mitigate, at least partially, the centuries-old all-pervasive injustices inflicted upon the S.C./S.T. communities and to enable them to participate in the process of development and social change. In other words, the acceptance of the reservation policy was tantamount to accepting the fact that the benefits to economic growth would not automatically ' trickle-down' to the weaker sections of society and still less to the socio-educationally disadvantaged groups like the S.Cs. and the S.Ts. This made positive discrimination in their favour by the state a historical necessity.

Against this background it is pertinent to review the nature and quality of the implementation of the reservation policy in India. Thus, Table 2 reveals the status of the implementation of job reservation in the central government services as also in the Public Sector Undertakings (PSUs) and the nationalised banks as on1 January 1987.

TABLE 2. PERCENTAGE OF SCHEDULED CASTES IN THE CENTRAL GOVERNMENT, PSUS AND AND NATIONLISED BANKS (1 JANUARY 1987)

Class/Grade	Total	SC	Per Cent
(A) Central Government			
A (I)	57,654	4,746	8.23
B (II)	75,419	7,847	10.40
C (III)	21,30,453	3,07,980	14.46
D (IV) (Excluding sweepers)	11,67,759	2,34,614	20.09
Total	34,31,285	5,55,187	16.18
(B) PSUS (total: 211)			
A	1,61,815	7,862	4.86
B	1,62,339	10,010	6.17
C	13,94,015	2,58,500	18.54
D (Excluding sweepers)	3,99,000	1,23,010	30.82
Total	21,17,169	3,99,382	18.86
Sweepers	38,900	30,150	77.51
(C) Nationalised Banks			
Officers	2,15,805	15,775	7.29
Clerks	4,49,1 44	61,891	13.77
Class IV	1,67,136	37,272	22.30
Total	8,32,085	1,14,938	13.81
Sweepers	17,794	8,740	49.11

Source: Government of India. Delhi: Ministry of Social Welfare.

What is the scenario in the educational institutions with respect to the reservation policy?

It is distressing to observe that in the year 1987, in as many as 41 universities in the country the share of the S.C. communities in the grades of professors, assistant professors and lecturers was 0.61, 1.04 and 3.16 per cent, respectively.

The position regarding filling up of the reserved posts in the category of Class I, Class II and Class III is also worse in these universities than that in the central government and PSU services.

It is the reservation policy that has enabled them to partially break the shackles of bonded labour. It is this policy which has been instrumental in creating in these communities a small middle class consisting of officials, lawyers, professors, managers, engineers, doctors and C.A., whose enhanced economic status has not only increased the pace of social mobility, but given some sort of mental stability and confidence to the communities as a whole. As a result, they have started to contribute to art and literature and thus seek cultural advancement. It is indeed gratifying that they are producing their own literature.

Impact of the NEP on Dalits

We mentioned at the beginning that the main thrust of the NEP is on the primacy of the 'market' implying thereby, a progressive erosion of the role of the 'state' in the economic affairs of the country. This transition, according to me, is very likely to have adverse consequences for the Dalits.

In a society characterised by the 'private ownership of means of production', the state primarily protects the interests of the ruling classes. These interests are not 'economic' alone, but also social, educational and cultural. Thus, the intervention of the state in the overall management of 'social relations' in an 'unequal' society generally implies championing the interests of the ruling classes. It is needless even to mention that in the Indian context 'ruling classes' further implies the so-called upper-castes, having greater command over the material and non-material resources. Consequently, the intervention of the state in favour of the ruling class who also happens to belong to the upper castes is bound to affect adversely the interests of the poor in general and the Dalits in particular.

Even in an unequal society, the ruling classes cannot remain totally neutral towards the minimal requirements of the vast majority of the poor. Thus, they have to take care of these socio-economically disadvantaged sections of the society through devising some economic and other policies and programmes intended to create some purchasing power in their hands. They have to do this for three reasons. One, maintenance of social stability requires that all socio-economic groups in the society develop a feeling that they stand to benefit from the overall development process in the country. Two, in a competitive democratic system, the ruling classes (and castes) are always constrained to obtain as large a support and sanction as possible with a view to widening their social base. Three, in a capitalist economy, creation of additional purchasing power is one of the objective conditions for sustaining, if not enlarging the size of the 'market', so vital for maintaining the rate of economic growth. The reservation policy meant for the S.C./S.T. communities (now effectively extended to the OBCs) is a case in point.

One of the major consequences of the NEP is the contraction of the public sector. Whatever rewards such a policy may bring for the economy, it is most likely to have an adverse effect on the fortunes of the S.C./S.T. communities. This is because the contraction of the public sector is certainly going to restrict the scope of the reservation policy which, in turn, is going to result in the erosion of job opportunities for the S.Cs. and S.Ts. In this context three pertinent questions may be raised. One, will the overall process of privatisation of the economy and all the attendant policies create enough jobs to compensate for the loss of jobs arising due to the contraction of the public sector? Two, assuming for a while that the private sector does so, what is likely to be the 'nature' of these prospective jobs? Three, and most important, what chance do the S.C./S.T. communities stand for getting a fair share of these jobs so as to compensate the adverse consequences of the erosions of the RP?

First, it is a matter of grave concern that during the last one-and-a-half decades or so the overall growth of the economy has not been accompanied by a proportionate increase in the level of employment. This may mainly be attributed to the decline in the elasticity of employment with respect to growth of the economy (Mundle, 1992; Kundu, 1993; Mungekar, 1993; and Gupta, 1994). Earlier, agriculture was the 'last resort' of employment; but over the years there is a growing tendency among the better-off farmers to substitute labour with machinery and all similar devices. As a consequence, the labour-absorption capacity of our agriculture is declining (Tyagi, 1981; Vaidyanathan, 1986; Bhalla, 1987). The organised sector as a whole is a great failure in contributing to employment generation. For instance, the total estimated employment in the organised public and private sectors rose from 26.73 million in 1991 to 27.37 million in 1994, i.e., by merely 0.64 million. Again, within the organised sectors, the performance of the manufacturing sector (both public and private) is just deplorable. Thus, between 1991 and 1995 this sector generated barely 0.08 million jobs (Government of India, 1997a). The small-scale industrial units which contribute enormously to employment generation are less likely to sustain the forces of overall competition, and as a result, may either slowly vanish or opt for such technological upgradation that may erode their employment generation capacity. The MNCs that are rushing to India are most likely to adopt capital-intensive techniques of production as they are/will be increasingly catering to the consumption requirements of the elites and therefore their coming does not brighten the employment prospects in the country. In fact, some even fear that too much emphasis on trade as an engine of economic growth may lead to 'deindustrialisation' of the country resulting in a fall in both growth and employment (Nambiar and Tadas, 1994). Further, the banking and insurance industries—the two major areas of the service sector—are being increasingly computerised, again leading to a trade-off between efficiency and employment.

Recently, this view was shared even by the Minister of Labour, Government of India when he expressed a serious concern over the continuously widening gap between job-seekers and the availability of jobs (Government of India, 1997b). Second, regarding the nature and quality of the jobs, it seems logical to argue that the jobs that the economy may create will demand relatively more technical skill and professional competence. I must hasten to add that I am not at all averse to our labour force acquiring higher technical skills and professional capabilities, in fact I am all for it. In view of what is discussed above the S.C./S.T. communities lag far behind in possessing these capabilities. This answers the third question, viz., how are these jobs going to be shared by the S.C./ S.T. communities? The chances of their sharing these jobs are indeed bleak. When the job interests of these dispossessed and disadvantaged groups are less than adequately protected even in the presence of a constitutionally prescribed (and hence mandatory) reservation policy, how will their interests be protected with the erosion of the very same reservation policy?

What then is the prospective scenario with respect to their job opportunities in the era of economic reforms? The answer seems to be inescapable. The Dalits will crowd themselves still more into the unorganised and informal sectors of the economy than they are today. This, in turn, will result in their economic marginalisation. How the NEP is likely to set in motion and also strengthen the process of marginalisation of the Dalits will be further evident once we understand.

One of the characteristics, one may even call them obligations, of the modern welfare state, is that it takes the responsibility of making available to the relatively poor sections of society certain services either free of cost or at lower-than-market prices. The rationale for such a policy stems from the failure on the part of a large section of society to enter the market for want of adequate purchasing power. Since the market is guided solely by the consideration of private profit, it does not care for those who are unable to enter it. Thus, the market is useless for the poor and the poor are useless for the market. This makes it obligatory for the welfare state to take special care of the relatively vulnerable sections of society through implementing specially designed policies and programmes such as (i) comprehensive social assistance/ security measures like old-age pensions and unemployment allowances, and (ii) spending on social services like health and education.

As mentioned in the beginning, consequent to the overall process of privatisation, the state is set to withdraw even more from its welfare obligations by reducing its expenditure on social sectors such as health, education and so on. This is and will continue to be justified on the ground of containment of fiscal deficit, a strict condition imposed by the International Monetary Fund (IMF) and the World Bank.

Thus, on the whole, in the post-reform period the expenditure on social services as a proportion of the GDP has either remained stagnant or at its worst, declined. In other words, taking into account the scope and severity of the prevailing vulnerability in our society, the expenditure on social services is far from adequate. Further, when adjusted against inflation it may prove to be even more inadequate. It is needless to mention that the greatest victims of the contradiction in the expenditure on social services are obviously the poor people in general and the Dalits in particular.

In 1995, the Planning Commission had mooted a proposal that only those S.C./S.T. students should qualify for the post-matric Government of India scholarships who secured more than 60 per cent marks in the SSC or equivalent examination. The proposal was dropped only because of some political intervention/consideration. Viewed in the light of the conditions in which the S.C./S.T. students are struggling to acquire education, the proposal not only amounted to a travesty of wisdom on the part of the Planning Commission, but also indicates the direction in which the wind has begun to blow.

The highly inequitous social system creating and sustaining an unequal opportunity structure will deprive the socio-economically and culturally disadvantaged and dispossessed groups such as the Dalits any opportunity of sharing meaningfully the benefits of this prospective economic growth. This will be essentially due to the erosion of the reservation policy on the one hand, and the growing process of commodification of social services, on the other.

REFERENCES

Ambedkar B.R. (1979), *Babasaheb Ambedkar: Writings and Speeches.* Vol. II. Bombay: Government of Maharashtra, Education Deptt.

Bhalla, Sheila (1987), 'Trends in Employment in Indian Agriculture, Land and Asset Distribution', *Indian Journal of Agricultural Economics* 42 (4) Oct—Dec: 537-60.

Government of India (1987-88), *Report of Commissioner for the S.Cs./STs.* New Delhi: Ministry of Social Welfare.

——— (1990a), *Report of the Study Group Appointed during the VII Five Year Plan to Look into the Progress of the S.Cs. and S.Ts..* New Delhi: Ministry of Social Welfare.

——— (1990b), *Agricultural Situation in India.* New Delhi: Ministry of Agriculture, June.

——— (1996), *Planning Commission, Draft Mid-Term Appraisal of the Eighth Five Year Plan: 1992-1997.* New Delhi: Government of India.

——— (1996-97), *Economic Survey: 1996-97.* New Delhi: Ministry of Finance, Economic Division.

——— (1997a), *Economic Survey.* New Delhi: Ministry of Finance.

——— (1997b), *Labour Bureau, Indian Labour Journal.* Simla; Ministry of Labour.

Gupta, S.P. (1994), 'Recent Economic Reforms and their Impact on the Poor and Vulnerable Sections of Society', NCAER, Mimeo, New Delhi.

Mundle, Sadipto (1992), 'The Employment Effects of Stabilisation and Related Policy Changes in India', Gandhian Journal of Labour Economics 35 (3) July: 227-37.

Mungekar, B.L. (1993), 'Investment, Growth and Employment in India, 1972-73 to 1987-88', *Indian Journal of Labour Economics* 36 (4) Oct-Dec: 589-98

Therborn, Goram (1984), 'The Prospects of Labour and the Transformation of Advanced Capitalism'. *New Left Review* 145, May-June.

Tyagi, D.S. (1981), 'Growth of Agricultural Output and Labour Absorption in India', *Journal of Development Studies* 18 (1) October. 104-14.

12

Rural Dalit Masses: A Case Study

Development and Dalit Masses

Here we will discuss briefly the developments in two states in western India, namely Maharashtra and Gujarat, and highlight the nature of contradictions and paradoxes underlying development. In an empirical survey, we had covered eight villages; four from Maharashtra and four from Gujarat. The Maharashtra villages (MVs) are: Kasbe Digraj and Tung from Miraj taluka of Sangli district, and Bargaon Nandur and Digras from Rahuri taluka of Ahmednagar district. The Gujarat villages (GVs) are: Vankaner and Mota from Bardoli taluka of Surat district, and Narsanda and Pij from Anand taluka of Kheda district.

All the four districts were involved in varying degrees in contributing to and shaping the social fabric of this region. Ideas of independence from foreign rule, social reform and moral uprightness of the individuals were quite popular and pronounced in this region. Protest against dominance and misrule was not an alien experience to the people of these districts (Omvedt, 1976; Hardiman, 1981). Political contacts and experiences of the nationalist workers and the freedom fighters helped many of them later, i.e., on the eve of Independence to consolidate their position in the Congress Party, the only party which had a broad mass base. The rich and vocal sections of the peasantry dominated the rural institutions like gram panchayat, cooperative societies, development banks, etc., albeit with the support of the lower ranks of peasantry (Jugale, 1987). The more influential and powerful the leader in the ruling party hierarchy, the more his village and the surrounding area benefited in terms of development schemes. Villages such as Kasbe Digraj of Sangli district and Bargaon Nandur of Ahmadnagar district provide a vivid testimony of this process. Facilities such as roads, electricity, banks, post offices, telephone, state transport, etc., are more developed in these politically advanced and influential areas. All eight villages covered in this study share certain common developmental attributes. All these villages have extensive irrigation facilities. They receive water through canals, tube-wells, rivers, rivulets, etc. Out of a total land of over 20,233 acres in eight villages, 9,641 acres (48 percent) are under canal irrigation. This has helped to increase agricultural production. Cash crops such as sugarcane, tobacco, etc. are now grown on an extensive scale. In recent years, lemon and grape orchards have also come up. A network of local and regional markets have enabled the farmers to sell their produce at favourable prices.

Beside these regulated marketing outlets, there are cooperatives of sugar and milk producers in these villages. The farmers are members of these cooperatives which are vertically linked to taluka and district-level organisations. These institutions have provided opportunities for village elites to gain political positions and influence. There are well-developed multipurpose cooperative societies in all four Maharashtra villages we surveyed. They are locally known as VIKAS agencies, an abbreviation for the Vividh Karyakari Sahakari Mandal (multipurpose cooperative society). Annual transactions of these VIKAS agencies or multipurpose cooperative societies run into several lakhs of rupees. They distribute annual 'gifts' to their members in the form of cash certificates, utensils or other household utility items, out of a surplus generated in the cooperative venture.

Land distribution is quite skewed. The advantage of cooperatives and the allied network has largely been secured by the upper and middle strata (UMS) of the peasantry. The UMS are known as the progressive farmers. In local parlance, they are referred to as 'Dhanik' (rich), 'Pragatishil' (progressive) and 'Mota Khedut' (big farmer). Most of the developments relating to crop-pattern, water management, agricultural technology, credit distribution, marketing, etc. have taken place in the last 15-20 years. Since the mid-1970s, this development has intensified, providing sharp contrasts between the rich and the poor in MVs and GVs. Rising productivity in agriculture, and its commercialisation has increased the net cash inflow in these villages. There is perceptible rise in the demand for consumer goods and services, especially from among the upper and middle strata. The latter group seem to be keenly imitating the lifestyle of their urban counterparts residing in the nearby towns like Bardoli, Surat, Anand, Vallabh Vidyanagar (in Gujarat); and Sangli, Miraj, Kolhapur, Ahmadnagar, Rahuri, etc. (in Maharashtra) (Breman, 1974; Punalekar, 1980; Shah, 1985).

In Kasbe Digraj and Tung together, between 2,000 to 3,000 migrant labourers live in the tents on village fields. These labourers have migrated from the drought-prone region, namely from the districts of Beed, Osmanabad and Latur from Marathawada region. There are some from the neighbouring districts of Karnataka state also. This number swells when the sugarcane-cutting season reaches a peak. Private doctors, numbering about 10 in this village make a good deal of money. Canal irrigation was introduced in these villages some 15 or 20 years ago and it has brought rapid prosperity to many farming households in this region. However, the ratio of cultivable land to grassland is quite low. Bargaon Nandur and Digraj villages have no worthwhile grassland at all. This does cause a great deal of hardship to the poorer households in obtaining fodder for their cattle.

In the study region, the rural poor can be classified into two groups: (i) the local, and (ii) the outsiders or the migrants. The locals are the longtime residents or natives of Kasbe

Digraj and Tung from Miraj taluka of Sangli district. The outsiders or the migrants are those who have migrated to these villages in recent times, mostly during the last 10-15 years. There are further two sub-groups among the migrants. These are (i) the early migrants, but now settled, i.e., those who have some permanent dwelling in a new village and have regular occupational relations with the local farming households; and (ii) seasonal migrants, i.e., those who move in and out of the village at regular intervals in correspondence with the agricultural season (mostly staying for six-eight months between October and June).

The Hindus are in overwhelming majority among the local poor households (91 percent). The Muslim households constitute about 8 percent. The rural poor are predominantly from the lower castes, comprising the artisan or service castes, the Scheduled Castes and the Scheduled Tribes, including the nomadic tribes. Over 92 percent of local poor households are landless. Some 8 percent have agricultural holding of less than one acre. The principal occupation of the head of the household is agricultural labour. Their other occupational activities are: non-agricultural, manual labour; service in the sugar factory or at a public works project; artisan work; petty trade; etc. Most of them are daily-wage labourers. They lack security of employment (Breman, 1985; Joshi, 1996; Katre, 1987). Only a handful of them have got jobs in relatively better-paid occupations like loaders and unloaders in a sugar factory, tractor drivers or as peons in a cooperative society. They get monthly wages with paid leave and holidays. They enjoy some status and respectability because they are a little more educated, and earn monthly wages or salary. This is particularly evident in village Kasbe Digraj and Tung, both from Miraj taluka (Maharashtra), and village Vankaner from Bardoli taluka (Gujarat).

Often the boys and girls of 10-12 years assist their parents in petty trade and even in agricultural labour. An early engagement of younger children in the above-mentioned activities serves a definite purpose of the poor households. For the families living below the poverty line, education is 'expensive', though formally free. Educational data amply reveal this situation. Nearly half of the respondents (heads of households) are totally illiterate, some 9 percent have reached the 11th standard and some have reached an even higher level of education.

Out of 411 households, 32 (8 percent) have less than one acre of land. The rest are landless. Out of these, 24 households cultivate their land. The rest do not cultivate it. Of these 24 cultivating households, 21 have irrigation facilities. The major source of irrigation is river water. Only five out of 32 landowning farmers have canal irrigation facility. This is despite the fact that all eight villages are well endowed with irrigation resources. A majority of the local poor households are without electricity (64 percent), though all the eight villages are electrified. Also, a majority get drinking water from the water taps owned by others (32 percent) or from the public well (37 percent). Only 16 percent of the households have their own water taps. It was alarming to note that nearly half of the local poor households experience starvation on some days during the year. Some 42 households, i.e., 10 percent (13 from Gujarat and 29 from Maharashtra) have to face starvation for more than 30 days during the year. This is despite the fact the some get 'cooked food' from their farmer-employers on various occasions. Pardhis who are nomadic tribals collect left-over food on marriage occasions in the well-off families.

All the study villages have Primary Health Centres (PHCs). These are wholly government-run institutions. Even then, more than two-thirds of the local poor households go to private doctors for their medical treatment (276 out of 411 households). Experience suggests that the PHC and other such public health systems are not yet widely utilised by the local poor households despite the fact that over one-fourth of them faced acute difficulties in health matters, and needed help and assistance. A majority of them (59 percent) still do not utilise the PHC or hospitals for the deliveries of babies. Child birth takes place at home at the hands of the local *dai* or midwife who is experienced but 'untrained'. Modern facilities including health systems are still 'miles away' both socially and culturally for these households. Why do the public health institutions remain unutilised by the marginal sections of rural society? This question underlying the interface between the poor and health institutions is indeed a complex one and needs deeper investigations to get at the circumstances behind inaccessibility. Dominant reasons seem to be: poor facility structures at these PHCs as well as the apathy and indifference of the medical and paramedical staff towards the members of poor households.

Since the introduction of cash crops and especially sugarcane production, there has been considerable influx of migrant labour in this region. From drought-prone, dry regions like Dharampur, Dangs, Songadh, Uchchal, Nizar, etc. in Gujarat state; and Beed, Latur, Osmanabad, Parabhani, Sholapur, Bijapur, Parner, etc. in Maharashtra state. As mentioned earlier, some neighbouring drought-prone talukas of Karnataka state also contribute to the supply of migrant labour to neighbouring irrigated villages in Maharashtra. As regards distance between the native place of the migrants and their destination point, i.e., the villages where they work; it varies from 35-40 kms, to over 250 kms. Sugarcane cutters (SCCs) constitute a sizable section of this migrant poor. The SCCs are mostly drawn from the dry and arid region adjoining this lush, green region such as our study villages. The SCCs come from nearby and also from far-off places. As mentioned earlier, the acute drought conditions prevailing recurrently in these areas compel many households to move out of their villages with cart, cattle and children. They seek employment through the contractors for sugarcane cutting or as daily-wage earners on public works. In the latter, they join individually in a gang which is provided work for road, nallah, or dam-building activities. Some join the labour cooperative societies which are 'cooperative' in name only.

The situation among the sugarcane cutters is worth examining (Katre, 1987; Breman, 1978). As mentioned earlier, the SCCs comprise more than 90 percent of the migrant labour in this region. In Sangli district alone, some 20-30,000 SCCs are employed during the crop-cutting season from October to May. Rahuri, Kopargaon and Srirampur talukas comprising a sugar belt in Ahmednagar district, employ over 40,000 sugarcane labourers. According to Jan Breman, some 50,000 men, women and children from Maharashtra work in the sugarcane fields of South Gujarat especially in the Chalthan, Palsana and Bardoli areas. He further writes:

> But what marks them out even more definitely as outsiders is the way they live and work, bonded together. The cane cutters are put up in temporary camps close to the field in which they are working. The camps can be seen from the road-rows of little makeshift huts, consisting of a couple of mats which are held aloft with a few sticks. These camps are regularly shifted and the seasonal labour force thus works its way throughout the area to be harvested, separated and apart from the village population... (Breman, 1978: 1317).

Employing the migrant labour for sugarcane harvesting operations has been the permanent feature of this region. This practice seems to be beneficial to the sugar factory management (SFM). The SFM relies on the contractors or labour brokers called *mukadams* in local parlance. Jan Breman has clearly established that labour recruitment through the *mukadams* is a clever move of the sugar factory management, He argues:

> The Mukadam system results in the seasonal migration taking place in a way which is controlled and which assures the sugar factories of a supply of the required number of the labourers at the right time for the least cost and without

> they themselves having to carry the risks attached to the process. In short, it is a cheap, reliable, efficient and workable system for making use of temporary labour on a grand scale (Breman, 1978: 1326).

These migrant labourers are 'strangers', 'outsiders' to the village people. No one gives them cash loans. Even local private doctors do not give them medicines, if they do not have money. 'They are here in this village for 10-15 days. Soon they will go to other "Fads" (cane-field). How can we trust them?'—said one doctor in Sangli district. So when the question of medical treatment arises, the SCCs go to local doctors along with their contractors. The contractors pay or promise to pay the doctor. Even shopkeepers in the village give grains on credit to the SCCs only after the contractor puts in a word. In some cases, the contractors settle their accounts with the doctors, shopkeepers and even liquor shop vendors. And later they deduct the money from the wage bills of the SCCs. 'We are mostly cheated in these transactions', said one labourer with a deep sense of anguish.

The SCC settlement is known as *basti* in common parlance. These *bastis* have no electricity, water supply, and even approach road. The SCC families have to face scarcities in a variety of things including foodgrains and firewood. The local labourers also do not always view the SCCs in a favourable light. They consider them as 'outsiders', intruding into their work and livelihood. The *bastis* of the migrant labourers are usually on the roadside or on the cleared sugarcane fields. Their contacts with local village institutions are fleeting, to say the least. Some SCC families bring their children along with them, as there is nobody at the native place to look after them. These children spend their time in tending cattle, playing or assisting their parents. They do not attend village schools. Neither the village elders nor the school teachers are bothered about non-participation of migrants' children in school education.

Canal irrigation was introduced in our study villages some 15 or 20 years ago and it has brought rapid prosperity to many farming households. However, the ration of cultivable land to grassland is quite low and declining year after year. Bargaon Nandur and Digras have no worthwhile grassland at all. This caused a great deal of hardship to poorer households in obtaining fodder for their cattle. It is clear from the evidence that agricultural modernisation has not brought any noticeable relief to them. In all spheres such as health, housing and education, there appears to be little advancement in the conditions of the agricultural labourers, the lowest strata of rural society in Maharashtra and Gujarat (Desai, 1987; Jain, 1985; Lobo, 1993).

There are numerous attempts within and outside to organise them. But so far all mobilisation efforts seem to have achieved little success. The state, through its various programmatic interventions is attempting to provide some relief to this class. There are a variety of developmental schemes aimed at improving the lot of the landless and poor peasantry. And yet, there is very little impact of these schemes/programmes on their living conditions. The most urgent and immediate questions before them is survival; earning livelihood on a day-to-day basis. They are in constant search of strategies of survival at the individual or household level. For instance, entire labour input in some households is so apportioned that at least there will be a minimum living for each. Use of child labour at home or in the field; use of female labour for an amorphous range of duties (from one's own households to domestic service in landowner's household), the keeping of some goats, sheep, fowls at home; rearing of the sick calf of the Dhaniama at his home; seasonal migration to a nearby village or town, etc., exemplify some typical ways of the rural poor to cope with problems of survival.

Why do the landless labourers remain the most neglected section of rural society? Why do they not come together and launch a collective struggle? These questions are significant, and to answer them, we need to closely examine the social, economic, and cultural contexts of their life including their work environment (Kurien, 1978; Punalekar, 1994). It is becoming increasingly clear that they essentially constitute a disaggregated mass which is fragmented into several caste groups with further divisions into religious sects and other primordial loyalties. There are no durable signs of their unity across class lines (Breman, 1978; P.M. Patel, 1981). They do not rise as a single, unified force in solidarity. And hence their demands do not get articulated with sufficient vigour and effectiveness. Also, there are occasions of mutual mistrust and misconceptions among the local and migrant workers about one another. Especially in seasonal, short-duration employment sectors like sugarcane cutting, mining, brick kilns, construction, or salt-pan work, such ill-will is distinctly surfacing. There are free-floating myths about the migrant labour in the minds of local villagers including the local landless labourers. The local labourers do not generally view the migrant labour in a positive way.

The local poor believe that the migrant labourers are much above them economically. 'They come from better off economic background; their staying power in the labour market is superior. They are cunning, shrewd and selfish. They are always for their own monetary gains and least concerned with the woes and discomforts of others working with them,'— such myths prevail. Their conditions at their native villages is not any better (Breman, 1985; Arjun Patel and Desai, 1992). Most of them barely manage to pull through the earnings they have gained while on migration. But even then, the local labourers are not able to see and get convinced about the real situation of the migrant labourers. Such notions or myths prevail among the local labourers and drive a wedge between the migrant labour and local labour; distancing them from one another. How are these myths floated and sustained? This is a question for separate enquiry. But we learn from our field experiences that some scrupulous elements like local contractors, Sarpanchs, sugar factory management officials, etc. concoct such stories and float these among the local population. One cannot also rule out the role of some disgruntled local labourers in spreading such myths.

The poor get divided, first in mutual perceptions and then in practice. The social and cultural distance between the two groups increases, and that further reduces the chance of their coming together and mobilising themselves as a united class. Seasonal employment, living separately in the camps (on fields or *gaothan/gauchar* lands, etc.), their concentration in a particular activity where there is hardly any chance to meet the local poor, and above all, the deliberate efforts of the contractors, *mukadams* and others from the employers' class are the known factors that are responsible for isolating and distancing the migrant labourers from the local labourers. Insecurities built into the work process also disengage the migrant labourers from interactions with the local or native labourers.

We observe that a small section of the cane cutters did speak well about their contractors. They felt a sense of gratitude towards them for providing them a chance to work and earn their livelihood. This was a miniscule section mostly comprising older people and those without any formal educational background. But the majority spoke negatively about their *mukadams* or contractors in a hush-hush voice. Similar mixed reactions were visible when the SCCs talked about their co-workers, local farmers and labourers, and the village community at large. A few older people wisely chose to remain silent on these issues. But there were quite a few young, educated SCCs who did not wish to conceal their anger and fury. They were agitated about their own forced migration, about inhuman working conditions, low wages and insecurities of all kinds. 'We are living like our cattle; dumb and dependent', said a labourer from Tasgaon taluka.

'These sugar factories are built on our sweat and blood. These sugar barons prosper and we languish year after year. This is a miserable life indeed,' added another young migrant labourer from Valva taluka.

Thus, there were clear signs of protest and militancy (Katre, 1987; Breman, 1978, 1994). Especially the younger generation from the SCC households was unwilling to submit to the highhandedness of the farmers and the contractors. Tensions in work, life and relationships were getting projected onto the domestic front also. There were instances of conflict between husband and wife, father and son on petty matters. There were physical fights also. All this was due to insecurity and instability built into the very mode of their migratory existence.

It is also evident that the situation of the ex-Untouchable castes has shown only marginal change in terms of social and cultural relations and behaviour of the village community. Even the members of the different Scheduled Castes (Mahars, Mangs, Chamars, Dhors, Vankars, Rohits, Meghwals, Bhangis, etc.) were not united among themselves socially and culturally. They believe in and uphold their separate identity based on social and occupational rankings. This fact of separation and disunity among the Scheduled Castes themselves: and between them and other lower Untouchable castes (Nhavi, Luhar, Suthar, Vanjari, etc.) demands deeper sociological attention. Though poverty was a common factor enveloping all or most of them and subjecting them to equally brutalising experiences, they were slow to learn the ways of closing their ranks and unite. As the present situation stands, both in Maharashtra and Gujarat, they seem to lack a sense of social solidarity and unity of purpose. They seem to exhibit differential social consciousness. Why this is so is a big question; and we can ill afford to further postpone its investigation.

There is another set of questions which need to be directed towards the ground-level manifestations among the rural poor. These questions are: Why do the rural poor including women hesitate to join development activities or express doubts about the outcome of such projects? Why do they desist from displaying a forward-looking, future-oriented outlook? Why are they so much tied to the questions of mundane, day-to-day living? These questions are important.

What is significant to note is the experience and the perceptions of the rural poor. Their views matter a great deal in formulating strategies to initiate 'development' which can meet their needs and interests. Their doubts and fears, their anxieties and agitation are rooted in their own past encounters and interaction with local structures of power, authority and control. This can easily be discovered through the reactions of the sugarcane cutters (SCCs) to prevailing conditions.

Let us now focus our attention on Scheduled Tribes (STs). The STs constitute over 14 percent of Gujarat and 7 percent of Maharashtra population. Major tribes are Bhils, Varlis, Thakurs, Dublas, Dhodias, Katkaris and Chodhras. Other significant tribal groups are Gamits, Nayakas, Tadvis, Dhankas, etc. An overwhelming majority of them live in rural areas, mostly in hills and forests. During the last 150 years, there have been substantial changes in the ecology and landscape of their habitat. Thanks to state planning and development efforts, tribals living in the command area or in villages having developed infrastructure are relatively better off. A few among them are getting closer to the mainstream peasant communities such as Marathas of Maharashtra and Patidars of Gujarat. Education has increased among some tribal groups like Dhodias, Chodhras. Gamits and Nayakas (STs) in southern Gujarat. Also, in Maharashtra, one observes a rise in the educational level of Thakurs and Mahadev Kolis (Shah, 1983, 1984; Punalekar, 1985a; 1985b).

The benefits of development including education have reached a small segment of this community. Only a few tribal households have advanced economically and socially. They have acquired a somewhat privileged position in their own social milieu and outside. A few of them have acquired a place in the mainstream political parties as well; giving them an opportunity to enjoy some share in political power too. They are the 'new' elites whose major attention is on improving their own socioeconomic and political profile. Evidence suggests that they have achieved some measure of success in the present social system. However, the common tribals who constitute a majority and belong to the lower economic strata are outside the vortex of these 'developments' (Desai and Choudhry, 1977; Punalekar, 1996).

We must note that tribal societies were relatively homogeneous some decades ago. Now they are getting internally differentiated and stratified. There is a distinct upper strata of the literate and educated tribals (Bose, 1981; Punalekar, 1985b; Shah, 1984). They come from the landowning groups with better access to input markets including seeds, fertilisers, credit, labour etc. Their closer acquaintance with (as well as membership in) other resource structures including cooperatives, has also helped them to strengthen their position. Among them, the households which have a larger share of development and prosperity in tribal regions belong largely to Dhodia, Kokna, Chodhra, Gamit and Mahadeo Kolis. Other groups such as Varlis, Dubias, Rathwas, Katkaris, etc. are socially and economically far behind. These backward groups live in relatively underdeveloped and sometimes inaccessible areas. Their struggle for existence is still very acute and sometimes grim. Their experience, with outsiders (be they contracts, traders, moneylenders, petty officials) is not altogether happy.

They are exploited in exchange and credit markets. They feel frustrated and agitated. This is evident in the transactions that take place in the *hats* or *hatwadas* (i.e., weekly markets). And, as mentioned earlier, whenever a 'development' project was launched in their territory, they became the first victim. Their ecological milieu is severely disturbed and their forest resources depleted. Their social and cultural relations are dislocated (Joshi, 1987; Mankodi and Gangopadhyay, 1983; Arjun Patel, 1994). In some cases, the tribals became 'oustees' meaning those who have been displaced; and were forced to shift to other places and community milieus where it took them years to readjust and resettle.

The effects, of dislocation on tribal communities are now known (for example, Koyana, Likai, Jaikwadi, and other smaller dams in Maharashtra and Gujarat). Needless to aver that the emergence of Naxalites and similar militant outfits among the tribals is largely rooted in these exploitative relations which rend to destabilise their society, economy and culture (Lobo, 1992: Punalekar, 1996; Joshi, 1996). The answer then is nor to fight and persecute Naxalites or other militants who are spearheading the movement; but to urgently address and resolve the basic socio-economic issues confronting the tribal masses.

In recent years, there has emerged a distinct group from among the tribals of Maharashtra and Gujarat, and that is of seasonal migrants. They live away from their village and family for over six months in a year. In Maharashtra, this trend is visible since the severe droughts in the state in the early 1970s. In Gujarat also, such migration has become a regular feature since the mid-1970s. Not only do these tribals migrate to irrigated villages for agricultural labour, but they have begun to migrate to towns and cities in search of their livelihood. In major towns and cities of Gujarat, the large congregation of such tribal migrant labour is seen in the city squares, vegetable market yards, railway stations, goods transport depots, etc. In Gujarat these markets are known as *chakla* market and the persons who assemble there to sell their labour are known as *chakla* workers. In fact, their labour share in urban services like loading, unloading, grass-cutting, construction of roads, buildings, etc. is considerable. This is a distinctly post-Independence phenomenon.

Bhils of Dhulia district work as casual labourers in Surat city; and Bhils of Panchmahals are seen in the urban labour markets at Ahmedabad, Anand, Nadiad, Baroda and Bharuch. Many of them migrate with their families. Obviously, their children's education suffers. But the question of survival precedes the question of education and other pursuits. What are their conditions of living in the urban areas? Do they get fair wages for their output? Does the settled urban population help them in coping with the problem of housing, health, water, and other social and cultural amenities? These and related questions need to be explored.

There is another social group, namely the nomadic or denotified tribes. Some of them were labelled as criminals during the British regime. Their number is considerable, both in Maharashtra and Gujarat. They are: Berad, Kaikadi, Kanjar Bhat, Banjara, Vadar, Vaghari, Gosavi, Joshi, Kolhati, Bhoi and Raval. In a changing socio-economic order, their problems of survival are becoming increasingly acute. Their day-to-day problems are too complex. Their traditional skills of trade, earth-digging, entertainment, repair services, etc. do not enable them much now to compete with modern technology and the service sector. The basis of their social relations with traditional clients is also getting eroded due to 'new' forces of production. Until recently there was no awakening among them. Even now, all nomadic groups have not come together. Also, perceptions of the common people and legal authorities have not sufficiently altered. To cite just one example, Paradhis of Maharashtra are still suspect in the eyes of the police *patil* and village headman. Vaghris and Chharas of Gujarat are still perceived as 'unreliable and untrustworthy'. So also are Kaikadis of Maharashtra who suffer several such humiliations and indignities.

Laxman Mane, himself a Kaikadi, indeed did a great service to the cause of his community by writing an autobiography *Upra* (1992). The literature world outside cold then know the woes and travails of the nomadic group. This also tells us how effectively a sociological account can be written by a literate and sensitive member of an oppressed community. *Upra* is reflective essay on living conditions of nomadic tribals. So are the autobiographical novels like *Balut* by Daya Pawar, *Athavaniche Pakshi* by Sonkamble, *Taral Antaral* by Shankarrao Kharat, *Katyavarchi Pot* by Uttam Bandu Tupe and *Majhya Jalmachi Chittarkathe* by Shantabai Kamle. They depict the lives of ordinary men and women from lower social groups. Literature of this kind provides vital sociological insights into the agonies and aspirations of marginal groups and their wounded consciousness (Punalekar, 1994).

The SCs, STs, nomads and others are now beginning to find their 'voice' and insist on rigorous implementation of constitutional safeguards, protective schemes, educational assistance, legal support and more vigorous monitoring of the existing schemes. Outside intervention including leadership can achieve but little in terms of political mobilisation. Internal awakening of the community itself can achieve a great deal, once they begin to reflect on their own conditions in the light of their relations and experiences with other relatively better-off, settled sections of the society.

Summing Up

This chapter outlines the rural situation in Maharashtra and Gujarat, the premier industrialising, fast-developing states in the Indian Union. Signs of growth and economic development are too clear to miss; they are distinctily visible. But this growth is lopsided, creating in its wake a series of contradictions and paradoxes. And that gives rise to another significant set of questions, namely those relating to social justice.

Rural development as evidenced in the countryside has bifurcated and broken the region in two parts; one is better endowed with externalities of irrigation facilities and developed infrastructure in input markets. It is richer in terms of production levels and productivity, buttressed further by a vigorous network of cooperatives and other institutions. A larger share of state resources seem to be concentrated in this part of the region. Political leadership at the state level is more attentive to their demands; so also others including the bureaucrats seem to concentrate on these pockets. The results are therefore 'promising', from their viewpoint.

On the other end of the spectrum are the villages in the underdeveloped region. They are dry, unirrigated and facing recurring drought and famine. People there are faced with the perennial question of survival and search for dependable means of livelihood. They have lands, but no means to irrigate them with any certainty. So they have to migrate and join a swelling army of casual labourers in the irrigated fields in their own district or outside. This migration stream from the arid, dry villages to green villages is becoming a permanent feature in the rural economy of both Maharashtra and Gujarat.

This migration is seasonal for some, and as years pass by, becomes a step in a permanent severing of their social and cultural linkages with their native village. They then live in the far-off host villages or in the town or city. We have seen that their conditions of living are indeed critical; whether they live in the open fields or in the city slums. Also, their conditions of work are critical, leaving them no space for creative, productive enterprise. Both their work and domestic life are full of tensions and unease, often leading to violence or self-abuse.

The question of survival obliterates all chances of meaningful participation in creative, constructive activities. As migrants, they are denied help and support in the host environment. Even the local poor families do not confide in or trust them. Rather, they are hostile and indifferent to the migrant families. Many myths supporting such chasms are prevalent in these rural areas, which further dim the prospects of their unity or solidarity. Alienated from the bonds of sympathy from the local populations, the migrant poor are further pushed into the network of their contractors or *mukadams*, who often take maximum advantage of such critical situations. Thus, the migrant labourers are subject to endless miseries and hardship.

Their womenfolk too suffer a great deal. They have to work along with their male counterpart, and share the family support burden amidst greater self-exploitation and abuse. The children suffer in their health and education. They cannot aspire for a settled, secure and steady life for themselves. Denial of education restricts their scope for social mobility.

[*Courtesy: Dr. Punalekar*]

13

Dalits and Higher Education

The economic opportunities are related to the educational attainments of people in modern society. The knowledge society has come of age. Therefore, redressing that exclusion requires a combination of policies. The Human Development Report 2004 has devoted a substantial part of its argument on the basis of the affirmative action policies pursued in India, Malaysia, USA and South Africa. Educational and occupational reservations have also made lasting impact on India's political system. The entire structure of political power has changed since independence, beginning with South Indian States. A new political leadership has emerged from among the Scheduled Castes, Scheduled Tribes and other backward classes (OBCs). In almost all states the beneficiaries of reservations occupy important positions in government and positions in lower levels of bureaucracy.

The little progress that the dalits have made during the five decades of post-independence period has started dwindling during the liberalization period of the last one decade. There are several policy changes that have affected the educational opportunities of the dalits. The post-independent public education was almost a continuation of the colonial mode of liberal education. The government has realised the lacunae and corrective measures such as creation of institutes of excellence like IITs, IIMs, new course structures, vocationalization of education have been initiated. The dalits have not realised the importance of these courses and therefore remained outside the purview of vocational education.

TABLE 1. EDUCATIONAL DEVELOPMENT OF SCHEDULED CASTES AT SCHOOL STAGE 1980-81 TO 2000-2001

(in '000)

Year	*Primary*	*Middle*	*Higher Secondary*
1960-61	(12.0)	(8.7)	(7.1)
1980-81	10981 (14.8)	2223 (10.7)	152 (10.5)
1985-86	13921 (15.9)	3619 (13.3)	1810 (10.9)
1991-92	16037 (16.0)	4693 (11.7)	2581 (12.6)
1995-96	19176 (17.9)	5445 (14.5)	2741 (11.9)
2000-2001	21195 (18.6)	6694 (15.6)	3812 (13.8)

Note: Figures in brackets indicate percentage to total enrolment in that category.

Source: Ministry of HRD, Government of India, 2002.

Higher Education: Accountability

The National Policy on Education 1986 and the programme of Action 1992 are very clear about the educational development of Scheduled Castes and Tribes. A separate chapter is devoted to the educational development of Scheduled Castes and Tribes where in the school education of the dalits is mentioned. There is no mention about higher education and particularly quality institutions like IIT's and IIM's. The government has already brought out the compulsory primary education bill 2003. All these initiatives indicate that the government is responsible for primary education of all the people in the country and only up to secondary education for dalits. Interestingly, the Scheduled Castes and Tribes Commission is also not aware of the fact that dalits are under-represented in professional and vocational education. The ministry of social justice and empowerment releases the post-matric scholarships to different states on the basis of the requisition for states. Apparently, they do not have a mandate to question the under representation of dalits in professional and vocational courses.

TABLE 2. ENROLMENT OF SC/ST IN HIGHER EDUCATION 2000-2001

	Scheduled Castes		*Scheduled Tribes*	
Class	*No.*	*% to total*	*No.*	*% to total*
Ph.D.,	3164	7.0	821	1.8
M.A.,	47898	11.4	12911	3.1
M.Com.,	7540	7.3	1713	1.6
M.Sc.,	11519	9.0	2416	1.9
B.A.,	434597	10.0	164303	3.7
B.Sc.,	18786	9.1	26922	1.9
B.Com.,	135545	9.1	26851	1.7
B.E.,	36533	8.7	13708	3.2
M.B.B.S.,	14209	9.5	5348	3.5

Source: Ministry of HRD, Government of India, 2002.

The educational progress of Dalits is of recent period. The first generation learners of dalits have realised the importance of education and have started encouraging their children to go for higher education. It is exactly here that the World Bank and the government of India wanted higher education to be provided through market. The Committee under the chairmanship of Sri Atal Bihari Vajpai with Mukhesh Amabani and Aditya Birla as members gave a report recommending the privatization and corporatization of higher education. There was no mention about the interests of the dalits. Probably the committee foresaw the implementation of GATS in education from 2005. Several private foreign institutions and universities have established their offices in India to admit students in courses that are considered to be important in the 21st century. Though the concept of privatization was in nascent stage in our education system for a long period of time, it has come out openly after liberalization in 1991. Several colleges and even universities have come up under the category of self-financing institutions. Interestingly all these institutions offer vocational and job oriented courses keeping in view the emerging opportunities in the globalised economy.

Opportunities

The educational development expansion of the scheduled castes can be divided into two periods. The pre-liberalization period and the post-liberalization period (1991 and after). The educational achievements of the first generation of dalits immediately after independence were related to the opportunities created by the state. Several state governments have started welfare hostels to promote school education. Very few opportunities were however, provided for vocational courses. Therefore, majority of the dalits have joined the mainstream courses of Arts and Sciences.

In the post-liberalization period, there is a revolution in science and technology, consequently it has influenced the communication and information networks. They have affected the education system also. The creation of WTO and GATS have brought in new opportunities of free mobility of resources and technology. This has facilitated the expansion of educational market in response to the needs of the expanding world market. The public sector started shrinking and the opportunities of employment in secure jobs have disappeared. The dalits have not perceived the danger of dwindling opportunities in public sector and the opening up of ever expanding possibilities in the globalised private sector. The global labour market has started influencing the educational programmes, particularly courses in electronics, computer science and related courses. Practically hundreds and thousands of courses are created to meet every small skill requirement of the job market. In fact the course structures have undergone a change. There are now two categories of courses. The short life courses and the long life courses. The long life courses require long period of time, resources and knowledge to enter the market. They are very expensive and the benefits are life long and useful to the entire society. The short life courses are very short in duration. They meet the immediate requirements of any tiny skill. The cost therefore is to be borne by the individual as it directly benefits the individual. But, its durability is limited. It runs the risk of short duration and therefore state does not take the responsibility of providing it on its own. It is exactly here the private sector is expanding to meet the requirements of the growing manufacturing and service sector. This has not been grasped by the dalits, who do not have a social network at the global level. But the groups who have a historical advantage in education have transformed themselves and already entrenched very much in the global market. This has an impact on higher education. It is now clear that no forward caste person will enter the liberal Arts and Science courses any more. On the other hand, all the liberal courses in government and aided colleges are filled in by the so called reserved categories and the private colleges are left out for the so called merit students.

Higher Education and the Threats of Privatisation

The higher education system in the USA is privately managed but the students get scholarships and studentships through government and other non-governmental agencies. This is happening today when the enrolment levels in higher education have reached 43 per cent. India can definitely emulate USA when it reaches at least the level of 20 per cent enrolment in higher education in general and at least 10 per cent for Dalits. The overall enrolment ratio at higher education in India today is only 7 per cent. Several disadvantaged groups have not reached the portals of higher education. Those who have reached the portals are far away from the vocational courses. The drop out rate at higher education is alarming in recent times. Some of the self financing courses that are offered in the private sector are not within the reach of the dalits. It requires lakhs of rupees to pay fees for a admission in course that may fetch a job in the private sector. The dalits are still fighting for the extension of affirmative action in private sector. There are very few dalits who are capable of enrolling in the courses mentioned above. But the future of higher education and the job market embellish in these emerging areas. The dalits need to understand this and develop their own educational strategies accordingly. Otherwise, they will hold Ph.D and other liberal Arts and Science degrees, but still remain unemployed. They cannot run the risk of spending their hard earned income and time on courses that do not bring any employment. They need to develop their own vision of education. Further, there are several academic and pedagogical problems with which the dalits suffer today. They need to overcome these deficiencies. It is necessary to work hard to improve the knowledge, skills and abilities in the emerging areas through hard work and social networking, while arguing with the government to extend the affirmative action also to private sector.

Summing Up

Strangely, India with several social and cultural diversities is going in for globalization of education for the elite without extending the same facilities to the historically disadvantaged groups. But, in a country like the UK, the government has realised the folly of following a policy of liberalization and privatization of higher education. They have realised the defect and are now saying that, "the expansion of higher education has not yet extended to the talent and best from all backgrounds. In Britain today too many of those born in to less advantaged families still see a university place as being beyond their reach, whatever their ability. Having a university education brings big benefits and while the government will continue to pay most of the cost involved in studying for a degree, it is also reasonable to ask students to contribute to this. But we need to make sure that no student is put off from going into higher education because they cannot afford the cost of studying while they are at university".

To conclude, the Government has to cope with the changing social scenario and ensure the welfare measures for Dalits. On the other hand, Dalits should also realize the grim position and should equip themselves with all courage to face the situation. After all, on the mercy of the State the solidarity of Dalit society can not perpetuate for long.

REFERENCES

Chalam, K.S., *Educational Policy for Human Resources Development,* Rawat, 1993.

George, P., Sacharopoulos and Harry Anthony Patrinos, *Returns to Investment in Education: A Further Update,* World Bank Policy Research Working paper, 2881, September 2002.

UNDP, *Human Development Report 2004,* Oxford, 2004.

Select Bibliography

Ambedkar B.R. (1979), *Babasaheb Ambedkar: Writings and Speeches.* Vol. II. Bombay: Government of Maharashtra, Education Deptt.

Ambedkar, B.R. (1946), *What Congress and Gandhi Have Done to the Untouchables* (Second edition). Bombay: Thacker & Co.

Ambedkar, B.R. (1969), *The Untouchables* (Second edition) Balrampur: Jelavan Mahavir.

Ambedkar, B.R. (1970), 'Federation Versus Freedom', *Bheem Patrika (Jalandar).*

Ambedker, B.R. (1948), *'Pakistan or Partition of India'* Tacker & Co. Ltd., Bombay, IIIrd Edition.

Bhalla, Sheila (1987), 'Trends in Employment in Indian Agriculture, Land and Asset Distribution', *Indian Journal of Agricultural Economics* 42 (4) Oct—Dec: 537-60.

Bhoyar, Divakar (1994), 'Dunkel, GATT and Bahujans', *Bahujan Sangharsh.* 30 April.

Caplan, Lionel (1987), *Class and Culture in Urban India: Fundamentalism in a Christian Community.* Oxford: Oxford University Press.

Census of India (1911), *Bengal Volume III, part 2; Bihar Volume III, Part 3: Orissa Volume III, part 15. Sikkim Volume III. part 18.* Calcutta: Manager of Publications. Government Press.

Chalam, K.S., *Educational Policy for Human Resources Development,* Rawat, 1993.

Chaturvedi, D.D. (1990), *Ancient India: An Introductory Outline,* New Delhi: Manohar.

Chaudhuri, Nagesh (1994), 'What Policy Should We Take Towards Dunkel?' *Bahujan Sangharsh,* 30 April, Editorial.

Chitnis, Suma (1981), *A Long Way to Go: Report on a Survey of Scheduled Caste High School and College Students in Fifteen States of India.* New Delhi: Allied Publishers.

Covett, V.A. (1972), *History of the Indian Nationalist Movement.*

Dange, S.A. (1949), *India from Primitive Communism to Slavery.* Bombay: Asia Publishing House.

Das, Bhagwan (1995), 'Socio-economic Problems of Dalits', in Bhagwan Das and James Massey (eds), *Dalit Solidarity.* Delhi: ISPCK.

Desai, Govind Bhai H. (1911), *Census of India.* Vol. XVI, *Baroda, Part I. Report.* Bombay: Bombay Presidency.

Frank Mordes (1973), 'Witness to An Erd; *Holt* (NY), pp. 47-48.

Frykenberg, Rober Eric (1989), 'The Emergence of Modern "Hinduism" as a Concept and as an Institution: A Reappraisal with Special Reference to South India', in Gunther, D. Sontheimer and Hermann Kulke (eds.), *Hinduism Reconsidered.* Delhi: Manohar.

Fuchs, Stephen (1981), *At the Bottom of Indian Society.* New Delhi: Munshiram Manoharlal.

Galanter, Marc (1968), 'Changing Legal Conceptions of Caste', in, Milton Singer and Bernard S. (eds), *Structure and Change in Indian Society.* Chicago: Aldine Publishing Co.

Gazetteer of Hoshiarpur District 1883-84. *Tribes and Castes.* Compiled and published under the Authority of Punjab Government, Lahore. The Civil and Military Gazetteers Press. Chapter III. by D. Mahtons.

George, P., Sacharopoulos and Harry Anthony Patrinos, *Returns to Investment in Education: A Further Update,* World Bank Policy Research Working paper, 2881, September 2002.

Government of India (1987-88), *Report of Commissioner for the S.Cs./STs.* New Delhi: Ministry of Social Welfare.

Gupta, S.K. (1985), *The Scheduled Castes in Modern Indian Politics: Their Emergence as a Political Power.* Delhi: Munshiram Manoharlal.

Gupta, S.P. (1994), 'Recent Economic Reforms and their Impact on the Poor and Vulnerable Sections of Society', NCAER, Mimeo, New Delhi.

Heimsath, C.H. (1964), *Indian Nationalism and Hindu Social Reform.* Princeton (New Jersay), p.342.

Hutton, J.H. (1933), *Census of India, 1931. Vol. I-India: Part I- Report.* Delhi: Manager of Publications, Government Press, Indian Statutory Commission Oral Evidence. 1929. Fourteenth Meeting, Madras. 1 March.

Hutton, J.H. (1951), *Caste in India* (Second edition). London: Oxford University Press.

Issae, Horld R. (1965), *'India's Ex-untouchables'*, Bombay Asia Publishing House, p.40.

Jatav, D.R. (1975), *'To the critics of Dr Ambedkar*, Jan Utthan Parishad, New Delhi.

Jatav, D.R. (1979), *Dr. Ambedkar's Role in National Movement*, Buddha Sahitya Samnela. New Delhi.

Jha, M. (1994), 'Problems of Scavengers in a Tribal City: A Case study of Ranchi, Chotanagpur', *Man in Asia* 2: 3-9.

Joshi, Barbara R. (1982), *Democracy in Search of Equality: Untouchable Politics and Indian Social Change*, Delhi: Hindustan Publishing Corp.

Juergensmeyer, Mark (1982), *Religion as Social Vision: The Movement Against Untouchability in 20th-century Punjab*. Berkeley: University of California Press.

Kamble, J.R. (1979), *Rise and Awakening of Depressed Classes in India*. New Delhi: National Publishing House.

Kananaikil, Jose (1986), *Scheduled Castes in Search of Justice. Part II: The Verdict of the Supreme Court*. New Delhi: Indian Social Institute.

Keer, D. (1962), *'Dr. Ambedkar: Life and Mission'*, Popular (Bombay).

Ketkar, S.V. (1909), *The History of Caste in India*. Vol. I. Ithaca: Messers Taylor and Carpentar.

Koilparampil, George (1982), *Caste in the Catholic Community in Kerala*, Kochin: C.I.S.R.

Lal, A.K. and A.N. Sinha (1995), *Letter to Shyam Lal from A.K. Lal and A.N. Sinha*. Patna: Institute Studies.

Lal, K.S. (1968), *Muslim Slave System in Medieval India*. New Delhi: Aditya Prakashan.

Lal, Shyam (1991), 'Origin of the Bhangis: A Hypothesis', *Eastern Anthropologist* (2): 83-98.

Malkani, N.R. (1961), *Report of the Scavenging Conditions Enquiry Committee.* Delhi: Ministry of Home Affairs, Government of India.

Mathew, Joseph. (1986), *Ideology, Protest and Social Mobility: Case Study of Mahars and Pulayas*. New Delhi: Inter-India Publications.

Mosse, C.D.F. (1986), 'Caste, Christianity and Hinduism: A Study of Social Organisation and Religion in Rural Ramnad.' Unpublished D.Phil. Thesis, University of Oxford.

Mukherjee, Prabhati (1988), *Beyond the Four Varna: The Untouchables in India.* Delhi: Motilal Banarsidass.

Mundle, Sadipto (1992), 'The Employment Effects of Stabilisation and Related Policy Changes in India', Gandhian Journal of Labour Economics 35 (3) July: 227-37.

Mungekar, B.L. (1993), 'Investment, Growth and Employment in India, 1972-73 to 1987-88', *Indian Journal of Labour Economics* 36 (4) Oct-Dec: 589-98

Natarajan, S. (1959), *A Century of Social Reform in India,* Asia (New Delhi).

Nath, Trilok (1987), *Politics of the Depressed Classes.* Delhi: Deputy Publications.

Oddie, G.A. (1969), 'Protestant Missions, Caste and Social Change in India', *Indian Economic and Social History Review* VI, September 259-91.

Omvedt, Gail (1994), *Dalits and the Democratic Revolution: Dr. Ambedkar and Dalit Movement in Colonial India.* New Delhi: Sage Publications.

Omvedt, Gail (1997), "Dalits and Economic Policy: Contributions of Dr B.R. Ambedkar". *Fourth World* 4 (1): 22-26.

Pathak, Bindeshwar (1991), *Road to freedom. A Sociological Study on the Abolition of Scavenging in India.* New Delhi: Motilal Banarsidass.

Pradhan, Atul Chandra (1986), *The Emergence of the Depressed Classes.* Bhubaneswar: Bookland International.

Rajgopalachari C (1946), *Ambedker Refuted,* Hind Kitab, Bombay, p.8.

Ram, Nandu (1988), *The Mobile Scheduled Castes: Rise of a New Middle Class.* Delhi: Hindustan Publishing Corporation.

Santhanam, K. (1946), *Ambedkar's, Attack,* The Hindustan Press, New Delhi, p.34.

Shah, Ghanshyam (1971), *Caste Association and Political Process in Gujarat.* Bombay Popular Prakashan.

Sharma, Srotriya C.L. (1971), *Jati Anvensan.* Part I. Phulera: H.D.V.V. Mandal, Samvat.

Teltumbde, Anand (1997), 'Impact of New Economic Policy on Dalits in India'. Occasional Paper Series 1, Pune: Department of Sociology, University of Pune.

Thapar, Romila (1985), 'Syndicated Moksha', *Seminar* 313, September: 14-22.

Therborn, Goram (1984), 'The Prospects of Labour and the Transformation of Advanced Capitalism'. *New Left Review* 145, May-June.

Thorat, Sukhdeo (1997), 'New Economic Policy and Its Impact on Employment and Poverty of the Scheduled Castes'. Occasional Paper Series 2, Pune: Department of Sociology, University of Pune.

Tripathy, R.B. (1994), *Dalits: A Sub-Hitman Society*. New Delhi: Ashish Publishing House.

UNDP, *Human Development Report 2004*, Oxford, 2004.

Index

□□□